Frommer's®

IRELAND'S
BEST-LOVED
DRIVING
TOURS

Ⓦ Wiley Publishing, Inc.

Written by Susan Poole and Lyn Gallagher

Published by AA Publishing

Published in the United States by
Wiley Publishing, Inc.
111 River Street, Hoboken, NJ 07030

Find us online at www.frommers.com

Frommer's is a registered trademark of Arthur Frommer. Used under license.

ISBN 978-0-470-22694-0

Cataloging-in-Publication Data is available from the Library of Congress.

Color separation by Daylight Colour Art, Singapore
Printed and bound by G Canale & C. S.P.A., Torino, Italy

Revised seventh edition published 2008
Revised sixth edition published 2006
Revised fifth edition published 2004
Reprinted 2002
Revised third edition published 2000
Revised second edition published in this format 1998
First published January 1992

Opposite: *South Cross detail, Kells*

CONTENTS

ABOUT THIS BOOK

This book is not only a practical guide for the independent traveller, but is also invaluable for those who would like to know more about the country.

It is divided into four regions, each containing between four and ten tours. The tours start and finish in the towns and cities which we consider to be the best centres for exploration. Each tour has details of the most interesting places to visit en route. Highlighted panels dotted throughout each tour cater for special interests and requirements and cover a range of categories – for those whose interest is in history, wildlife or walking, and those who have children. There are also panels which highlight scenic stretches of road along the route and which give details of special events, crafts and customs.

The route directions are accompanied by an easy-to-use map at the beginning of each tour along with a simple chart showing how far it is from one town to the next in miles and kilometres. These can help you to decide where to take a break and stop overnight, for example. (All distances quoted are approximate.)

Before setting off it is advisable to check with the tourist information centre (addresses are given after the symbol [i] at the end of town entries) at the start of the tour, for recommendations on where to break your journey and for additional information on what to see and do, and when best to visit.

Tour Information
See pages 185–92 for addresses, telephone numbers and opening times of the attractions mentioned in the tours, including telephone numbers of tourist offices.

Hotels and Restaurants
See pages 160–79 for a list of recommended hotels and restaurants en route for each tour.

Business Hours
Banks: there are many bureaux de change in Ireland, but banks are the best place to change money. Opening hours vary, but most are open 10am–4pm, with some extended hours, including limited Sat morning opening, in Northern Ireland. Foreign exchange counters in the main airports give good rates: Belfast International, 5am–8pm, may vary; Dublin, open Business Hours, Foreign exchange at Dublin Airport: daily; hours vary according to bureau location: 5.30 or 6am–9pm, 10pm or midnight; Shannon, open daily 6am–10pm; Cork, open Mon–Fri 6.45am–8pm, Sat–Sun 9am–6.30pm. There is also a wide network of automatic cash points where you can use credit and bank cards.

Post offices: in the Republic, standard post office opening times are generally Mon–Fri 9–5.30; Sat 9–1. The General Post Office in O'Connell Street, Dublin, is open Mon–Sat, 8–8. Post boxes are green; Republic of Ireland stamps must be used.

In Northern Ireland, standard opening times are Mon–Fri 9–5.30, and Sat 9–12.30. Northern Ireland post office opening hours: Belfast City Post Office on Bridge Street is open Mon–Sat 9–5.30 (from 9.30am Tue), Sun 9–12, 1–5.

Throughout Northern Ireland sub post offices also close one other afternoon each week. Post boxes are red; British stamps must be used.

Credit Cards
Throughout Ireland American Express, Visa and MasterCard are generally accepted. Personal cheques can be cashed using a Eurocheque card. A few bed and breakfast establishments may expect to be paid in cash.

Currency
The currency of the Republic of Ireland is the euro, divided into 100 cents, with notes in denominations of 5, 10, 20, 50, 100, 200 and 500, and coins in denominations of 1, 2, 5, 10, 20 and 50 cents, plus 1 and 2 euros.

Northern Ireland uses the pound sterling, divided into 100 pence, with notes in denominations of 5, 10, 20, 50 and 100 and coins in denominations of 1, 2, 5, 10, 20 and 50 pence, plus £1 and £2. Large companies and businesses around the border will often accept either.

Customs Regulations
Standard EU customs regulations apply when travelling between the Republic or Northern Ireland and another EU country, and if crossing the border between the two. Travellers may import or export goods for their personal use, up to certain limits depending on whether the goods were bought in ordinary shops (tax paid) or duty-free shops.

Electricity
220 volts AC (50 cycles) is standard. Sockets for small appliances are the three-pin flat or two-pin round wall types.

Embassies and Consulates
Embassies in the Republic: Australia: Fitzwilton House, Wilton Terrace, Dublin 2 (tel: (01) 664 5300); Canada: 65 St Stephen's Green, Dublin 2 (tel: (01) 417 4100); UK: 29 Merrion Road, Dublin 4 (tel: (01) 205 3700); US: 42 Elgin Road, Dublin 4 (tel: (01) 668 8777).

Consular offices for Northern Ireland: Australia High Commission, Australia House, The Strand, London WC2B 4LA (tel: 020 7379 4334); Canada: Honorary Consul, Unit 3, Ormeau Business Park, 8 Cromac Avenue, Belfast BT7 2JA (tel: 028 9127 2060); New Zealand: Honorary Consul, Ballance 118A, Lisburn Road, Glenavy, Crumlin, BT29 4NY (tel: 028 9264 8098); US: US Consul General, Danesfort House, 223 Stranmillis Road, Belfast BT9 5GR (tel: 028 9038 6100).

Emergency Telephone Numbers

In both the Republic and Northern Ireland, dial 999 for police, fire or ambulance.

Entry Regulations

When planning your trip to Ireland, remember that the Republic of Ireland and Northern Ireland (which is part of the UK) may have different passport and visa requirements. For this reason, you should check before you leave your home country.

Health

There are no special health requirements or regulations for visitors to the Republic or Northern Ireland. It is best to take out medical insurance, though EU visitors are covered by a reciprocal agreement. British visitors should contact the post office for an EHIC (European Health Insurance Card) form.

Motoring

For information on all aspects of motoring in Ireland, including accidents, breakdowns, car hire and speed limits, see pages 158–59.

Public Holiday

(R) Republic only
(NI) Northern Ireland only
1 January – New Year's Day
17 March – St Patrick's Day
Good Friday & Easter Monday
1st Monday in May – May Day

Last Monday in May (NI)
1st Monday in June (R)
12–13 July – Orangemen's Day (NI)
1st Monday in August (R)
Last Monday in August (NI)
Last Monday in October (R)
25 December – Christmas Day
26 December – St Stephen's Day (Boxing Day)

Route Directions

Throughout the book the following abbreviations are used for roads:
M – motorways
Northern Ireland only:
A – main roads
B – local roads
Republic of Ireland only:
N – national primary/secondary roads
R – regional roads.

Telephones

To call a number, in Ireland, first dial the International access code: Australia 0011; Canada 011; New Zealand 00; UK (for the Republic only) 00. Then dial 353 for the Republic or 44 for Northern Ireland, and then the full number (omitting the first zero of the area code).

For international calls out of Ireland dial 00, then the country code: Australia 61; Canada 1; New Zealand 64; UK 44; US 1.

Traditional pub music session

Then dial the full number omitting the first zero.

Call boxes are mostly glass and metal. Phones using cards (bought at newsagents) are widely available.

Time

Both the Republic of Ireland and Northern Ireland follow GMT, or GMT plus 1 hour from late March to late October.

Tourist Offices

Republic of Ireland Tourist Board (Bord Failte): Suffolk Street, Dublin 2 (tel: (01) 605 7799).
Northern Ireland Tourist Board: St Anne's Court, 59 North Street, Belfast, BT1 1NB (tel: 028 9023 1221).
Tourism Ireland now has joint tourist offices abroad, which include:
Australia: 5th Level, 36 Carrington Street, Sydney, NSW 2000 (tel: (02) 9299 6177).
Canada: 2 Bloor Street West, Suite 1501, Toronto, Ontario M4W 3E2 (tel: (1-800 223 6470)
UK: 103 Wigmore Street, London W1U 1QS (tel: 08000 397000).
US: 345 Park Avenue, New York, NY 10154 (tel: 800 223 6470).

MUNSTER

The province of Munster is made up of the counties of Waterford, Cork, Kerry, Limerick, Clare and Tipperary. Its fertile ever-changing landscapes form a microcosm of Ireland.

Soaring, surf-fringed cliffs rise above tiny coves and sandy beaches. Mountains, awash with colours of rhododendrons and the delicate hues of heather, are slashed by deep gaps and scenic passes. The Knockmealdown and Comeragh ranges guard east Munster, while to the west the peaks of Macgillycuddy's Reeks include Ireland's highest, 3,400-foot (1,036m) Carrauntoohill. The Slieve Mish range marches out to the tip of the Dingle Peninsula, and the Galtees, Slieve Felims, and Silvermines straggle across the interior.

A variety of fish fill Munster's rivers: the mighty Shannon that draws a watery line along the boundaries of counties Kerry, Clare, Limerick and Tipperary; the Lee that rises in the hills of Gougane Barra and flows eastward to split into two forks that make an island of Cork city's centre; the tidal Blackwater whose scenic beauty has earned it the title of the 'Rhine of Ireland'; and the Suir, Slaney and Nire whose waters trace their way across eastern Munster.

Fertile fields are ringed by stone walls and verdant woodlands. Small fishing villages along the coast and prosperous inland market towns dot the landscape. Three of Ireland's largest industrial cities and most important ports – Waterford, Cork and Limerick – ring the coastline, while inland lies the great Golden Plain of Tipperary.

The beautiful Italian Gardens on Garinish Island benefit from the warming effects of the Gulf Stream (Tour 6)

Ancient ringforts, dolmens and cairns predate recorded history, while massive castles, monasteries and round towers speak of Christians, Vikings and Normans. The stone promontory fort of Dunbeg stands guard on the Dingle Peninsula, while adjacent fields contain the still-intact beehive huts of early Christians. The lofty Rock of Cashel is a reminder both of the days of Celtic kings of Munster and of the coming of Christianity.

The breathtaking scenery and the juxtaposition of history with progress leave the visitor with an almost overwhelming sense of the enduring nature of the region. There is a feeling that time has not stood still in this ancient land, but is marching on into eternity, its past a solid foundation for the future.

Tour 1

The strange barren landscape of the Burren is the most evocative sight of this region, though the towering grandeur of the Cliffs of Moher forms another unforgettable vista. For history lovers, Clare is a county of castles. Ennis, which readily claims the affection of the visitor, is the base for the tour.

Tour 2

From the Viking city of Limerick, this tour takes you west along the banks of the Shannon estuary, tracing the footsteps of the mighty Desmond clan who left massive castles in their wake. The route turns south, where history merges with culture in northern County Kerry and continues east and north for medieval ruins in Newcastle West and the picturesque beauty of Adare.

Tour 3

Turning east from Limerick city, it is not such a long way to Tipperary town, in the heart of that county's Golden Vale. Further east is the great Rock of Cashel, with its impressive ruins and folk village, then on to Thurles, Roscrea and Nenagh.

Dunguaire Castle looks out over Kinvarra Bay (Tour 1)

Tour 4

Tralee is the gateway to a tour of the antiquities of the Dingle Peninsula, through tiny seaside villages and over the breathtaking Connor Pass to Dingle town. Prehistoric forts, beehive huts and a drystone oratory that has stood watertight for over 1,000 years are only a few of the relics of this magical place.

Tour 5

The 107-mile (172km) Ring of Kerry takes top billing on this tour as you travel from one scenic wonder to the next. Mountains, lakes, sandy beaches and offshore islands form an unforgettable panorama, and Killarney town has its own fair share of splendid lakes, antiquities and legends.

Tour 6

From Kenmare, this tour takes you south to Glengarriff and the semitropical Italianate gardens on Garinish Island. It continues along the wild seascapes and mountain passes of the Beara Peninsula.

Tour 7

This tour takes you to Blarney to kiss the famous stone and northwest through historic towns before turning east then south for Cahir's Norman castle, the spectacular drive across The Vee, Lismore's fairy–tale castle perched above the Blackwater river, and Youghal's harbour, haunted by Sir Walter Raleigh.

Tour 8

Turning south then west from Cork, the splendours of West Cork unfold along this tour. Delightful little coves and sandy beaches are backed by wooded hills. A turn inland takes you through a mountain to remote Gougane Barra.

Tour 9

After exploring historic Bantry, with its great house and attractive harbour, the route takes you to picturesque Skibbereen, with a side trip to tiny Baltimore, a village which has seen more than its fair share of violence, and circles the unspoiled peninsula that stretches as far as Mizen Head, the southernmost mainland point of Ireland.

Tour 10

Waterford is the starting point for a journey along dramatic coastal cliffs and coves, past picturesque castles, panoramic mountain views, and lush farmland. The Vee opens up unforgettable views of heather-covered mountains and bogs and Tipperary's fertile landscape.

Clare

The pleasant town of Ennis, the capital of County Clare, winds around low hills astride the River Fergus. It was at the forefront of the struggle for emancipation, and has strong associations with Daniel O'Connell and Eamon de Valera. The Riches of Clare Exhibit in the Clare Museum has enthralling displays on all aspects of Clare life.

2/3 DAYS • 159 MILES • 256KM

ITINERARY

▶ *Take the N85 for Lahinch. After 9 miles (14km) turn left at Inagh on to the R460 for Milltown Malbay. After another 9 miles (14km) turn right on to the R474 for Milltown Malbay.*

❶ Milltown Malbay, Co Clare

The coastline of County Clare is better endowed with cliffs and rocky foreshore than with beaches, but there is good bathing at White (or Silver) Strand. Close by is Spanish Point, which owes its name to the unhappy fate of shipwrecked sailors from the Spanish Armada, executed by Sir Turlough O'Brien in 1588.

Milltown Malbay feels like a seaside resort, even though it is a little inland. It is an important centre for traditional music.

▶ *Take the N67 to Lahinch.*

❷ Lahinch, Co Clare

The busiest resort in Clare, Lahinch earns its reputation from its splendid beach, good for bathing and popular for surfing. The name Lahinch comes from the Irish name for peninsula, as it has water on three sides. Its name today is perhaps most often associated with the championship golf course.

Across the bay lies Liscannor, birthplace of John Phillip Holland, the man who developed the submarine into a working naval vessel in 1900. In appreciation of his achievement, the US Navy erected a commemorative stone at the small fishing harbour.

▶ *Take the R478 for 6 miles (10km) to the Cliffs of Moher.*

❸ Cliffs of Moher, Co Clare

These awe-inspiring bastions of rock rise sheer from the sea to a height of nearly 670 feet (200m) and run relentlessly for 5 miles (8km). The great Irish naturalist Robert Lloyd Praeger, writing in the 1940s, suggested: 'If you want to feel

The precipitous Cliffs of Moher, home to flocks of sea birds

very small, go out in one of the canvas curraghs on a day when a ground swell is coming in from the ocean, and get your boatman to row you along the base of those gigantic rock-walls. The rollers and their reflections from the cliffs produce a troubled sea on which your boat dances like a live thing, like a tiny cork, and the vast dark precipice above, vertical and in places overhanging, seems to soar up to the troubled sky. It is a wonderful experience.'

Generations of visitors have been impressed by the monumental quality of these cliffs. In 1835 Sir Cornelius O'Brien MP built O'Brien's Tower as an observation point on the highest point of the cliffs and overlooking a rockstack called Breanan Mor.

After restoration, the tower reopened in 2007 to coincide with the opening of the New Visitor Experience. This exciting centre has been tunnelled into the ground so as not to mar the view, and the vast cavern includes themed areas relating to the cliffs, with interactive exhibits and such virtual experiences as an aerial trip over Clare and Atlantic Edge, which simulates a step onto the cliff face.

i *New Visitor Experience (seasonal)*

RECOMMENDED WALKS

The best way to appreciate the full grandeur of the Cliffs of Moher is on foot. A walking guide for the path starting at O'Brien's Tower is available from the visitor centre. The Burren Way stretches for 20 miles (32km) along the 'green roads' of this magical limestone landscape, passing many ruined churches and stone forts and monuments along the way. The Mid Clare Way is a 60-mile (100km) route from Quin that encircles Ennis and traverses some beautiful and varied landscape.

SPECIAL TO...

There are varying accounts of just how many dolphins inhabit the Shannon Estuary and waters off Co Clare – some say 50, some say 100 – but whatever their number, they have become a major attraction. Enquire locally about dolphin-watching cruises.

▶ *Continue on the **R478**, turning left to bypass Lisdoonvarna, on the coastal route, **R477**, by Black Head to Ballyvaughan, 25 miles (40km).*

---

4 **Ballyvaughan,** Co Clare
Ballyvaughan is an attractive village, focused on a large harbour used for a small fishing fleet, for sailing and for boat trips to the islands. Close to the village is a cluster of holiday homes in traditional style, known as 'Rent an Irish Cottage', which is a popular feature of this area. As a

---

FOR CHILDREN

The Burren is widely known for its potholes and caves and Aillwee Cave, south of Ballyvaghan, is perfect for a memorable family visit. Guided tours are informative and often amusing, and passages are safe and lit throughout. Another cave worth visiting is Doolin Cave, near Lisdoonvarna, which opened in 2006 and contains the longest stalactite in the northern hemisphere.

---

centre for contemporary and traditional craftspeople, the village is a good place to look for quality souvenirs.

▶ *Take the **N67** up Corkscrew Hill for 10 miles (16km) to Lisdoonvarna.*

5 **Lisdoonvarna,** Co Clare
Lisdoonvarna has long been synonymous with the art of

SCENIC ROUTES

The descent to Ballyvaughan, down Corkscrew Hill, provides a wonderful combination of the extraordinary Burren rock formations with the little village of Ballyvaughan, its whitewashed cottages and harbour and the wide expanse of Galway Bay beyond. Kinvarra and Finavarra Head are to the right, Gleninagh Mountain and Black Head to the left.

Perfumery at Caron. In a lovely remote location, it also features visual presentations in its floral centre and herb garden.

FOR HISTORY BUFFS

In 2002, to mark the 1,000th anniversary of the inauguration of Brian Boru as High King of Ireland, a special heritage trail, The Footsteps of Brian Boru, was launched. It highlights 31 important sites associated with the monarch who routed the Vikings and led a prosperous and cultured society, as well as his descendants, the O'Brien clan. Many of those sites are within the area of this tour, but the Brian Boru Visitor Centre, is a little to the east at Killaloe. An excellent colour brochure, available from tourist information centres, gives full details, plus lots of fascinating historical information.

▶ *Take the Corofin road, R476, for 4 miles (6km), then turn left on to the R480 for Ballyvaughan. Turn right and follow the N67 to Kinvarra.*

The wild and treeless Burren landscape is eerily beautiful

'matchmaking', and festivals are held to persuade traditionally reluctant bachelor farmers to the altar. The town has a great reputation for fun and good company, which is at its height in September when the harvest is gathered in. It also has Ireland's only active spa. The Spa Wells Health Centre has a Pump House and a variety of health treatments.

▶ *Take the R476 for 5 miles (8km) to Kilfenora.*

6 Kilfenora and the Burren, Co Clare

You will already have passed through part of the Burren, but here at Kilfenora, the Burren Centre puts this unique landscape and its plants into context. May is the best time to see the wild rock garden of flowers that covers the Burren, crowding together in crevices or covering the limestone outcrops in profusion. It is not only the abundance of the plants that makes the Burren so special, as bright blue gentians blossom in the shallow turf and mountain avens, clear white with golden centres, tumble across the limestone terraces. The Burren also harbours a profusion of rare varieties. Species normally found only in the Arctic or at high altitude, such as the alpine saxifrage, appear in the Burren, but so does the denseflowered orchid, which is a Mediterranean plant. Twenty-two varieties of orchid grow here, favouring a unique ecosystem created by a combination of factors, including fast drainage into the limestone, mild, moist weather conditions, the absence of grasses and the control of hazel scrub by goats. Drawing on this natural, fragrant bounty is the Burren

7 Kinvarra, Co Galway

Kinvarra is a fishing village in Galway Bay, and the hill above gives splendid views of these much-loved Irish waters. Dunguaire Castle – the 7th-century seat of the King of Connacht, Guaire Aidhneach, a man of celebrated hospitality – stands on a promontory in Kinvarra Bay. The 17th-century tower house and bawn that now stands here was built by his descendants, the O'Heynes.

Southeast of Kinvarra, near Gort, is Thoor Ballylee, where Yeats lived, a place of great symbolic importance to the poet. You can climb the 'narrow winding stair', and see an audiovisual presentation on Yeats's life and times. Yeats often visited Coole Park, home of Lady Gregory, co-founder of

The house-painter's art – an appropriate mural for this shop in Kinvarra

the Abbey Theatre in Dublin. The house, where many of the figures involved in the literary renaissance met, was demolished in 1941, but the beautiful woods that appear in much of Yeats' work are in state care and the former stables contain an interpretative centre and tearoom.

▶ *Turn right for Gort. After 4 miles (6km) bear left, and go through Tirneevin to Gort. Take the N18 for Ennis and after 6 miles (10km) follow the R462 for Tulla. Half a mile (1km) further on, turn right on to the R532 for Ennis, then after 2 miles (3km) turn left for Quin.*

8 Quin, Co Clare
A Franciscan friary, of which altars and tombs, a graceful tower and cloister remain, was built by the MacNamaras in the 15th century, on the site of a 13th-century castle. It also incorporates the buildings of a large Anglo-Norman castle. Close by, Knappogue Castle is

typical of hundreds of medieval castles that are scattered throughout Clare, many of them the preserve of the MacNamara family. The present castle has Georgian and Regency extensions. Set in pretty gardens within its well-planted demesne, it combines the atmosphere of sturdy stronghold and comfortable home.

Craggaunowen is close to Quin, too. An enterprising historical project has been built up around Craggaunowen Castle, a restored 16th-century tower house with replicas of furniture and tools of the period. The project lifts the lid off many of the skills of the past, including the construction of wattle-and-daub buildings, and weaving and cooking techniques. There is a reconstruction of a *crannóg*, or defensive lake dwelling, used by the Celts in the 6th and 7th century. Another replica is that of the boat St Brendan the Navigator is said to have used for his legendary transatlantic voyage in the 6th century. In 1977 Tim Severin sailed the Atlantic in this replica, proving that St Brendan could have

discovered America centuries before Columbus's landfall.

▶ *Take the Limerick, road R469, turning right after 4 miles (6km) on to the R462. After 6 miles (10km) turn right on to the N18 for Bunratty and Ennis.*

SPECIAL TO...

Medieval banquets have become a very popular ingredient of many holidays in the Shannon region. In the atmospheric surroundings of Bunratty, Knappogue or Dunguaire, medieval feasts or banquets are served with pageantry, costume, music and rhyme, with the emphasis on plenty of fun.
Bunratty Folk Park has a Traditional Irish Night in the Corn Barn.

9 Bunratty, Co Clare
One of Ireland's most popular tourist destinations, Bunratty's completely restored Norman-Irish keep sits four-square by the main road, its stout defences, including three

'murder holes' over the main door, defying entry. In fact, this is the most inviting of castles and, furnished with Lord Gort's magnificent medieval collection, it gives a colourful insight into the life of a 15th-century keep. In the grounds is Bunratty Folk Park, which re-creates 19th-century life, both in the small cottages and houses of the region, and in a village street. The scenes are enlivened with traditional crafts in action – bread-making, candle-making, thatching, milling and basketweaving. Ballycasey Craft Workshops for contemporary craftsmen and women are close by.

Towards Limerick is Cratloe, where a mighty oak forest once supplied the timbers for Westminster Hall in London and the Grianan in Ulster. Cratloe Woods House, a good example of the Irish longhouse dating from the 17th century, is the family home of descendants of the O'Briens.

▶ Take the **N18** for 14 miles (23km) back to Ennis.

Bunratty Castle combines history with entertainment

BACK TO NATURE

Ireland's rarest and shyest wild animal, the beautiful pine marten, is now plentiful only in County Clare, its numbers drastically reduced in the last century because of demand for its coat. A night hunter, it can occasionally be seen in the headlights of cars. A favoured haunt is Dromore Wood, 5 miles (8km) north of Ennis, a habitat of semi-natural woodland, and wetland that includes lake and marsh.

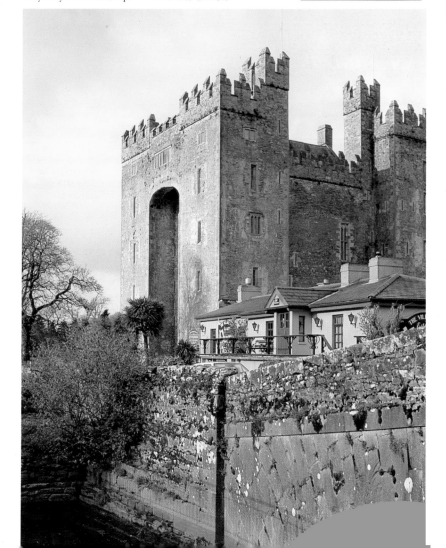

River Shannon
Rambles

2 DAYS • 112 MILES ▲ 179KM   The Celts were the first to recognise Limerick's strategic position when they built a fort at the lowest ford of the River Shannon. In the 18th century the city developed its present form, but then suffered a period of decline in the 20th century. Renovation has now restored much of its earlier style, notably at The Georgian House on Pery Square. King John's Castle and its excellent visitor centre tops the attractions. St Mary's Cathedral, founded in the late 12th century by the King of Munster, is filled with antiquities.

(See also Tour 3.)

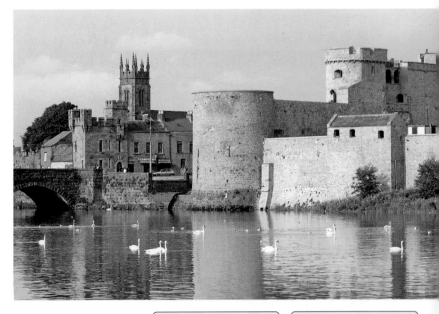

In military use from 1200 to 1922, King John's Castle gives a magnificent insight into Limerick's eventful history

ℹ️ *Arthur's Quay, Limerick*

▶ *Take the **N69** west for 17 miles (27km) to Askeaton.*

FOR HISTORY BUFFS

Limerick's history comes to life in King John's Castle, aided by costumed characters. Built in the 13th century as an instrument of royal authority and a military stronghold, it has been converted into an international visitors' centre. The centre has an audiovisual overview of Limerick's long history, and historical exhibits and archaeological remains covering some 800 years. The excavation of archaeological treasures beneath the castle floor has provided added fascination since the dig began in 1990.

BACK TO NATURE

About 11 miles (18km) west of Limerick on the N69, turn south for 2 miles (3km) on a signposted, unclassified road to reach Currahchase Forest Park. This was the estate of poet Aubrey de Vere (1814-1922). The grounds contain fine landscaped gardens and an arboretum with exotic plants, as well as the tombstone that marks his pet cemetery. A nature trail leads through the estate, one of the finest in Ireland, past native Irish trees and plants, and the picnic area is an ideal spot for lunching in the open.

❶ Askeaton, Co Limerick
A Middle Ages stronghold of the Desmond clan, Askeaton sits on the River Deel. Alive with echoes of the past, ruined Desmond Castle inhabits a rocky islet in the river, right in the village centre. Its last defending Earl of Desmond fled to the Kerry Hills when the castle and the town fell to British troops in 1580. The impressive Great Banqueting Hall measures 90 feet by 30 feet (28m by 9m) and at the south end there is a small chapel.

On the east bank of the river, cloisters enclosed by black marble pointed arches and supported by cylindrical columns are all that is left of a 15th-century Franciscan friary.

At Kilcoran, to the east, the Celtic Theme Park and Gardens features re-created historic buildings.

❸ Glin, Co Limerick
The Fitzgeralds, powerful Earls of Desmond, dominated this village, and ruins of their Castle of Glin still overlook the Shannon estuary. It was fiercely defended in 1600 but fell to the English forces after two days of intense fighting.

Glin Castle is a mixture of 18th-century and Victorian Gothic architecture

The Desmond holdings here have passed without interruption for more than seven centuries to the present Knight of Glin, whose home, Glin Castle (not to be confused with the Castle of Glin), contains a fine collection of Irish paintings, furniture and decorative arts. The Castle (now a hotel), pleasure grounds and walled garden are open to the public.

About 1 mile (1.5km) west of the village, look for the Gothic-style Glin Castle Gate Lodge, a pleasant tea-room and craft shop, where cast-offs from the castle are often scattered among craft items.

The castellated building overlooking Glin pier is Hamilton's Tower, a 19th-century folly built by one Dr Hamilton to give employment to Irish famine victims.

▷ *Continue west on the **N69** for about 4 miles (6km) to Tarbert.*

❹ Tarbert, Co Kerry
A car ferry across the Shannon to Killimer in County Clare departs from the wooded headland that juts into the river's estuary at this quiet little village, a real timesaver for travellers who want to avoid Limerick traffic.

▷ *Take the unclassified coastal road to Ballylongford, then the **R551** to Ballybunion.*

▷ *Follow the **N69** to Foynes.*

❷ Foynes, Co Limerick
The most scenic portion of the coastal drive along the Shannon begins in this small seaport, though these days, its waters play host to luxury yachts as well as commercial ships. The first steamship to depart its docks was a blockade runner providing uniforms made in Limerick for Confederate forces during the American Civil War. During the late 1930s and 1940s, Foynes was the home port for a transatlantic sea plane service, and the renowned Flying Boat Museum presents an audio-visual show along with mementoes of those pioneering days in the world of air travel.

▷ *Continue west on the **N69** for another 8 miles (13km) to Glin.*

5 **Ballybunion,** Co Kerry
The ruins of Ballybunion Castle stand on Castle Green in this popular Atlantic coast resort town. It is the fine beach, however, that draws visitors, as well as the network of souterrains (subterranean passages) near Castle Green, and invigorating clifftop walks.

Just north of the town are the remains of a promontory fort overlooking Doon Cove. The 18-hole golf course is an attraction for amateurs and professionals alike.

▶ *Continue southeast via the R553 to Listowel.*

Castle ruins point skyward above Ballybunion's beach

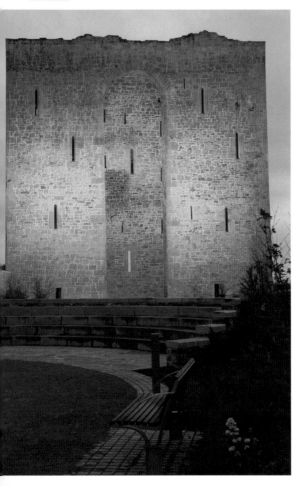

The town of Listowel grew up around its medieval castle

▶ *Take the **R555** southeast to Abbeyfeale.*

7 Abbeyfeale, Co Limerick
In the foothills of the Mullaghareirk Mountains, this little market town grew from the Cistercian abbey founded here in 1188. The only traces of the abbey have since been incorporated into the Catholic church building. The town square has a statue of Father William Casey, parish priest and leader of the tenant farmers' fight against landlordism in the mid- and late 1800s.

▶ *Take the **N21** northeast to Newcastle West.*

8 Newcastle West, Co Limerick
Adjacent to the town square of this bustling market town are the ruins of a Knights Templar castle dating from 1184. Burned in 1642, its two 15th-century halls, peel tower, keep, bastion and curtain wall have survived. While the Great Hall is largely in ruins, the Desmond Banqueting Hall is almost perfectly preserved, complete right down to a vaulted basement, and now serves as a cultural centre for recitals, concerts, lectures and exhibitions.

You can see Irish Dresden porcelain being made at the factory and showroom in Dromcolliher, some 9 miles

6 Listowel, Co Kerry
The castle in this bustling market town was the last to hold out against Elizabethan forces in the Desmond rebellion. When it finally fell in 1600, the entire garrison was put to the sword. Two fine Gothic-style churches dominate the town square, and the old Protestant church has been converted into an information centre. Take a look at a wonderful bit of plaster fantasy, the 'Maid of Erin' figure on the Central Bar that sits on one corner of the square. Local craftsman Pat McAuliffe and his son created this monument and other works around the town and in Abbeyfeale.

It was from a window of the Listowel Arms Hotel on the square that Charles Stewart Parnell, campaigner for Home Rule, made one of his last public appearances just three weeks before his death in 1891. The Garden of Europe in the town's park was established in 1995 and its 12 areas represent the countries that formed the European Union at that time. It contains trees and shrubs from those nations, plus Ireland's only public holocaust memorial. Lord Kitchener was born at Gunsborough in 1850.

ℹ *St John's Church (seasonal)*

(15km) southeast of town via the R522.

▶ Follow the **N21** northeast for 8 miles (13km) to Rathkeale.

9 Rathkeale, Co Limerick
The poet Edmund Spenser and Sir Walter Raleigh first met in Rathkeale at Castle Matrix, built in 1440 and named after an ancient Celtic sanctuary that once occupied this site. The castle has furnishings authentic to its era and an outstanding library with many rare books. There is also a unique collection of documents about the 'Wild Geese', Irish chieftains and soldiers who fought with European armies in the 17th and 18th centuries.

▶ Continue northeast via the **N21** to Adare.

10 Adare, Co Limerick
With its neat thatched cottages and broad main street, Adare is

One of the delightful cottages that have made Adare one of Ireland's prettiest villages

likely to come closer to the romantic image of the 'quaint little Irish village' than any other in the country, although its appearance is decidedly English. Credit for its beauty must go to the third Earl of Dunraven, who had a passion for early Irish architecture and local improvements.

The ancestral home of the Dunravens, Adare Manor, stands at the northern edge of town and is now a luxury hotel. In the heart of the hotel's golf course are the ruins of a castle on the banks of the River Maigue, a Franciscan friary dating back to 1464 and the 15th-century Desmond family

chapel (check with the golf club before visiting).

In the village, remains of a 14th-century Augustinian friary sit near the fine 14-arch bridge across the River Maigue. The Adare Heritage Centre in Main Street has interesting displays on the area's unique history, including realistic models and an audiovisual show (in several languages). Guided tours leave from here in summer.

i Heritage Centre (seasonal)

▶ Take the **N21**, then exit on sliproad left to join the **N20** back to Limerick.

Ancient Castles
& Lake Odyssey

Limerick is a large and lively city with a long history of momentous events. (See also Tour 2). The Limerick Museum in St John's Square tells the story from the Stone Age onwards, and the famous Hunt Museum, in Rutland Street, holds more than 1,000 Irish antiquities and examples of medieval art.

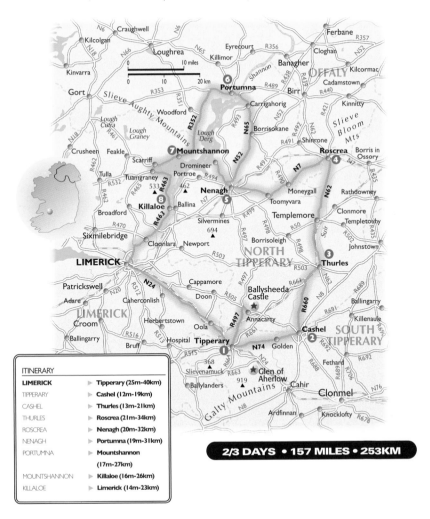

2/3 DAYS • 157 MILES • 253KM

i *Arthur's Quay, Limerick*

▶ *Take the N24 southeast for 25 miles (40km) to Tipperary.*

❶ Tipperary, Co Tipperary

In the heart of Ireland's fertile Golden Vale, Tipperary town is an important dairy farming centre. It figured prominently in the 19th-century Land League campaigns to legalise land ownership for Irish tenants, and today it is a thriving market town, and an excellent base for hill walking in the nearby Slievenamuck and Galty mountains. The major point of interest in town is St Michael's Church, Gothic in design and noteworthy for its fine lancet windows and west door.

About 8 miles (13km) north of town via the R497 and R505, the well-preserved circular keep of Ballysheeda Castle stands on a hillside 1 mile (1.5km) north of Annacarty village. South of Tipperary, via the R664, is the Glen of Aherlow, one of Ireland's most scenic places. From the car park there's a path leading to several viewpoints.

▶ *Follow the N74 to Cashel.*

❷ Cashel, Co Tipperary

Ecclesiastical ruins on the Rock of Cashel dominate the town of Cashel (see Tour 10), but also of interest are the Cashel Folk Village, and the ruins of the Dominican friary, which was rebuilt in 1480 after destruction by fire, both in Chapel Lane. Be sure to see the lovely 13th-century east window. The Bishop's Palace, set in enclosed grounds in Main Street, was built for Protestant archbishops

Bru Boru Heritage Centre is an imaginative presentation of Irish crafts and culture

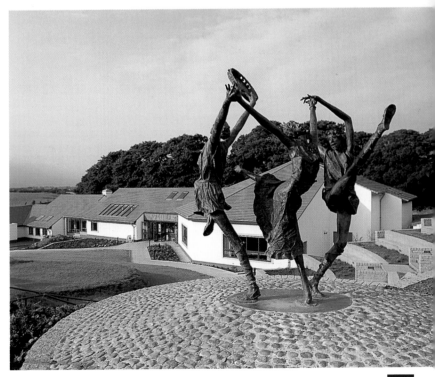

and is a splendid example of 18th-century architecture. It is now a hotel. Bru Boru, at the foot of the Rock, is a heritage and cultural centre which showcases Irish music and dance.

ⓘ *Heritage Centre, Main Street*

▶ *Take the **R660** north for 13 miles (21km) to Thurles.*

8 Thurles, Co Tipperary
It was in the Hayes Hotel in this old Anglo-Norman town that the Gaelic Athletic Association was founded in 1884. Bridge Castle, at the western end of the Suir river bridge, and Black Castle, near the town square, are remnants of Butler clan castles. In the 19th-century Catholic cathedral the lavish use of marble, especially in the altars, gives a special beauty to the interior.

St Mary's Famine Church is now home to a museum with rare items relating to the famine and a military collection.

Holycross Abbey, a 12th-century Cistercian centre, set on the east bank of the Suir, 4 miles (6km) southwest of Thurles, has been restored as the parish church.

FOR HISTORY BUFFS

Two rectangular keeps, remnants of the castles built by the powerful Butlers in Thurles, are reminders of the town's turbulent past. In the 10th century, the Irish and Norse fought fierce battles here, and when Strongbow's Anglo-Norman troops attacked in 1174, the Irish initially repelled them, but were unable to prevent them building a castle to control traffic on the River Suir.

▶ *Take the N62 north for 21 miles (34km) to Roscrea.*

4 Roscrea, Co Tipperary
One of Ireland's Heritage Towns and a good base for climbing and hill walking in the nearby Devil's Bit and Slieve Bloom mountains. Its most outstanding attraction is the Roscrea Heritage Centre in an annexe to Damer House, a town house dating from the early 18th century, set within the walls of an 11th-century Norman castle and narrowly saved from demolition in the mid-1970s. There are panoramic views from the top of the gate tower, and, inside, the magnificently carved staircase is stunning. The house is lavishly decorated and furnished and holds mementoes of life in the town through the ages. Available from the Heritage Centre is a booklet detailing a walking tour that incorporates the ruins of St Cronan's Church and Round Tower, and a High Cross, all of which date back to the 12th century.

At Monaincha, 2 miles

The bell tower of Thurles Catherdal stands 125 feet (38m) high

(3km) southwest of town, are the remains of a 12th-century church with 16th-century additions and an elegant High Cross from a former monastery.

▶ *Take the N7 southwest for 20 miles (32km) to Nenagh.*

5 Nenagh, Co Tipperary
Originally a Norman settlement, Nenagh served as a mid-19th-century garrison town, and finally evolved into a prosperous market town with many traditional shopfronts. One of the town's major features is the circular keep of Nenagh Castle, a mostly 1860 structure incorporating portions of a larger castle built in the early 1200s. The 100-foot-high (30m), 53-foot-wide (16m) keep, with walls up to 20 feet (6m) thick, formed part of the curtain wall of the earlier castle. Winding stairs set into the thickness of the wall lead to the roof. Nenagh's Heritage Centre is located near the castle in the old Governor's House and county gaol. There is a marvellous 'Lifestyles in Northwest Tipperary' exhibition, as well as visiting art and photographic exhibits. Nenagh Friary, in Abbey Street, was founded in around 1250 and features a 13th-century church.

Six miles (10km) northwest of Nenagh, via the R494, then the R495, Dromineer, on Lough Derg, is a lively centre for fishing, sailing and watersports.

ℹ️ *Heritage Centre (seasonal)*

SCENIC ROUTES

Six miles (10km) south of Nenagh, via the R500, look for the signposted turnoff for Step viewing point, near Silvermines village, at the foot of the Silvermines Mountains. The drive up to the viewing point is very scenic, and it culminates in panoramic views – the perfect place for a picnic.

towers at each corner and the lovely formal gardens.

About 7 miles (11km) south of Portumna via the N65 and the R493, the village of Terryglass, on the shores of Lough Derg, has a lovely old stone church and ruins of a 13th-century castle. There are boats for hire and facilities for lakeside picnics.

BACK TO NATURE

Portumna Forest Park is a marvellous 1,000-acre (405-hectare) wildlife sanctuary that counts red and fallow deer among its many inhabitants. There is an observation tower beside the lake, and several other viewing stands, a nature trail and a picnic area.

▶ *Go west on the R353, then on the R352 past Lough Derg to Mountshannon.*

FOR CHILDREN

At the little town of Mountshannon children can embark on an island adventure – hire a boat at the pier to visit the mysterious holy island of Iniscealtra.

▶ *Head northwards on the N52, then turn left on to the N65 and continue for 19 miles (31km) to reach Portumna.*

FOR CHILDREN

Lough Derg is a natural paradise for children. Its many islands and tiny inlets invite exploration, fishing is excellent, and watersports and boating are favourite pastimes for locals and visitors alike. The best places for access and facilities on the lough are Dromineer, Portumna, Mountshannon and Killaloe.

The massive keep of Nenagh Castle is mostly Victorian

6 **Portumna,** Co Galway

This small lakeside town at the northern end of Lough Derg is a popular centre for fishing the lake and the River Shannon, as well as a major base for cruisers. The impressive ruins of Portumna Castle stand in its demesne, laid out as an attractive forest park, on the edge of town. Built in 1609 by the Earl of Clanricarde, it was destroyed by fire in 1826, but has been restored and is open to the public. Of special interest are the Renaissance doorway with gunholes on one side, the Jacobean gables, the square

7 **Mountshannon,** Co Clare

The River Shannon, in the course of its 230-mile (370km) rambles, forms several lakes, of which Lough Derg is the largest, stretching some 25 miles (40km) in length and sprinkled with numerous islands and islets. The drive down its western shore is lovely.

At the little town of Mountshannon, hire a boat at the pier to visit the Holy Island of Iniscealtra and the remains of an early Christian settlement, including a round tower and no less than five churches. Brian Boru reputedly built one of the churches, while others date back to the 7th century, and since the late 17th century, the island has been a place of pilgrimage.

crucifix possibly formed by a Viking convert. There are traces of a ringfort on the southeastern side of Crag or Cragliath hill.

Killaloe has been declared a heritage town, and its Brian Boru Heritage Centre tells a fascinating story.

The Shannon remains an important feature of the town, with fishing and watersports.

i *Killaloe Heritage Centre, The Bridge (seasonal)*

▶ *Follow the* R463 *southwest to return to Limerick.*

▶ *Continue southwest on the R352 to Tuamgraney, then turn southeast on to the R463 to reach Killaloe.*

8 Killaloe, Co Clare

This charming little village stands at a fording point of the River Shannon at the lower end of Lough Derg. The churchyard of St Anne's is said to be the ancient site of Kincora, the palace of Irish King Brian Boru and his O'Brien descendants. In the church grounds, St Molua's Oratory, estimated to be 1,000 to 1,200 years old, reposes in safety after being rescued when its Friar's Island home was threatened by submersion in a hydroelectric development. The 12th-century Church of Ireland St Flannan's Cathedral is noteworthy for its ornately carved Irish Romanesque doorway. It has an Ogham (ancient Celtic writing) stone that also has runic writings and a crude

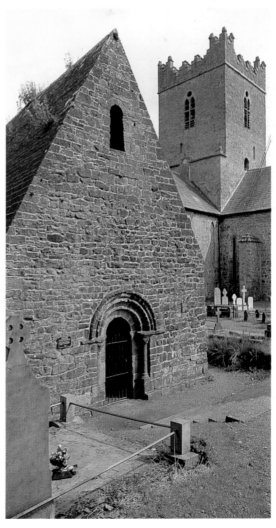

Killaloe village has an important ecclesiastical heritage

Beehive Huts &
Coastal Splendours

Known for its Rose of Tralee Festival in late August, Tralee is an important business centre and the principal gateway for the Dingle. Its many attractions include historic streets, fine churches, the County Kerry Museum (including a 'time travel experience'), and the National Folk Theatre, Siamsa Tíre.

2/3 DAYS • 97 MILES • 156KM

Kerry Head
Ballyduff
Causeway   Listowel   Athea
Ballyheige
Ballyheige Bay
Corca Dhuibhne
(Dingle Peninsula)
Rough Point
Ardfert   Abbeydorney   Abbeyfeale
357
Brandon Bay
Tralee Bay
Gallarus Oratory ⑪   950   Castlegregory ②   **TRALEE**
Cnoc Bréanainn ★
Baile an Fheirtéaraigh ⑩
CONNOR PASS   R560   ①   Castleisland
Camp   852   N86
Dun Chaoin (Dunquin) ⑨   ⑤ ④   Baurtregaun   N70
Anascaul ⑫   N86   Castlemaine   Scartaglin
An Bhlascaod Mhór (Great Blasket)   Ceann Trá (Ventry)   An Daingean (Dingle)   R561   Inch ⑬   Milltown   ⑭ R561   KERRY
Ceann Sléibhe (Slea Head)   Killorglin
Dunbeg & Fán (Fahan) ⑧   ⑥⑦   B a y   Glenbeigh   Beaufort   Killarney   Rathmore
D i n g l e   Doulus Head   Macgillycuddy's Reeks   Lough Leane
Valencia Island   Cahersiveen   I v e r a g h   P e n i n s u l a

[i] *Ashe Memorial Hall, Denny Street, Tralee*

FOR CHILDREN

A great attraction for children is the narrow-gauge Tralee/Blennerville railway that runs along part of the long-abandoned Tralee/Dingle line on a 5-mile (8km) round-trip.
At Blennerville is a restored windmill, while at the Tralee end, adjacent to the platform, is the Aqua Dome, a palace of water-based fun.

▶ *Take the N86 west, with the Slieve Mish mountains on your left, to Camp.*

FOR HISTORY BUFFS

Five-and-a-half miles (9km) northwest of Tralee via the Ballyheige road (R551) is imposing Ardfert Cathedral, which dates from the 13th century. A niche in the building holds the 13th- or 14th-century effigy of a bishop unearthed here in 1830, and there is an ogham stone in the graveyard. The tiny village of Fenit, 8 miles (13km) west of Tralee via the R558, is thought to be the birthplace of St Brendan the Navigator (AD484–577), who, according to some, may have reached the shores of America long before Christopher Columbus.

❶ Camp, Co Kerry

Turn off the main road west to reach Ashe's pub, the epitome of an old-time Irish pub.

Near the village, Cathair Chonroi, a prehistoric dun, is one of the oldest places named in Irish literature. The climb to see it is rewarded with remains of the protecting wall and some great views.

▶ *Go back for a ½ mile (1km) before turning left on to the R560. Soon turn right to Castlegregory.*

❷ Castlegregory, Co Kerry

There are fine beaches at Castlegregory, which sits at the

The dramatically beautiful Slieve Mish Mountains

bird sanctuary, which attracts such exotic species as the Bewick's swan from Siberia.

▶ *Return to the R560, and turn right signposted 'Dingle, Connor Pass'.*

8 Connor Pass, Co Kerry
Climbing between the Brandon and central Dingle groups of mountains, this drive passes through some of Ireland's most spectacular scenery. On a fine day, there are vast panoramas of mountains, sea, lakes and valleys – on a not-so-fine day, mist and clouds can turn the narrow, winding road into a real driving challenge.

Just past the village of Stradbally, you cross the deep Glennahoo Valley and begin the climb to the 1,500-foot (460m) summit of the Connor Pass, with spectacular views of valleys strewn with boulders and, about a mile from the summit, tiny Pedlar's Lake. The road upwards winds along the base of great cliffs. From

the lay-by at the summit, there is a fine view of Dingle Bay and Dingle town to the south, with several small lakes in the deep valley to the left; the north aspect takes in the wide sweeping bays of Brandon and Tralee.

▶ *Continue southwest for 5 miles (8km), descending to An Daingean (Dingle).*

The drive across the Connor Pass, in either direction, has some of the most magnificent mountain views in Ireland

neck of a spit of land dividing Tralee and Brandon bays, with more along the drive from Camp. Birdwatchers will want to turn left just before reaching the town to visit Lough Gill

4 An Daingean
(Dingle), Co Kerry

County Kerry's chief port in the old days of Spanish trading, and a walled town in the Elizabethan era, Dingle town today is a busy little market, fishing and tourism centre with a boat-building industry right on the harbour. Dingle is in the heart of a Gaeltacht district in which Irish is the everyday language, but, of course, everyone can speak English too.

Dingle is a centre for specialised tours, including riding, cycling and archaeological ones. The town itself is compact, with tiny streets that climb upward from the seafront with several excellent shops, and there are boat rides out into the bay to see Dingle's resident dolphin (see For Children).

On the western edge of town, the Ceardlann na Coille craft village is a cluster of small cottages housing shops and workshops that sell handcrafted leather goods, Uilleann pipes, knitted goods, and the work of weavers and a cabinetmaker.

One of the town's most impressive collections of Irish-interest publications and records can be found in the front shop section of An Café Liteartha in Dykegate Lane. For traditional music and song that stems from a long-time family tradition, look for the red-and-white pub on Bridge Street with the Irish name UaFlaibeartaig, which translates to O'Flaherty's. It is a warm, informal setting, as traditional as the music itself, its walls sporting the sort of haphazard collection of pictures, posters and other assorted items that have accumulated over the years. Most pubs have music on summer nights; try Mac Cárthaigh's, An Droichead Beag and John Benny Moriarty's.

ℹ️ *The Quay*

▶ *Drive due west on the **R559** for 6 miles (10km) through Baile an Mhuilinn (Milltown) to Ceann Trá (Ventry).*

Wonderful unspoilt beaches are dotted around the Dingle peninsula

FOR CHILDREN

What could be more fun for the younger ones than a boat ride out into Dingle Bay to watch Dingle's friendly Dolphin, Fungie. He playfully follows the boats that leave from the town quays to ferry visitors out to his watery home, cavorting with scuba divers, and sometimes taking a flying leap over a small boat. On dry land, near the harbour, Dingle Oceanworld is a state-of-the-art aquarium that includes an undersea tunnel.

5 Ceann Trá (Ventry),
Co Kerry

According to legend – and a 15th-century manuscript now in the Bodleian Library at Oxford, in England – Ventry beach was the scene of a fierce battle when the King of the World, Daire Doon, attempted to invade and conquer Ireland. He and his vassal monarchs, however, suffered a massive defeat at the hands of the King of Ireland, Fionn MacCumhaill, and his loyal Fianna band.

The village nestles at the head of Ventry Harbour, with the slopes of Mount Eagle and Croagh Marhin as a backdrop and a 5km (3-mile) safe, sandy beach.

The black, beetle-like boats you will see upturned on the beach are currachs, the traditional canvas-covered vessels painted with tar that have been used by fishermen in these waters for centuries.

▶ *Continue southwest on the **R559** to Dunbeg.*

6 Dunbeg, Co Kerry

A relic of the Iron Age, Dunbeg Fort perches on a high promontory above Dingle Bay, its landward side surrounded by earthen trenches, and its 22-foot (7m) thick wall riddled with an elaborate souterrain (inner passage). Originally, there was an inner enclosure and a skilfully built inner house. But time has taken its toll, and some of its stones long ago tumbled into the sea. There's also a good visitors' centre with refreshments.

The beehive huts at Fahan are an evocative relic of prehistoric times

▶ *Turn north, still on the R559,*
for 2 miles (3km) heading for
Dún Chaoin (Dunquin).

SCENIC ROUTES

The drive along the R559 from Ventry to Slea Head has a wide diversity of scenic pleasures, at times hugging the sides of sheer cliffs high above Dingle Bay, and at others passing through stony fields reaching up sloping mountains.

▶ *Cross the R559 to the Fahan*
archaeological grouping.

7 Fahan, Co Kerry

In farmyards on the southern slopes of Mount Eagle, across from Dunbeg, unmortared beehive cells, or clochans (huts), are reminders of the prehistoric people who made their homes here and, quite possibly, built the promontory fort. It is a revelation to stoop down and enter one of these unique structures that are as watertight today as when they were built.

From more recent history is the Famine Cottage, former home of a family that departed for the New World during the famine.

▶ *Continue west on the R559*
for 2 miles (3km) to Ceann
Sléibhe (Slea Head).

8 Ceann Sléibhe (Slea Head), Co Kerry

At the very tip of the Dingle Peninsula are the high cliffs of

The jagged coastline at Slea Head, on the Dingle Peninsula

FOR HISTORY BUFFS

About 3 miles (5km) above the main road (R559) at Fahan, an ancient road is lined with stone huts and other remains of ages past. The nearby Celtic and Prehistoric Museum at Kilvicadownig has an incredible collection, including a complete fossil of a baby dinosaur skeleton and the world's largest fossil of a woolly mammoth's skull and tusks.

Slea Head – the westernmost mainland point in Europe. It is from here that you get the most sweeping view of sheltered coves below and Na Blascaoidí (the Blasket Islands) across the water, sometimes called 'the last parish before America'.

An Bhlascaod Mhór (the Great Blasket), the largest of these seven offshore islands, was for many years home to a hardy band of islanders who inhabited the one small village. In 1953, when a living wage could no longer be wrested from fishing, its population was moved to the mainland and given government grants for small farm holdings on the peninsula. A day trip to the islands from Dún Chaoin is an experience of tranquillity and scenic beauty unequalled anywhere else in Ireland.

9 Dún Chaoin (Dunquin), Co Kerry

Dunquin Pottery, on the road between Slea Head and Dunquin, is one of the many excellent potteries on the Dingle Peninsula. Its speciality is hand-thrown, ovenproof stoneware in shades of sand, browns and blues. Boats from Dunquin harbour make intermittent trips out to the Blasket Islands (see Slea Head) during summer months, and arrangements can often be made with individual boatmen when there is no sailing scheduled.

The Blasket Centre at Dunquin has an art gallery and audiovisual presentation, and highlights the extraordinary literary contribution of island writers Tomás O Crohan, Maurice O'Sullivan and Peig Sayers.

▶ *Follow the R559 north, then*
east to Baile an Fheirtéaraigh
(Ballyferriter).

10 Baile an Fheirtéaraigh (Ballyferriter), Co Kerry

The old schoolhouse is now home to Chorca Dhuibhne Museum, where well set out displays on the area include artefacts from the National Museum of Ireland.

The West Kerry Co-op office, just off Main Street, issues an excellent illustrated guidebook to the Dingle Peninsula, with great detail on its many antiquities. The Co-op began in 1968 in an effort to stem the out-going tide of young people who could not be supported by the large areas of untillable ground, and to perpetuate the unique culture and heritage of the Gaelic-speaking region. The Co-op imported a special deep-ploughing machine to break up the layer of iron ore that lay just beneath the surface and turn it into productive acres. Vast areas have been reclaimed, and the Co-op's remit has widened to include upgrading tourist facilities, and administering the Gaelic summer-school programme, in which students of all ages lodge with local families to learn their language.

Louis Mulcahy has a pottery studio on the outskirts of town, turning out many unique items with special glazes. Giant jugs and vases, unusual lamp bases and beautiful wall plaques supplement the more practical dinner services and cookware.

Two miles (3km) southwest of Ballyferriter, turn north on to an unclassified, signposted road to reach the site of the 16th-century fortress Dún an Oir, the so-called 'Golden Fort', built within an ancient promontory fort at Smerwick. The harbour here was the disembarkation point for an expedition of Spanish and Irish, along with their families and other retinue, who arrived in September of 1580 and constructed a fort to support the cause of the Catholic Irish against the Protestant English. It was bombarded from land and sea by English forces until eventually the fort capitulated, but over 600 were slaughtered – men, women and children – once they were disarmed. Poet Edmund Spenser (most famous

for *The Faerie Queene*), and possibly Sir Walter Raleigh were participants in the battle, which came to be known as the 'Massacre of Smerwick Harbour'. There is an excellent safe beach here.

▶ Follow the **R559** northeast for 2 miles (3km) and turn right at the signpost to Gallarus Oratory.

11 Gallarus Oratory, Co Kerry

This marvellous example of early Irish architecture is perhaps the most impressive of the peninsula's antiquities. Built in an inverted boat shape, it has remained completely watertight for more than 1,000 years, its unmortared stones perfectly fitted. At the crossroads just above Gallarus, turn left for Cill Maoilchéadair (Kilmalkedar), a 12th-century ruined church. In the church is the famous Alphabet Stone, a standing pillar carved with both Roman and Ogham characters. The east window of this medieval church is known locally as 'the Eye of the Needle' through which one must squeeze to achieve salvation.

▶ Proceed via an unclassified road to Baile na nÁith (Ballynana), turning southeast on to the **R559** to Baile an Mhuilinn (Milltown) and An Daingean (Dingle), then drive east for 10 miles (16km) on the **N86** to Anascaul.

FOR CHILDREN

The Freshwater Experience, 3 miles (5km) east of Dingle, is a 15-acre (6-hectare) park with lakes, a wildfowl reserve, nature trails and a reconstruction of an ancient Celtic lakeshore dwelling. This is also a working trout farm, with man-made ponds where you can catch your own dinner.

including kitchen middens. In summer, there is sometimes horse-back riding across the firm sand and through the gentle surf. From the cliffside drive, west of the village, views out over the Iveragh Peninsula across the water are nothing short of spectacular.

▶ *Continue east along the R561 for 12 miles (19km) to the little town of Castlemaine.*

14 Castlemaine, Co Kerry
In the town, immediately after turning left on to the Tralee road (N70), turn left again and look for the unclassified road signposted 'viewing park' less than a mile (1.5km) further on. There is a viewpoint about 2½ miles (4km) along this road, with splendid views of Castlemaine Harbour and beyond the Laune Valley to Killarney. A second viewpoint, a little further on, looks north to Tralee Bay, Tralee town, and the Stack's Mountains.

▶ *Reach the N70 and drive north to return to Tralee.*

12 Anascaul, Co Kerry
Look for the South Pole Inn as you enter the village. It is named in honour of the former proprietor, Tom Crean, a member of the Scott Antarctic expedition. Beautiful Anascaul Lake is well worth a short detour.

▶ *Heading south, then east on the R561, pass through Red Cliff to reach Inch.*

On Dingle's western extremity, Dunquin (and its sheep) looks out across Blasket Sound

13 Inch, Co Kerry
The wide, 4-mile (6km) long sandy beach on this spit at the head of Castlemaine Harbour is one of the best bathing beaches on the peninsula. The high dunes backing the beach have yielded archaeological evidence of ancient dwelling sites,

RECOMMENDED WALKS

On the Dingle road west of Anascaul, park the car for a short, easy walk north along a signposted road that leads to lovely Anascaul Lake set in a boulder-strewn hollow. Hardy walkers with two or three hours to spare can continue around the lake and strike out across the hills of the Beenoskee Mountains to Stradbally and Castlegregory.

SCENIC ROUTES

The drive from Anascaul to Castlemaine through Red Cliff and Aughils via the R561 follows a narrow, winding road with fantastic views south across Castlemaine Harbour. Stop to admire the view from one of the tiny lay-bys along the way – it is extremely dangerous to stop the car anywhere else and block the road.

SPECIAL TO...

The Rose of Tralee International Festival, which is in full swing for six days and nights in late August, is a fierce, but entertaining competition to see which of the beauties of Irish lineage from around the world best fits the time-honoured description from the famous song '...lovely and fair as the rose of the summer.' This gathering is much more fun than other beauty contests, which are usually taken very seriously indeed. The Rose of Tralee is a festival of light-hearted fun and frolic that includes parades, pipe bands, street entertainment and inter-festival singing competitions for the Folk Festival of Ireland. The whole thing culminates at the end of the week in the crowning of the Rose.

Killarney &
The Ring of Kerry

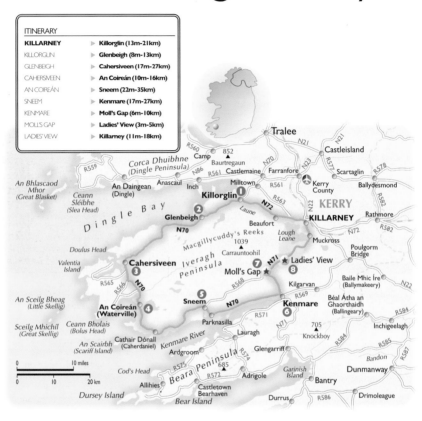

An abundance of natural **2 DAYS • 107 MILES • 172KM**
beauty has drawn visitors to Killarney and its lakes for centuries.
The scenic network of Lough Leane, Muckross Lake and Upper
Lake, in a broad valley west of Killarney, is the single most
powerful magnet for visitors. Killarney was
once a quiet little market town, but today its narrow,
congested streets can make for nerve-racking
driving – it is, however, a perfect
town to explore on foot.

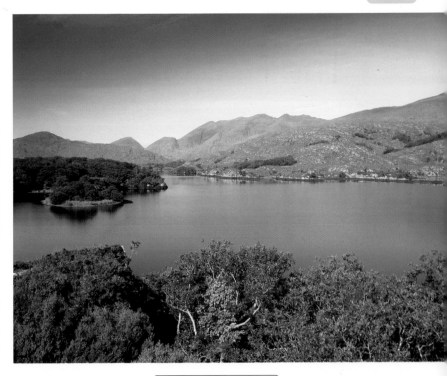

▶ *Take the **N72** northwest for 13 miles (21km) to Killorglin.*

RECOMMENDED WALKS

There's a good walk from Killarney to the ruins of Ross Castle (about 1½ miles (2.5km) on a long peninsula out on to the Lower Lake. Built in the 14th century, it was a prominent fortification during the Cromwellian wars in the 17th century. An exhilarating walk is that over Gap of Dunloe, for which you should allow a minimum of three hours.
The Kerry Way, a splendid walk of approximately 134 miles (214km), has been laid out for dedicated walkers. It begins at Killarney National Park and extends around the Iveragh Peninsula. The tourist office in Killarney has full details.

SPECIAL TO...

Wilma's Killorglin Farmhouse Cheese is made at Ardmoniel, just outside Killorglin, by the O'Connor family.
What started out as a hobby for John O'Connor's Dutch wife Wilma has grown into a business that sells cheese throughout Ireland and the UK. Visitors are welcome to visit the farm and see the cows being milked (at 8.30am and 2pm).

FOR HISTORY BUFFS

In ancient times, the Hill of Aghadoe just outside Killarney was the seat of the Celtic Archdruid. *The Annals of Innisfallen*, a chronicle of Irish history from the 11th to the 13th century, was recorded by dedicated monks on one of the Lower Lake's 30 islands.

Upper Killarney Lake, with the Macgillycuddy mountains in the distance

❶ Killorglin, Co Kerry
Perched on hills above the River Laune, Killorglin is an ideal starting point for the Ring of Kerry drive, a 112-mile (180km) scenic drive with an ever-changing panorama of mountains, lakes, cliffs, sandy beaches and craggy offshore islands. The route skirts the edges of the Iveragh Peninsula to Kenmare, then circles back over the mountains via Moll's Gap and Ladies' View to Killarney. Make this a leisurely drive with an overnight stop in order to savour all the magnificent scenery along the way.

In mid-August, this rather quiet little town is abuzz with the three-day Puck (Poc) Fair. It dates from 1613, and things get off to a rousing start when a tremendous male (or puck) goat is crowned King of the Fair. In the somewhat rowdy atmosphere, pubs stay open around the clock, and every sort of street entertainment goes on non-stop. This is also a traditional gathering place for the country's travelling people, who come to engage in some hard-driving horse trading. The origin of the Puck Fair is a matter of dispute: some say a goat bleated to alert a shepherd boy of approaching enemy forces and he, in turn, alerted the town about impending attack. The argument that the festival dates back to the worship of the Celtic god, Lug, gains credence when linked to the Gaelic word for August – Lughnasa, or festival of Lug.

▶ *Turn southwest on to the* **N70** *to Glenbeigh.*

2 **Glenbeigh,** Co Kerry
Look for the Kerry Bog Village Museum adjoining the Red Fox Inn on the main street. Bogs have played an important role in Ireland, and this is an authentic depiction of the lives of the peatbog communities.

▶ *Follow the* **N70** *southwest to reach Cahersiveen.*

3 **Cahersiveen (Cahirciveen),** Co Kerry
The drive along the southern shore of Dingle Bay from

Glenbeigh to this small town at the foot of the Bentee Mountain is one of island-dotted coastal scenery and fields studded with prehistoric stone ringfort ruins, with clear views of the Dingle Peninsula across the water. At Cahersiveen, Valentia Island comes into view. There is a ferry service, and it is accessible by car via a causeway at Portmagee. The island is noted for its mixture of superb cliffs, mountains, seascapes and vividly coloured subtropical flowers.

Brooding mountains – and the weather – overwhelm the pretty village of Waterville

One mile (1.5km) northeast of Cahersiveen, on the N70, Carhan House was the birthplace of Daniel O'Connell (1775); Cahersiveen's Heritage Centre includes displays on Ireland's beloved 'Liberator'.

BACK TO NATURE

If the seas are calm and you are a birdwatcher, join one of the cruises that take you out to the rocky islands that make up the Skelligs. Landings are limited because of erosion and because this is a bird sanctuary. The smaller of the two, An Sceilg Bheag (Little Skellig), is a major breeding ground for gannets. More accessible is Puffin Island which has breeding puffins as well as Manx shearwaters. Boats go from Valentia Island. The Skellig Experience Heritage Centre focuses on monastic and birdlife on the Skelligs.

▶ *Drive south on the **N70** to Waterville (An Coireán).*

4 **Waterville,** Co Kerry
Set on a strip of land that separates Ballinskelligs Bay from the island-sprinkled Lough Currane, this popular resort and angling centre is also

SCENIC ROUTES

From Waterville, the N70 follows the coast, then rises some 700 feet (215m) above sea level at Coomakista Pass, with breathtaking views of the bay, the Skellig Islands, and the coastline. It was on Sceilg Mhichíl (Skellig Michael), a rocky hulk that rises 700 feet (215m) above the sea, that a colony of early Christian monks built a retreat of stone beehive huts. It is now a UNESCO World Heritage Site. From Castlegrove, the road turns inland through wild and gorgeous scenery before returning to the sea at Sneem.

internationally known for its superb golf course. Mountains rise from the lake's eastern and southern shores, and on Church Island there are ruins of a 12th-century church that was dedicated to the 6th-century holy man, St Fionan.

▶ *Continue south, then east on the **N70** for 22 miles (35km) to reach Sneem.*

5 **Sneem,** Co Kerry
On the drive east on the N70 from Waterville to Sneem, just east of Caherdaniel (Cathair Dónall), is Castlecove, where, about 1½ miles (2km) north of the road you will see Staigue Fort, one of the country's best-preserved Iron-Age stone forts. The circular stone walls, 13 feet (4km) wide and 18 feet (5.5km)

Sheltered by encircling hills, Sneem nestles at the head of an inlet of the Kenmare River

high, have held over the centuries without the benefit of mortar, and along their interior are several flights of stairs in near perfect condition.

Just beyond the Coomakista Pass, about 1 mile (1.5km) beyond Caherdaniel on the Derrynane road, is Derrynane House, set in the wooded National Historic Park. This is where 'The Liberator', Daniel O'Connell, lived for most of his political life, and the house is now a museum containing all sorts of O'Connell memorabilia.

The park covers some 300 acres (120 hectares), incorporating semi-tropical plants and coastal trees and shrubs, as well as dramatic coastal scenery.

The pretty little town of Sneem, where the Ardsheelaun River estuary joins the Kenmare River, is a popular angling centre for brown trout and salmon, and its fine sandy beaches provide safe swimming. Sneem is also the last resting place of Father Michael Walsh, a parish priest in the area for 38 years in the 1800s and immortalised as 'Father O'Flynn' in an Irish ballad.

Anyone interested in eco-friendly energy should visit Kerry Alternative Technology, a 40-acre (16-hectare) farm that is home to ten permanent and six temporary residents who use wind, water and solar power, grow organic vegetables, compost their waste and are developing bio-diesel production for their vehicles.

▶ *Continue east on the N70 for 17 miles (27km) to Kenmare.*

6 Kenmare, Co Kerry
The drive from Sneem along the banks of the Kenmare River has lovely views of the Caha and Slieve Miskish mountains on the opposite shore. Kenmare faces the broad Kenmare river estuary, with impressive mountains behind.

Known as Ceann Mara (Head of the Sea) by the ancients, today it is a lively resort and heritage town. It is also noted for its fine salmon, brown trout and sea fishing, safe swimming, local walks and climbs, homespun woollen industry and lace. (See Tour 6.)

[i] *Kenmare Heritage Centre (seasonal)*

▶ *Turn north on to the N71 to reach Moll's Gap.*

7 Moll's Gap, Co Kerry
The drive north to Moll's Gap is one of rugged mountains and stone-strewn valleys. The viewing point at this gap affords sweeping views of Macgillycuddy's Reeks and of Ireland's highest mountain, the 3,408-foot (1,039m) Carrauntoohil. The restaurant and craft shop make this a good refreshment stop.

▶ *Follow the **N71** northeast for 3 miles (5km) to Ladies' View.*

8 Ladies' View, Co Kerry
This mountainside viewing point overlooks the broad valley of the Killarney lakes. Queen Victoria and her ladies-in-waiting so enthused about this view that it was promptly named in their honour.

Nine miles (14.5km) north on the return to Killarney, are the well-preserved ruins of Muckross Abbey. The abbey dates from 1448 and was built on the site of an earlier religious establishment. About a 10-minute walk from the abbey, Elizabethan-style Muckross House, Gardens and Traditional Farms are surrounded by landscaped gardens that slope down to the lake. Built by a wealthy Kerry MP in 1843, it was sold to Americans in 1911, and presented as a gift to the Irish people in 1932. The house is furnished in the manner of the great houses of Ireland, while the basement portrays the busy life of the servants.

Muckross Traditional Farms form a working museum which farms the land using methods that were used in the 1930s. There are three separate farms, complete with animals, fully equipped workshops, a forge and an interesting furnished farm labourer's cottage.

The gardens include a Victorian Walled Garden with glasshouses, craft workshops, a restaurant and gift shop.

About 1 mile (1.5km) before Muckross House, a signpost on the N71 directs you to a scenic footpath up a mountain slope to the 60-foot (18m) Torc Waterfall in a beautiful wooded area. Continue upwards to the top of the falls for magnificent views.

▶ *Continue for 11 miles (18km) northeast on the **N71** to Killarney.*

FOR CHILDREN

Most children love being on the water, so what better way for them to see the Lakes of Killarney than aboard one of the watercoaches that leave the Ross Castle slipway several times daily to cruise the Lower Lake. They are sure to be fascinated by the mystical legends of the lake related by the boatmen as they glide past Innisfallen Island, O'Sullivan's Cascade, Tomies Mountain, Darby's Garden, the old copper mines, Library Point and many other points of interest.

The lakes and woodland of the Killarney National Park stretch out below Ladies' View

Kenmare & The
Beara Peninsula

The attractive town of Kenmare, at the head of Kenmare Bay, is a thriving market town and tourist centre, and an excellent base for exploring the Iveragh and Beara peninsulas which extend westwards on either side of the bay.

Its own attractions include The Kenmare Heritage Centre and Lace Centre and one of Ireland's most impressive stone circles, known locally as the Druid's circle, beside the River Finnehy.

1/2 DAYS • 86 MILES • 137.5KM

ITINERARY	
KENMARE	▷ **Glengarriff (18m–29km)**
GLENGARRIFF	▷ **Adrigole (12m–19km)**
ADRIGOLE	▷ **Castletown Bearhaven (9m–14km)**
CASTLETOWN BEARHAVEN	▷ **Allihies (12m–19km)**
ALLIHIES	▷ **Eyeries (10m–16km)**
EYERIES	▷ **Ardgroom (4m–6.5km)**
ARDGROOM	▷ **Kenmare (21m–34km)**

i Heritage Centre, Kenmare
(seasonal)

RECOMMENDED WALKS

Walk out along the Glengarriff road (N71) from Kenmare and turn right at the signpost for the pier. Try to go when the tide is in, as the views of the Kenmare River are at their most impressive then. The river, with its backdrop of surrounding mountains and drifts of graceful swans, presents a view of tranquillity and natural beauty and is ample reward for the short walk.

▶ *Drive south for 18 miles (29km) on the N71 to reach Glengarriff.*

❶ Glengarriff, Co Cork

The 18-mile (29km) drive from Kenmare to Glengarriff (Rugged Glen) is known as the Tunnel Road. Two tunnels, one the longest in Ireland, bore through the Caha Mountains, and the road alternately climbs around mountain heights and dips into deep valleys.

FOR HISTORY BUFFS

Cross the bridge over the River Finnehy at Kenmare to find an impressive stone circle and dolmen. There are 15 stones in the circle, which measures about 50 feet (15m) across. In its centre is the dolmen, a megalithic tomb where upright stones support a large, flat capstone. Kenmare has been designated a Heritage Town as a 'planned estate town'. There is a visitor centre in the square which includes exhibitions of lacework and the story of the Nun of Kenmare.

Lying in the heart of a secluded valley surrounded by mountains, Glengarriff's sheltered position nurtures luxuriant Mediterranean flowers and plants such as fuchsia and arbutus. Its harbour is dotted with wooded islands. On Garinish Island you will find the world-famous Italian gardens, laid out between 1910 and 1913 by John Annan Bryce and Harold Peto. The lovely little island was a favourite of George Bernard

Stormy skies add an extra touch of mystery to the ancient standing stones at Kenmare

Shaw, who came here to write much of his *St Joan*.

There is a licensed waterbus to take you across to the island on a short but scenic trip. There are also a number of independent ferry operators. Compare prices before you decide which to take.

Glengarriff is also one of the few places in the country that preserves some specimens of the ancient mixed forests that once covered much of Ireland, best seen at Glengarriff Forest Park, on the northern edge of the village. A little more exotic is the Bamboo Park, impossible to miss behind its Japanese gateway. Delightful paths meander between plantings of bamboo, palms and other tropical species, which thrive in the balmy climate here, and there are some wonderful views over the bay.

Along with the boatmen advertising trips to Garinish Island, the main street is lined with shops selling Irish crafts.

Glengarriff lies at the head of the Beara Peninsula, a

30-mile (48km) long finger of land between Bantry Bay and the Kenmare River. It is bisected by the Cork/Kerry county border running along the Caha mountain range that forms the backbone of the peninsula. A drive around this wild, sparsely populated peninsula constitutes the remainder of this tour.

i Town Centre (seasonal)

▶ Drive southwest on the R572 to Adrigole.

2 **Adrigole,** Co Cork
From Glengarriff, the road follows the shoreline of Bantry

Lush vegetation cloaks the hillsides around Glengarriff

Bay, winding along the rocky coastal strip at the foot of the Caha Mountains, with 1,887-foot (575m) Sugarloaf Mountain on the right. At Adrigole Bridge, the spectacular Healy Pass (named after Tim Healy, the first Governor-General of the Irish Free State) crosses the mountains and is an alternative (and shorter) route to Kenmare and Killarney.

Some 3 miles (5km) west of Adrigole, Hungry Hill, highest of the Caha range, rises 2,251 feet (686m), with a rocky shelf halfway up its face with two lakes that feed a 700-foot (214m) cascade into the valley below – especially spectacular after rain.

▶ Continue southwest for another 9 miles (14km) on the R572 to Castletown Bearhaven.

3 **Castletown Bearhaven,** Co Cork
Sheltered by the elongated Bere (Bear) Island just offshore, Castletown Bearhaven, now a fishing port, was once a British naval base. On North Street, the Call of the Sea offers an imaginative exploration of local maritime history, including the naval heritage, fishing, smuggling and Vikings, plus displays on the local copper mining industry.

There is a regular ferry service out to the island, where some forts still remain, manned from time to time by Irish forces. On a hillside near the old waterworks, look for a group of boulder burials and a fine stone circle, the latter on the western side of the hill.

Less than 2 miles (3km) west of town, facing Bere Island, are the remains of 16th-century Dunboy Castle, in spacious grounds overlooking the inlet. Its star-shaped fort was the stronghold of O'Sullivan Bere, the last Irish leader to hold out with Spanish allies against the British forces led by Sir George Carew in 1602. After a long siege, during which the garrison refused to surrender until the walls were completely shattered, the fort was all but destroyed. The ruins have been excavated for easy exploration.

Fifteen miles (24km) further west, Ireland's only cable car connects Dursey Island with the mainland. The beautiful, long, mountainous island is rimmed by high cliffs and is the site of a gannetry.

▶ Continue southwest on the R572 to its junction with the R575, which turns north to Allihies.

4 **Allihies,** Co Cork
The road from Castletown Bearhaven continues southwest to Black Ball Head before turning northwest to reach Allihies through a gap in the hills. This was once a rich copper-mining centre that formed the basis for the Puxley family fortunes. The 19th century was its most prosperous period, although some work continued right up to 1962. There are picturesque ruins on the scarred hillsides, but they should be explored with extreme caution, since the

Rejoining the main road, the R571, the drive into Kenmare follows Kenmare Bay, with scenic views along a striking section of the journey.

▶ *Remain on the* **R571** *for 21 miles (34km) back to Kenmare.*

old workings, with unguarded shafts, can be very dangerous.

Seascapes seen from the hills are breathtaking, the strand is safe for swimming, and just north of the village there is an old Mass rock.

▶ *Follow the* **R575** *northeast to Eyeries.*

⑤ **Eyeries,** Co Cork

From Allihies, the road leads northeast along the wide sea inlet of the Kenmare River through rugged scenery to the little village of Eyeries, set back from the sea on a pretty bay.

A little to the east, at Ballycrovane, there is an inscribed Ogham pillar stone thought to be the tallest in western Europe, at more than 17½ feet (5.18m) high. In general, Ogham stones served as gravestones and the script on them records details of the person who is buried.

One of Ireland's most striking wayside shrines looks south from the summit of the Healy Pass over the Caha Mountains

▶ *Continue northeast on the* **R571** *for 4 miles (6.5km) to Ardgroom.*

⑥ **Ardgroom,** Co Cork

Just beyond the little village of Ardgroom, you cross into Kerry, where there is yet another fine stone circle in Canfie, on the Lauragh road.

Lauragh, at the northern end of the Healy Pass, has a scenic ridge walk along a horseshoe of peaks surrounding the valley in which the village stands.

Near by is almost totally enclosed Kilmakilloge harbour, where boats can be hired to sail the safe waters. A little beyond Lauragh, signposts direct you inland to Cloonee Loughs, which is worth a detour.

Island City,
Magic Stone

Spreading out along a long valley, Cork is the Republic's second city, with an atmosphere and character all of its own. It has a lively arts scene, excellent shopping and such attractions as the Crawford Art Gallery, the Old Gaol and the famous St Anne's church at Shandon. (See also Tour 8)

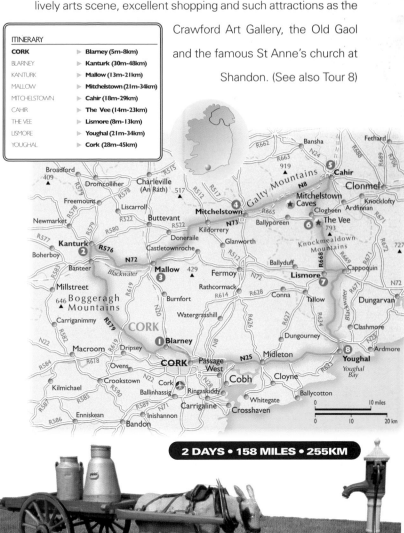

2 DAYS • 158 MILES • 255KM

i *Grand Parade, Cork*

FOR HISTORY BUFFS

Between 1848 and 1950 over six million people emigrated from Ireland; 2.5 million left through the port of Cobh, 15 miles (24km) east of Cork. The Queenstown Story, a multimedia exhibition, details the life of the port. Convict ships, transatlantic steamers and other ocean liners all departed from here, and the ill-fated *Titanic* called here before setting out across the Atlantic. The Titanic Trail is a daily walking tour of maritime history sites.

RECOMMENDED WALKS

There is a fine riverside walk in Cork which leads between rows of old trees, with seats and rustic shelters sprinkled along the way. The river widens into Cork Harbour, and on the opposite bank fine town houses climb up the hills of the Montenotte and Tivoli residential sections. The small fishing village suburb of Blackrock is at the end of the marina, with Blackrock Castle (now a restaurant) on a little promontory jutting out into the River Lee.

▶ *Cross Patrick Street bridge and turn left for a 5-mile (8km) drive northwest on the N20. Turn left onto the R617 to reach Blarney.*

❶ **Blarney,** Co Cork
The well-preserved ruins of Blarney Castle, built in 1446, draw visitors not just for their history, but also for the magical powers attributed to the famous stone embedded in its parapet wall. The legend of its powers rose from Queen Elizabeth I's frustration in dealing with Cormac MacCarthy, Lord of

The climb to kiss the Blarney Stone renders many visitors speechless rather than eloquent

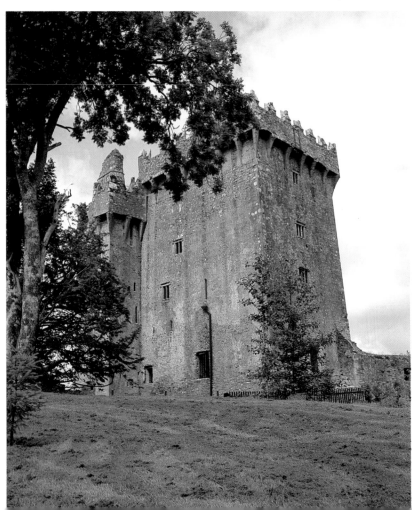

Blarney, and his smiling flattery that veiled wiliness with eloquence. Her declaration that 'This is nothing but Blarney – what he says, he never means!' added a new word to the English language and probably gave rise to the legend of the 'gift of eloquence' associated with the stone. Kissing the magical stone, however, involves climbing 120 steep steps to lie on your back and hang over an open space.

About 200 yards (180m) from the castle is the superb Scottish baronial mansion, Blarney Castle House, set amidst lovely 18th-century gardens.

Blarney Woollen Mills are also worth a visit.

i Town centre

▶ *Go west from Blarney on the R617 and a few miles from the village turn northwest on to the R579 for the 28-mile (45km) drive to Kanturk.*

2 Kanturk, Co Cork
One mile (1.5km) south of town, unfinished Kanturk Castle was begun in 1609 by Irish chieftain MacDonagh MacCarthy, who planned it as the largest mansion in Ireland, with a large quadrangle and four-storey towers at each corner. Alarmed at its size and strength, the English Privy Council ordered work to cease, declaring that it was 'much too large for a subject'. The roofless, stout walls and towers have survived in remarkably good condition.

▶ *Drive southeast on the R576 to its junction with the N72, then turn east for 9 miles (14km) to reach Mallow.*

3 Mallow, Co Cork
Set on the Blackwater River, Mallow was a popular spa town during the 18th and early 19th centuries; its lively social life gave rise to the famous song, *The Rakes of Mallow.* The fine fortified house, built in the

16th century to replace 12th-century Mallow Castle, itself burned in 1689 on the orders of James II, now stands in fairly complete ruins in its own park by the river crossing.

From the Tourist Office in Cork or Youghal ask for the Blackwater Drive map, which shows a wealth of historic relics.

About 9 miles (14km) north of Mallow, via the N20, the little town of Buttevant was the venue for the world's first steeplechase in 1752, run between its church steeple and the one in Doneraile. Buttevant was the model for 'Mole' in Spenser's *The Faerie Queene.*

On the outskirts of town are the remains of Ballybeg, an Augustinian Canons' Regular House, enclosed by low stone walls, that date back to 1237. The ruins include a dovecot with ranks of stone nesting boxes inside.

▶ *Take the N72 northeast, then turn left on to the N73 for 21 miles (34km) to Mitchelstown.*

4 Mitchelstown, Co Cork
This is a tidy, attractive land-lord-planned town founded in the early 19th century. Ten miles (16km) northeast of town via the N8, are the signposted Mitchelstown Caves, an underground wonderland of passages

Mitchelstown Caves are thought to be the largest system of river-formed caves in Ireland

and high-ceilinged chambers, including the biggest chamber in the British Isles. The Old Caves were used as a refuge for the 16th-century Earl of Desmond, with a price on his head. There are escorted tours through 2 miles (3km) of the fantastic netherworld, with its fine stalactite formations.

▶ *Follow the N8 for 18 miles (29km) northeast to Cahir.*

5 Cahir, Co Tipperary
Cahir Castle occupies a small islet in the River Suir, a natural site for fortifications as far back as the 3rd century. The present castle was built in the 13th century but was severely damaged during the 16th and 17th centuries. Oliver Cromwell besieged it in 1650 and sent in surrender terms. Historians argue as to whether or not the terms were accepted immediately but they did surrender before the walls were battered again, and the castle thus remained in sound condition. It has been restored almost to its original condition, and there is an excellent audiovisual show in the 1840 courtyard cottage.

On the southern edge of town, Cahir Park is a lovely area

of riverside woodland and shrubs, with a 2km (just over a mile) trail, fishing, a picnic site and walks to Swiss Cottage. This lovely building dates from the early 1880s, and its elegant interior contrasts with the rustic exterior and thatched roof. (See also Tour 10.)

▶ *Head south on the R668 through Clogheen to begin The Vee mountain pass road en route to Lismore.*

6 The Vee, Co Tipperary and Waterford
The viewing points along this drive through a gap in the Knockmealdown Mountains provide spectacular panoramic views of Killballyboy Wood, Boernagore Wood, the Galty Mountains, the Golden Vale of Tipperary, Bay Lough and the Comeragh mountain range. (See also Tour 10.)

▶ *Continue south on the R668 for 8 miles (13km) to Lismore.*

7 Lismore, Co Waterford
This historic little town, site of an ancient monastic centre of learning, is beautifully situated on the Blackwater River. Its most outstanding sightseeing

attractions are Lismore Castle, whose gardens and art gallery (in the castle's west wing) are open to the public, the Protestant cathedral, with grave slabs from the 9th and 11th centuries, and the modern Romanesque-style Catholic cathedral. An outstanding audiovisual show in The Heritage Centre depicts the town's history. The Centre has booklets detailing interesting town walks. (See also Tour 10.)

SCENIC ROUTES

About a mile (1.5km) from the Cappoquin bridge, the scenic 10-mile (16km) route to Youghal follows the Blackwater River, with deeply wooded stretches as well as superb views of the broad river and the opposite banks. Great houses of the 19th century and earlier are dotted along the route, and about 2 miles (3km) south of Cappoquin, the large house high above the east bank is the remodelled wing of ancient Dromana Castle, where traces of the old gardens sloping down to the river can still be seen.

The fairy-tale appearance of Lismore Castle is second only to the fascinating facts of its history and illustrious occupants

ℹ️ *Heritage Centre*

▶ *Take the N72 east for 4 miles (6km) to the bridge on the outskirts of Cappoquin and turn right on to an unclassified road to a T-junction. Turn right on to the road signposted Youghal that follows the Blackwater River south to the sea, then turn right on to the N25 south for the short drive into Youghal.*

8 Youghal, Co Cork
This picturesque fishing harbour and seaside resort is filled with mementoes of its past. Sir Walter Raleigh lived here, and legend has it that this is where he first smoked tobacco from the New World and planted the first potato in Irish soil. Myrtle Grove, his Elizabethan house, is at the top of Nelson Place.

A Tourist Trail booklet available from the Heritage Centre details a signposted walking tour of the town, which includes the historic Clock Tower in the town centre that was erected in 1771 as a gaol.

The Heritage Centre also contains displays on the history of the town. A short distance away, there are fragments of the old town walls, constructed in 1275 and added to up until 1603. During summer months there are harbour and river cruises as well as deep-sea fishing charters.

As the Blackwater River broadens near its entrance to the sea north of Youghal, look for the extensive ruins of 13th-century Molana Abbey, situated on what was once an islet. Although it has become rather overgrown, the site has the ruins of a church, cloisters and conventual buildings, as well as what is believed to be the burial place of the Norman knight Raymond le Gros.

Eight miles (13km) east of Youghal, via a signposted turnoff from the N25, the pretty little seaside village of Ardmore grew from the 7th-century settlement founded by St Declan. It has a fine group of ecclesiastical remains, including one of the most

perfectly preserved round towers in Ireland. There are also bracing cliff walks along the sea's edge.

i *Heritage Centre, Market Square*

▶ Follow the **N25** west for 28 miles (45km) to return to Cork.

Sunset over a deserted Youghal beach, on the south coast

BACK TO NATURE

About 5 miles (8km) west of Youghal on the N25, the entrance to Glenbower Wood is at the Thatch Inn in Killeagh village. Its nature trail is a 1½-mile (3km) loop that can be walked in about half an hour, or fully savoured for an hour or two. The wood is set in a glen through which the River Dissour rushes, and at one point an earthen dam was built to power the village corn mill, forming a lovely lake. Native trees include hazel (considered to have magical powers to ward off evil), sessile oak, alder, scrub oak, holly, birch and rowan. Tree plantations are mostly Norway spruce, Western hemlock and Sitka spruce. The profusion of ferns includes hard fern, bracken fern, hart's tongue and the male shield fern.

FOR CHILDREN

The Fota Wildlife Park, east of Cork, is a child's paradise, inhabited by an engaging animal population that includes zebras, cheetahs, kangaroos, giraffes, ostriches, antelopes, gibbons and monkeys, as well as rare and endangered species. Young children will also enjoy Leahy's Fun Farm at Midleton, which has farm animals, playgrounds, boat rides, and other amusements. Teens would prefer Bartizan Game World (tel: 021 4633323) on Youghal Road, Midleton.

SPECIAL TO...

The old Cork waterworks, in a scenic spot beside the River Lee, have been transformed into the Lifetime Lab. The buildings have been refurbished and now house restored steam engines and boilers, plus fascinating and fun interactive displays about energy, waste and water, showing how the environment can be changed by the way we make everyday choices. There's also a themed playground for hours of fun.

Cork's
Coastal Villages

Its great age and its location in a long, marshy valley have fashioned Cork City into what a native son once aptly described as 'an intimate higgledy-piggledy assemblage of steps, slopes, steeples and bridges'. Parallel to the Western Road is the Mardyke, a mile-long (1.5km) tree-shaded walk bordered by Fitzgerald Park, the site of the Cork Museum. (See also Tour 7.)

2 DAYS • 143 MILES • 229KM

i Grand Parade, Cork

RECOMMENDED WALK

Cork has a Tourist Trail marked out for visitors and a copy can be obtained from the Tourist Information Office.

FOR CHILDREN

Children will relish all the beaches and boat rides of West Cork, but if it rains try taking the little ones along to Chuckies Playzone (tel: 021 4344112) in Cork City's Doughcloyne Industrial Estate, open daily from 10am to 6pm.

▶ Take the **N27/R600** *south for 16 miles (26km) to Kinsale.*

❶ **Kinsale,** Co Cork
The fishing and boating village of Kinsale has figured prominently in Ireland's history since it received its charter in 1334. A decisive British victory here in 1601 led to a mass exodus of Irish royalty known as the 'Flight of the Earls'. The 15th-century Desmond Castle served as a prison and a work-house during its long history, but since 1997 has been the home of the International Wine Museum. Displays tell the story of Ireland's links with wine-producing countries of Europe and beyond.

FOR HISTORY BUFFS

When Don Juan d'Agila arrived in Kinsale from Spain in 1601 with a large force to assist the Irish rebels against the English, an Irish victory seemed certain, even though the English Lord Deputy, Mountjoy, threw some 12,000 soldiers into the siege of the town. Irish chieftains O'Donnell and O'Neill marched their troops down from the north to mount a rear offensive against the English. This might well have succeeded had not word reached Mountjoy of their strategy, enabling him to successfully rout both Irish and Spanish. South of the town, you can visit the remains of King James Fort (or Old Fort), which housed the Spanish.

The narrow promontory of the Old Head of Kinsale shelters the popular yachting centre of Kinsale Harbour, to the east

Near Summer Cove, there are extensive, well-preserved remains of Charles Fort, built around 1677, with spectacular views of Kinsale harbour.

Seven miles (11km) south via the R600 and R604 is the Old Head of Kinsale, where a ruined clifftop castle overlooks the spot where the *Lusitania* was sunk in 1915 by a German submarine.

i Pier Road

SPECIAL TO...

The lively town of Kinsale is internationally known for its gourmet restaurants featuring cuisines from around the world, with local seafoods and meats in various guises on all the menus. Look for restaurants displaying the Kinsale Good Food Circle emblem. Or come for the Autumn Flavours Festival of Fine Food and Fun in October.

▶ Continue on the **R600** for 22 miles (35km) southwest to Clonakilty.

SCENIC ROUTES

For a scenic alternative route from Kinsale to Clonakilty, turn southeast at Timoleague on the R601 and drive along Courtmacsherry Bay. The fishing village of Courtmacsherry nestles between the bay and the thick woods behind. Continue south to Butlerstown, where there are marvellous seascapes and views of the Seven Heads, a rugged peninsula with seven jutting headlands. Follow the unclassified road west to North Ring, then head north along the shores of Clonakilty Bay, to reach Clonakilty.

2 **Clonakilty,** Co Cork

Ten miles (16km) from Kinsale, on the Clonakilty road, Timoleague Castle Gardens were laid out more than one and a half centuries ago. Timoleague Abbey is a well-preserved ruined Franciscan friary, which in its day was an important religious centre.

At Clonakilty, castles dot the shores of the bay; the Catholic church is a fine example of Gothic architecture. The Michael Collins Centre has been developed by Tim and Dolores Crowley, related to Collins through Tim's grand-mother. Their farm is now home to various exhibits that relate the life and times of Michael Collins, including a replica of the section of road where Collins was ambushed and killed. Tours of other places connected with Michael Collins can be arranged, and there's a festival each August.

ℹ️ 25 Ashe Street

FOR CHILDREN

A West Cork town of the 1930s to 1950s has been re-created at 1:24 scale at the West Cork Model Railway Village, and while kids can enjoy peering into the buildings and watching the trains, adults can appreciate the accurate historical content and workmanship.

▶ Continue southwest on the **N71** to Ross Carbery.

3 **Ross Carbery,** Co Cork

At the head of Ross Carbery Bay, this picturesque little town

The gentle hills and tranquil waters of Ross Carbery

was the site of a medieval Benedictine monastery in the 6th century, founded by St Fachtna, and was famous for its school. A few remains of its foundation can be seen near the church, which stands on the site of an ancient cathedral.

One mile (1.5km) east of town are the ruins of Benduff Castle, and a little further on, the beautiful demesne of Castlefreke. Two miles (3km) west of town, the fine Drombeg stone circle can be seen from the Glandore road, R597, and near by is Fulacht Fiadh stone trough, an ancient Celtic cooking pot in which water was brought to the boil with stones heated in a fire.

▶ Take the **N71** west to Leap.

4 **Leap,** Co Cork

This pretty little village sits at the head of a narrow inlet where the River Leap (pronounced 'lep') enters Glandore harbour. Stop in at the Leap Inn in the main street to experience an authentic Irish country inn that has been run by the same family for generations; the dining room serves good, solid, traditional Irish favourites.

Climb the hill above the village for beautiful harbour views, and drive to nearby Unionhall on a scenic road that follows the harbour as it widens to enter the sea.

▶ *Continue west on the **N71** until Skibereen, then take the **R593** for Drimoleague and the **R586**. Turn north for Dunmanway, a total distance of 17 miles (27km).*

5 **Dunmanway,** Co Cork

The famous Gaelic Athletic Association figure, Sam Maguire, was born near this early 17th-century linen industry plantation town and is buried in St Mary's cemetery. The town pitch bears his name.

There are fine forest walks at Clashnacrona Woods, 3 miles (5km) southwest of the town on the R586, and at Aultagh Wood, which lies 4 miles (6km) north on the R587.

▶ *Take the unclassified Derrynacaheragh road northwest, then turn left on meeting the **R585** and continue to Kealkill. Turn northeast on the **R584** through the Pass of Keimaneigh to reach the Gougane Barra road.*

The Gougane Barra Forest Park is a haven of peace and wildlife

6 **Gougane Barra Forest Park,** Co Cork

Gougane Barra was Ireland's first forest park, and is one of the few to have a drive-around trail as well as forest trails. The River Lee rises in Gougane Barra lake, a corrie lake surrounded by thickly wooded crags. Before moving on to the marshes of Cork, St Finbar had a hermitage in this remote spot. St Finbar's Holy Island, connected to the shore by a causeway. Pilgrimages are made to the hermitage each September.

▶ *Drive northeast on the **R584** to Macroom, turning left on to the **N22** to enter the town.*

7 **Macroom,** Co Cork

This is the main market town for the Gaelic-speaking region to the west. Macroom Castle, off the square, dates from the 13th century and was a seat of the MacCarthys of Muskerry. Oliver Cromwell granted it to Admiral Sir William Penn, whose son William spent much of his childhood here and later founded the US state of Pennsylvania. Little remains of the castle, but its entrance has been restored.

[i] *Castle Gates, The Square (seasonal)*

▶ *Take the **N22** east for 25 miles (40km) and return to Cork.*

Unspoiled
Peninsulas

Bantry sits at the head of one of Ireland's most beautiful bays, with a sheltered harbour that reaches right into the town centre, where the narrow streets and lovely broad square are lined with shops and houses that have changed little over the centuries.

The beautiful landscaped grounds of Bantry House are open to the public, and the French Armada Interpretive Centre, holds items from the disastrous invasion of 1796.

1/2 DAYS • 96 MILES • 156KM

ITINERARY	
BANTRY	▶ **Drimoleague (11m-18km)**
DRIMOLEAGUE	▶ **Skibbereen (8m-13km)**
SKIBBEREEN	▶ **Schull (14m-23km)**
SCHULL	▶ **Mizen Head (18m-29km)**
MIZEN HEAD	▶ **Durrus (21m-34km)**
DURRUS	▶ **Bantry (24m-39km)**

Killarney National Park

Kilgarvan

Baile Mhic Íre (Ballymakeery)

Kenmare

Béal Átha an Ghaorthaidh (Ballingeary)

Macroom

Ceann Bholais (Bolus Head)

Parknasilla

R571

705 Knockboy

Inchigeelagh

Lee Crookstown Kilmichael

Cathair Dónall (Caherdaniel)

Kenmare River

Lauragh

An Scairbh (Scariff Island)

Ardgroom

Glengarriff

Bandon

Enniskean

Cod's Head

Beara Peninsula

685 R572

Adrigole

Garinish Island

Dunmanway

R586

Allihies

Castletown Bearhaven

BANTRY

R586 ❶

Drimoleague

Timoleague

Dursey Island

Bear Island

Bantry Bay

Sheep's Head Peninsula

Durrus ❺

Leap

Ross Carbery

Clonakilty

Muntervary/ Sheep's Head

Dunmanus Bay

R591

Ballydehob

R592

Schull ❸

N71

Skibbereen ❷

Clonakilty Bay

Mizen Peninsula

407

Toormore Goleen

Mizen Head ❹

Crookhaven

Roaringwater Bay

Baltimore

Castletownshend

Galley Head

Toe Head

Oileán Cléire (Clear Island)

0   10 miles
0   10   20 km

FOR HISTORY BUFFS

High seas and storm conditions spelt defeat for the French Armada that anchored in Bantry Bay on 21 December, 1796. Fired with the fervour of their own successful revolution, they had responded eagerly to the entreaties of revolutionary Wolfe Tone to join with United Irishmen to end the British occupation of Ireland. The fleet lost its flagship and commanding officer in a storm at sea, and eventually gale-force winds drove 20 of the great ships back out to sea. When there was no let-up in the weather, the Armada and a heartbroken Tone sailed back to France. Bantry House has an exhibition about the failed endeavour.

Beautiful Bantry House Gardens enjoy an unparalleled setting on the shores of Bantry Bay

RECOMMENDED WALKS

There are fine forest walks in Barnegeehy Woods, about 3 miles (5km) south of Bantry via the Ballydehob road (N71).

[i] *The Old Courthouse, The Square, Bantry (seasonal)*

▶ *Take the N71 south and turn left for Drimoleague, east via the R586.*

❶ Drimoleague, Co Cork
The Roman Catholic church in this small town is noteworthy for its architecture, a modern box-like structure with a solid, unbroken wall on one side, and glass on the other. Castle Donovan, north of town and now in ruins, is a relic of the late 15th and early 16th centuries.

▶ *Turn south on to the R593 to Skibbereen.*

SPECIAL TO...

This West Cork region is alive with festivals and special events during the summer months. There are regattas in Castletownshend in July, and Baltimore, Schull and Crookhaven in August. Events include the Taste of West Cork Food Festival in Skibbereen in September, storytelling festivals on Cape Clear in May and September, Bantry's West Cork Literary Festival in June/July and the Baltimore Wooden Boat and Seafood Festival in May.
The entire area is also a mecca for anglers, with sea angling, and salmon fishing in the River Ilen at Skibbereen. Trout are the prize at lakes Garranes and Driminidy near Drimoleague.

❷ Skibbereen, Co Cork
This progressive town sits on the River Ilen just where it broadens and then empties into

Baltimore Bay. Its long history of independence has produced two battling bishops – one who died fighting Elizabethan forces in 1602 and another who was hanged in 1650 during the Cromwellian conflicts. The Maid of Erin monument in the town square was erected in 1904 by the Young Ireland Society. The Pro-Cathedral, a fine Grecian-style edifice built in 1826, is well worth a visit. Surprisingly picturesque, the old gasworks building has been beautifully restored and converted into the Skibbereen Heritage Centre, which includes a Great Famine exhibition and information on nearby Lough Hyne. Guided walks are also available.

You can see garden design in progress at the superb Liss Ard Gardens, 200 acres of woods, meadows, lakes and waterfalls that will mature in 30 to 50 years. Pathways thread through scenic and tranquil areas dotted with art works.

Abbeystrewery Abbey, dating from the 14th century, lies in ruins 1 mile (1.5km) west

Abbeystrewery is a sad and atmospheric place, with its mass famine graves amidst the overgrown abbey ruins

of town, the setting for mass famine graves that bear silent witness to one of Ireland's most tragic eras.

Castletownshend, 5 miles (8km) southeast of Skibbereen via the R596, is a pretty little village with only one street that slopes rather steeply down to the sea. This was home to Edith Somerville and Violet Martin Ross, two Victorian ladies whose humorous *Experiences of an Irish RM* has kept the English-speaking world chuckling. They lay buried in the Church of Ireland grounds, their lively spirits no doubt still haunting the halls of their beloved Drishane House at the upper end of the village. Just outside town, on a ridge overlooking the sea, Knockdrum ringfort has an underground passage (souterrain) and a stone with megalithic cup marks.

Eight miles (13km) southwest of Skibbereen, the little

fishing village of Baltimore also has a stormy history, attested to by the ancient castle of the O'Driscolls, now in ruins on a rock overlooking the harbour. Despite the presence of that powerful clan, in 1631 Algerian pirates captured some 200 town residents for sale to North African slave traders and massacred most of those left behind. Poet Thomas Davis's *The Sack of Baltimore* gives a vivid account of the raid.

There are fine views of the bay and Sherkin Island from the tall whitewashed navigational beacon a short distance outside the village, and there is a regular boat service to Sherkin Island, which defines the westward side of Baltimore Bay. Silver Strand is typical of several good swimming spots among the island's many coves. Near the pier stand ruins of another castle of the O'Driscolls, destroyed in 1537, and on the eastern end of the island are the remains of a friary founded by one of the O'Driscolls in the 15th century for the Franciscan Order of Strict Observance.

Southwest of Sherkin is Oileán Cléire (Clear Island), one of the four Gaeltacht (Irish-speaking) areas in the Cork/Kerry region, with a regular boat service from Sherkin and mailboat service from Baltimore. You will be well rewarded by a visit to the Cape Clear Heritage Centre. There is also a small bird observatory that has tracked the migrations of a host of interesting species. Just south of the island, on the southernmost offshore point in Ireland, Fastnet Rock Lighthouse stands as a major navigational aid to mariners. It was built in Cornwall in 1906 from local granite, disassembled and refitted on to Fastnet Rock, each block dovetailed into the next to withstand the fierce seas.

BACK TO NATURE

About 4 miles (6km) southwest of Skibbereen is Lough Hyne, the country's most important marine nature reserve. Its pollution-free waters, 30°C (54°F) warmer than the sea, form a natural habitat for several thousand species of marine animals and plants. Many southern, or Lusitanian, species common to the Mediterranean and surrounding area thrive here, as do others peculiar to Ireland and Britain. At low tide, search the shore for intriguing marine creatures such as jewel anemones, sea squirts and gobies. From the lake shores, you can observe patches of different-coloured seabed, which change with the intensity of grazing by the fascinating marine population.

There is always activity on the water at Schull harbour

RECOMMENDED WALKS

At the head of Lough Hyne, look for the path that climbs up through woodlands to the hilltop. The panoramic view is breathtaking, looking down over the Hundred Isles, down the length of the peninsula to Mizen Head, and east as far as Kinsale.

ℹ️ *Town Hall, North Street*

▶ *Take the N71 west to Ballydehob, then turn southwest on to the R592 to reach Schull.*

3 Schull, Co Cork

The scenic drive west from Skibbereen follows the River

Ilen and then the shore of Roaringwater Bay to Ballydehob, a picturesque little harbour that has attracted scores of crafts-people, whose workshops may well prompt a shopping stop. During World War II a German war plane crashed on the slopes of Mount Gabriel, which is now topped by a tracking station. Beautiful Cuss Strand, 2 miles (3km) from Ballydehob, offers excellent swimming.

Further on, Schull's virtually enclosed harbour is a haven for fishing and pleasure boats. This delightful little town usually has music in the pubs and a variety of special events during summer months. In the village, the Church of Ireland church (no longer in use) incorporates some interesting medieval remains, and in the grounds of the Community College, a 60-seat planetarium is the only one in the Republic of Ireland.

There is also a regular ferry service to Clear Island from Schull harbour.

▶ *Follow the **R592** to Toormore, then turn left on to the **R591** to Goleen. At Goleen take an unclassified road to Mizen Head.*

4 Mizen Head, Co Cork
This part of the peninsula route calls out for a leisurely drive as it sweeps around beautiful Toormore Bay to Goleen, where a lovely secluded beach invites a break for a swim. From Goleen, you can either drive straight out to Mizen Head via a minor road off the R591 or make a short side trip to the village of Crookhaven, where the charming harbour is a favourite with yachtsmen, before proceeding on to land's end.

The fine sandy beaches of Barley Cove are worth the side trip to this popular resort spot. The drive on to Mizen Head is one of breathtaking seascapes and high vertical cliffs against which breaking white-foamed waves beat ceaselessly. Exercise extreme caution, however, as the clifftops end abruptly with a straight drop. Mizen Head Visitor Centre is housed in the former lighthouse-keeper's house and engine room and includes a Navigational Aids Simulator, automatic weather station and award-winning displays.

▶ *An unmarked road strikes north at Barley Cove, but is rough driving. The recommended route is to return to Goleen and rejoin the **R591** north to Toormore, then head*

The ever-changing seascapes of the Mizen Peninsula culminate in this spectacular headland

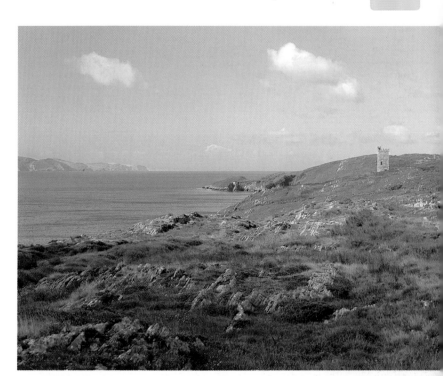

northeast for the scenic drive to Durrus, 21 miles (34km).

FOR CHILDREN

While most children will enjoy the coastal scenery and wooded stretches along the drive, they will welcome stops for a swim and romp on the fine beaches at Goleen, Barley Cove, Ahakista, and Kilcrohane. Surfers will find good waves at Barley Cove.

---

5 **Durrus**, Co Cork

Situated at the head of Dunmanus Bay, this village is the gateway to the narrow, 15-mile (24km) long Sheep's Head Peninsula. A minor, unnumbered road leads southwest along the coast to the wooded inlet of Ahakista, where there is good swimming at sandy beaches. You will see the Air India Memorial commemorating the loss of the passengers and crew of the plane that crashed off this coast in 1985. Then it's on to Kilcrohane, which also has a good beach. Adventurous souls may want to continue southwest to the car park from where you can walk out across the rocky headland to Sheep's Head.

▶ *From Durrus, take the unclassified road west to Kilcrohane, then take the road known as Goat's Path across Seefin Mountain for the drive along the southern shore of Bantry Bay. Just past the village of*

RECOMMENDED WALKS

It is an easy walk from the summit of the Goat's Path road up to the top of Seefin Mountain. The small effort will be rewarded by even more extensive views of the peninsula and coastline, since Seefin is almost twice the height of the road summit.

The Sheep's Head Peninsula has a wonderful rocky coastline, backed on its sheltered southern slopes by luxuriant hedgerows and gardens

Tedagh, turn left on to the N71 for the short drive back to Bantry.

SCENIC ROUTES

The drive from Durrus down Sheep's Head Peninsula — especially the Goat's Path road just outside Kilcrohane that leads across the mountains — is the most scenic part of the route. When you reach the summit, stop to enjoy the extensive panorama east over County Cork and west to the Beara Peninsula and parts of County Kerry. The narrow but well-surfaced road is especially beautiful in autumn when gorse (dwarf furze/whin) covers the mountains and countryside with golden yellow flowers.

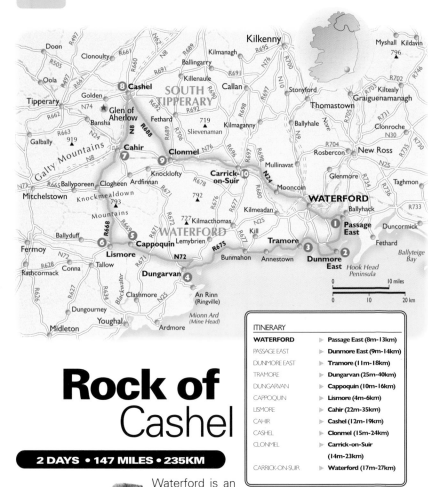

Rock of
Cashel

2 DAYS • 147 MILES • 235KM

Waterford is an important seaport and cultural centre and reflects much of Ireland's history. Reginald's Tower, on The Quay, dates back to 1003, and Waterford Treasures is in the old Granary on Merchant's Quay. There are traces of the old Viking city walls, a fine cathedral and the famous Waterford Crystal Glass Factory, and summer river cruises are great attractions. See also Tour 15.

ⓘ *41 The Quay, Waterford*

SPECIAL TO...

In September, a lighthearted gathering of amateur companies from around the world and from all parts of Ireland converges on Waterford for the annual International Festival of Light Opera. For 16 nights there are performances of such musicals as *Brigadoon* and *Showboat*, all to a very high standard.

▶ *From Waterford head east on the R683 to Passage East.*

❶ **Passage East,** Co Waterford

This quaint riverside village with its whitewashed cottages, narrow, winding streets and a car-ferry service to Ballyhack, County Wexford, was the landing point for Henry II, who arrived in 1171 with 4,000 men in 400 ships to receive oaths of loyalty from Irish chieftains who wished to hold on to their lands. The hill just above the village provides splendid views of the head of Waterford harbour.

On the road to Dunmore East are the ruins of Geneva Barracks, relics of a colony of goldsmiths and silversmiths from Switzerland who sought refuge from religious persecution in 1782. Their planned town of New Geneva failed, and by 1785 was abandoned. The barracks became a prison for insurgents (or 'croppies') of the 1798 rising, subjects of the ballad 'The Croppy Boy'.

▶ *Follow an unclassified coastal road south, join the R684 and turn left for Dunmore East.*

❷ **Dunmore East,** Co Waterford

Neat thatched cottages perch on steep hills above the harbour of this pretty little village that is a popular summer resort and sea-angling centre. Pleasure boats and fishing vessels fill the picturesque harbour. The bay is divided into cliffs and coves, with good walks to Creadan Head to the north, Black Knob promontory to the south, and Swines Head at the southern end of the peninsula. There are also several safe sandy beaches in the area.

Dunmore East offers the Irish idyll in pretty, traditional-style holiday homes

▶ *Take an unclassified coastal road to the junction with the R685, turn left, then left again at the junction with the R675 and continue to Tramore.*

FOR CHILDREN

There are exciting diversions for children in Tramore. Splashworld has water-based fun, with slides, flumes and white-knuckle rides, while Laserworld provides a high-tech game with special effects, set in a Celtic maze.

---

❸ **Tramore,** Co Waterford

This lively seaside town is one of the southeast coast's most popular resorts, with a wide, 3-mile-long (5km) beach, its waters warmed by the Gulf Stream. Attractions include a 50-acre (20-hectare) amusement park, a race course, miniature golf, and an 18-hole golf course. Watersports, particularly surfing, are popular here, and The Surf and Wildlife Visitor Centre incorporates a surf school and related facilities with exhibitions on wildlife and surfing history, guided eco-hikes, and a performance venue.

The giant clifftop 'Metal Man' statue at Great Newtown Head, was erected as a navigational landmark for sailors, and legend has it that any unmarried female who hops around it three times will hop down the aisle within 12 months.

On the coastal drive to Dungarvan, the little fishing village of Bunmahon has a good sandy beach surrounded by jagged cliffs that rise to about 200 feet (60m), with interesting rock formations at their base.

[i] *Railway Square (seasonal)*

▶ *From Tramore, follow the **R675** coastal drive southwest to take you to Dungarvan.*

Sand and rocks between Dungarvan and Tramore

There is scarcely a mile of this tour that could not be described as a scenic route. The R675, the coastal road from Tramore to Dungarvan, dips and winds through the quaint little fishing villages of Annestown and Bunmahon, with spectacular seascapes of soaring cliffs and quiet little coves. A short detour to the wide, curving beach at Clonea Strand is worthwhile. The Vee drive (see also Tour 7) from Lismore to Clogheen, on the R668, winds and twists along mountainsides covered with heather to the V-shaped pass in the Knockmealdown Mountains, with lay-bys giving sweeping views of Tipperary's Golden Vale, before descending to the little town of Clogheen.

Between the pass and Clogheen, look for the stone cairn on the northern slope, where Samuel Grubb of Grace Castle was interred upright overlooking his landholdings. This drive is especially spectacular in the spring when the mountainsides are ablaze with rhododendron flowers.

4 Dungarvan, Co Waterford

Dungarvan sits on the broad, natural harbour where the Colligan river meets the sea. Along the quays you can see remnants of Dungarvan Castle, dating from 1186, surrounded by fortified walls. On St Augustine Street you'll find the excellent and very active Dungarvan Museum, with interesting local displays, a splendid photographic collection and a space devoted to visiting exhibitions from other major museums.

Five miles (8km) south of town on the R674 is the village of An Rinn (Ringville), where Irish is the daily language and is taught in an acclaimed language college. Further east, Helvick Head rises to

230 feet (70m) and shelters a picturesque small harbour.

i The Courthouse

FOR CHILDREN

Further south on the coastal drive, Clonlea Strand, some 2 miles (3km) east of Dungarvan, flies the European blue flag for its clean beach, and there are ample refreshment facilities.

▶ Take the **R672** and then the **N72** west to Cappoquin.

5 Cappoquin, Co Waterford

The broad Blackwater River makes a 90-degree turn to the west at Cappoquin, and provides scenic riverside drives and some of the best salmon fishing, trout angling and coarse fishing in Ireland.

Cappoquin House and Gardens command fine views over the River Blackwater. The house, built in 1779, used to face the town, but later the entrance was turned round and the façade is now enhanced by informal gardens and handsome trees which extend towards the river.

Ballysaggartmore Gatehouse is a fitting entrance to romantic Lismore Castle

▶ Follow the **N72** for 4 miles (6km) to Lismore.

6 Lismore, Co Waterford

Set on the Blackwater River, Lismore is one of Ireland's Heritage Towns, a definitive example of an Estate town. It's proud history is portrayed in the Lismore Heritage Centre, in the fine Courthouse building, where the story of the town from AD636 is related through an award-winning multilingual audiovisual presentation.

The most prominent feature is Lismore Castle, which looms over the town and river, looking for all the world like a fairy-tale castle. It was built by King John in 1185 on the site of a 7th-century monastery that was a renowned seat of learning. The castle was presented to Sir Walter Raleigh, who sold it to Richard Boyle, Earl of Cork, in 1602. His son, Robert, the noted chemist and author of Boyle's Law, was born here. Since 1753 it has been the Irish seat of the Dukes of Devonshire, and the gardens and art gallery are open to the public.

The medieval Protestant cathedral dates from the 17th century. It has soaring Gothic vaulting and still retains in its west wall 9th- and 11th-century grave slabs from an earlier church. The modern (1888) Catholic cathedral is Romanesque in style. Lady Louise's Walk along the river and the interesting Town Walk are well signposted.

Five miles (8km) south of Lismore, via the N72, the little town of Tallow was the birthplace of famed 19th-century sculptor John Hogan. Panoramic views open up from 592-foot (180m) Tallow Hill, and there are ruins of an ancient fortified Fitzgerald keep located ½ mile (1km) west of Tallowbridge.

Six miles (10km) west of Lismore, via the R666, the village of Ballyduff is a popular angling centre.

i Heritage Centre

▶ *At the eastern end of the bridge in Lismore take the R668 which follows the Blackwater River northwards, and then climbs to the pass in the Knockmealdown Mountains known as The Vee and descends to Clogheen, then on to Cahir.*

7 Cahir, Co Tipperary

Cahir Castle, with its massive great hall, grim dungeon, and thick protective enclosing walls, is a superb restoration of the 1142 castle set on a rocky islet in the River Suir. It is also one of Ireland's best-preserved castles. Furnishings in the residential apartments are authentic reproductions of the period. The Articles ending the long Cromwellian wars were signed here, and in modern times it has served as the setting for such films as *Excalibur* and *Barry Lyndon*.

Other interesting buildings include the 13th-century abbey, founded by a Norman knight, which is being restored, and the delightful little Swiss Cottage. Cahir is also a centre for walking and climbing.

A few miles northwest of Cahir, the N24 (the road to Tipperary town) leads to a left turnoff heading to the lush Glen of Aherlow, a secluded glen that was once a major route between the counties of Tipperary and Limerick and the scene of ancient battles. Later, Irish insurgents and outlaws took refuge in the thickly wooded valley that runs between the Galty Mountains and Slievenamuck Hills.

Even the myths, legends and history pale beside the actual sight of the Rock of Cashel

BACK TO NATURE

The mile-long (1.5km) nature trail in Glengarra Wood is a delight for those interested in rare and exotic trees and plants. To reach the wood, drive 8 miles (13km) southwest of Cahir via the N8, and turn right on to the signposted and unclassified road, then continue 2 miles (3km) to the car-park. There are nature walks along the Burncourt river and through forest groves, where Douglas fir, ferns and native heathers, Western hemlock, rowan, holly, birch, arboreal rhododendron, Bhutan pine from the Inner Himalayas of eastern India, and many other plants and trees can be seen.
Native birds such as the treecreeper, the tiny goldcrest, wren, robin, chaffinch, magpie, jay and the introduced pheasant make this their home, as do a herd of fallow deer.

i Castle Car Park (seasonal)

▶ *From Cahir, follow the N8 due north to Cashel.*

8 Cashel, Co Tipperary
Dominating the landscape is the awe-inspiring Rock of Cashel which soars 200 feet (60m) above the surrounding plains. Since ancient Celtic times, its summit has been connected with royalty and mysticism. Cormac's Chapel, the Round Tower, St Patrick's Cathedral, and a replica of St Patrick's Cross (the base of which may actually have been a pre-Christian sacrificial altar) are among the ruins, all in good condition. At the foot of the Rock, the Bru Boru Heritage Centre presents traditional Irish entertainment. See also Tour 3.

i *Heritage Centre (seasonal)*

FOR HISTORY BUFFS

In the 5th century, a cashel, or stone fort, was erected on the lofty Rock of Cashel, and it was here, legend has it, that St Patrick came to preach to the King of Munster, using the humble shamrock as a symbol of the Christian Trinity. In 1101, Murtough O'Brien presented the Cashel of the Kings to the Church. In 1127, Cormac MacCarthaigh, King of Desmond, built the little chapel, a miniature gem of Romanesque style. King Henry II came here to receive homage from Irish princes; Edward the Bruce held a parliament here; and the first Protestant service was conducted here.

▶ *Take the R688 southeast for 15 miles (24km) to Clonmel.*

9 Clonmel, Co Tipperary
Set on the banks of the River Suir, Clonmel is the main town of County Tipperary, and is home to the South Tipperary County Museum, where lively exhibits span prehistoric to modern times.
   It was in Clonmel that the world's first public transport system was established by Charles Bianconi in 1815, based at Hearn's Hotel in Parnell Street. This interesting aspect of Clonmel's history is reflected in the Museum of Transport in Gortnafleur Business Park.
   Some parts of the Franciscan church in Abbey Street date back to the 13th century, and 19th-century St Mary's Church near by has a fine high altar. The town's streets are lined with beautiful restored shopfronts.

RECOMMENDED WALKS

From Clonmel, you can walk the 12-mile (19km) towpath to Carrick-on-Suir.

One of Clonmel's charming streets is framed by the arch of the great West Gate

▶ *Take the N24 east to Carrick-on-Suir.*

10 Carrick-on-Suir, Co Tipperary
This scenic town is on the River Suir, and its Ormonde Castle is the only Elizabethan fortified mansion of its kind in Ireland. A principal seat of the Butlers, it is said to have been built by 'Black Tom', Earl of Ormonde, to host Elizabeth I, who subsequently cancelled her proposed visit.
   The Heritage Centre, housed in the former Protestant Church, contains many memorials to various Ormonde earls, plus local artefacts and a collection of church plate.
   The Tipperary Crystal workshop and showroom are on the N24.

i *Heritage Centre, Main Street*

▶ *Take the N24 back to Waterford.*

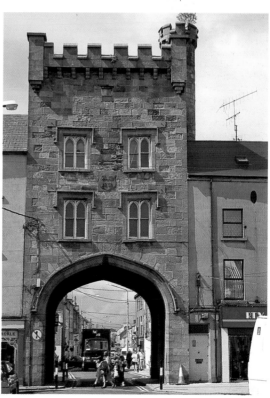

LEINSTER

Leinster might well be called the 'Royal Province' of Ireland. Its 12 counties have harboured rulers from the days of the prehistoric clans who constructed the great burial mound at Newgrange to the High Kings of Ireland who ruled from the Hill of Tara, from Viking and Norman conquerors, to appointees of English kings and queens. Indeed, with Irish chieftains battling against invaders and each other, it seemed best to concentrate beleaguered Crown forces in 'The Pale', a heavily fortified area around Dublin.

At Clontarf, just outside Dublin, the great Irish High King Brian Boru defeated the Vikings in 1014. In 1649, Oliver Cromwell arrived with his dreaded 'Ironside' forces and proceeded to march from Dublin to Drogheda, where he slaughtered thousands of men, women and children. And in 1690, William of Orange's decisive victory at the Battle of the Boyne had a profound effect on Ireland's history that echoes down the centuries to the present day.

South of The Pale, County Wexford bears the scars of Viking occupation followed by Normans, who first landed in Ireland along this county's coast. Cromwell and the insurgents of 1798 left their imprint too. The lush countryside of Kilkenny lured the Normans, who dotted the landscape with castles and built a dignified town that soon rivalled Dublin as an administrative centre.

Inland, Athlone stands guard over County Westmeath's rural, lake-dotted landscape and the River Shannon that divides it from Connacht. Along the banks of that great waterway in County Offaly are the remains of one of Ireland's most awe-inspiring ecclesiastical settlements, Clonmacnoise. Kildare's Hill of Allen is thought to have been the winter quarters of Fionn MacCumhail's legendary Fianna warriors, but these days the county is known for its stud farms and Curragh race course.

Kilkenny Castle reflects the history and importance of this lovely town (Tour 14)

The lushness and variety of Leinster's landscape are as much a delight to today's visitors as they were to past conquerors, many of whom sprinkled it with great mansions and gardens. The lake-filled midland counties draw avid anglers and boating enthusiasts on the Shannon, and the peat bogs of counties Laois and Offaly form part of the most important bogland in Europe, with global significance. Along the coast are curving bays and sandy beaches, as well as nature reserves inhabited by a wide range of wildlife.

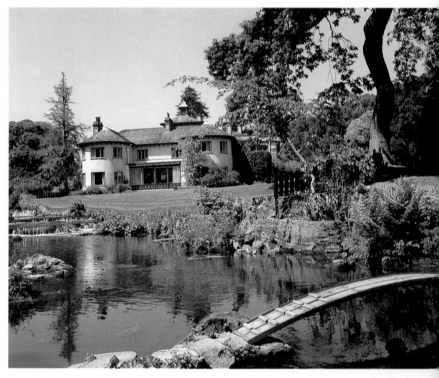

Tour 11

From the historically important Athlone and its modern-day riverboating, this tour takes you to the former garrison town of Mullingar, whose proximity to good trout lakes makes it an excellent angling centre. Then you travel to Tullamore, home of a world-famous distillery, and on to Birr, with its castle and garden. The monastic ruins of Clonmacnoise lend a spiritual aspect to your travels, as do the ruins at Clonfert.

Tour 12

This is a historic drive through Ireland's past, in pleasant countryside rich in megalithic and early Christian monuments, including the intriguing passage grave of Newgrange, exquisite high crosses at Monasterboice, Slane and its associations with St Patrick and the Hill of Tara, redolent of the heroic age of the High Kings of Ireland. The tour ends with the site of the Battle of the Boyne in 1690, where

King William met King James to finish a conflict of national and European significance.

Tour 13

From Dublin, the tour visits bright coastal towns which owe much of their character to Victorian enthusiasm for the seaside. The route winds its way into the mountains, and visits Glendalough, one of Ireland's most captivating combinations of history and landscape. The scenery is a combination of bog, lake and mountaintop, and a highlight of this tour is the profusion of glorious gardens, justifying the claim that this area is 'the Garden of Ireland'.

Tour 14

Norman castles, ecclesiastical ruins and tales of medieval witches haunt Kilkenny, starting point for this tour. History and active river commerce meld happily in New Ross on the River Barrow. Further along the river, prehistory has left its mark

Mount Usher Gardens (Tour 13) on the River Vartry

just outside Carlow town in the form of an impressive dolmen. Kildare's horse country will appeal to followers of the sport of kings, and the gardens near Portlaoise have universal appeal. Celtic kings and St Patrick draw you on to Cashel.

Tour 15

Founded by Vikings, invaded by Normans, conquered by Cromwell's troops, and a hotbed of insurgence, Wexford is an excellent tour base: north to the country's famed beaches, then inland for more history, before turning south to the river town of New Ross. Continue south to Waterford, another Viking stronghold and the east coast's most important port, then a ferry ride takes you to the enchanting Hook peninsula through villages undisturbed by 'progress', and on to a noted bird refuge and a holy island.

Monastic Ruins
& The Midlands

Athlone is an important commercial and holiday centre, and a junction for road, rail and river traffic. Its marina on the Shannon has fleets of smart river cruisers for hire, and Athlone also has good facilities for anglers and golfers. Athlone Castle, overlooking the bridge, provides marvellous town views and has an interesting visitor centre. There is much to see in the vicinity.

1/2 DAYS • 141 MILES • 227KM

ITINERARY		
ATHLONE	▶	**Mullingar (44m-71km)**
MULLINGAR	▶	**Tullamore (22m-35km)**
TULLAMORE	▶	**Birr (23m-37km)**
BIRR	▶	**Clonmacnoise (22m-35km)**
CLONMACNOISE	▶	**Ballinasloe (14m-23km)**
BALLINASLOE	▶	**Athlone (16m-26km)**

SCENIC ROUTES

Leave Athlone on the N55 northeast, and about 2 miles (3km) outside town turn right on to the R390. At Ballymore, some 12 miles (19km) northeast of Athlone, look for the remains of a 14th-century Anglo-Norman fortress. Continue on the R390 for 4 miles (6km) to the 602-foot (183m) high Hill of Ushnagh. This was a place of religious importance during pagan times, as it was the accepted centre of the universe, and from the summit there are fine views of Ireland's vast central plain.

There are burial mounds and an earthen fort, and on the southwest side of the summit, Aill na Mireann (The Stone of Divisions) is thought to mark the boundaries of all five ancient provinces of Ireland.

Mullingar Cathedral is famous for its mosaics and its ecclesiastical museum

RECOMMENDED WALKS

On Lough Ree's western shore, about 8 miles (13km) from Athlone, Rinndown Peninsula juts out into the lake just east of the village of Lecarrow. Follow the unnumbered road from Lecarrow until it becomes a track leading to the lakeshore. The heavily wooded path passes ancient ruins from the 13th century that combine with the dense shade to create a somewhat spooky atmosphere. The walk takes in the remains of St John's Castle (so named for the Knights of St John who once occupied it) and a church with its outbuildings.

i Athlone Castle, St Peter's Square, Athlone

▶ Take the **N55** northeast from Athlone to the town of Edgeworthstown, then turn southeast on to the **N4** for the drive to Mullingar.

0 **Mullingar,** Co Westmeath
En route to Mullingar, stop by in Edgeworthstown, the village named after the Edgeworth family. The father of the family was a noted inventor and author, and his daughter Maria became one of Ireland's leading women writers. She holds a special place in Irish affections for her work among the suffering during the famine years. A friend of Sir Walter Scott, her best known work was *Castle Rackrent*.

If you plan to eat steak in Ireland, Mullingar, the county town of Westmeath, is the place to do it, in the heart of Ireland's cattle-raising area. Mullingar's long history includes a position of prime importance as a barracks town for the British military. It was here, during the Williamite Wars, that British commander de Ginkel rallied his forces for the 1691 Siege of Athlone. The imprint of those years is stamped on the town's face even today in the form of large, grey, rather formidable buildings. The present-day personality of the town, however, in no way reflects its somewhat grim past, and Mullingar is an excellent base for seeing the Westmeath lakes, most of which offer excellent brown trout fishing.

The Cathedral of Christ the King, designed by Ralph Byrne, has outstanding mosaics of St Patrick and St Anne near the high altar that are the work of Russian artist Boris Anrep. Permission must be obtained from the sacristan to see the ecclesiastical museum.

In July, Mullingar celebrates eligible bachelors from all over the world, with the International Bachelor Festival.

A little way south on the Tullamore road is Belvedere House, Gardens and Park. The 18th-century mansion is an architectural gem, and interpreters bring convincingly to life the stories and scandals from its history. The grounds, on the shore of Lough Ennell, include woodland, lakeshore walks, Ireland's largest folly, and walled gardens with a wonderful collection of rare and unusual plants. The stable block now houses exhibitions, a visitor centre and a multimedia show, and there's an animal sanctuary and children's play area near by.

Travel in almost any direction from Mullingar and you will find the lakes that have made this region famous for trout. Lough Ennell is about 6 miles (10km) to the south, with a championship golf course overlooking the lake and the ruins of ancient Lynn Church on its northeastern shore.

Three miles (5km) north of town, Lough Owel is a sailing and sub-aqua centre, and there are good swimming facilities. About 6 miles (10km) north of town, Lough Derravaragh is a beautiful, irregular-shaped lake with thickly wooded shores. It plays a central part in one of Ireland's most tragic and beloved legends, since it was one of three lakes on which the Children of Lir were doomed to spend 300 years when their wicked stepmother turned them into swans. To this day, swans on Irish waters are under the protection granted to all swans by the grieving father.

Tullynally Castle's rather grim exterior belies its splendid interior and works of art

For good views of the lakes and plains, Rathconnell Hill is just 2 miles (3km) northeast of Mullingar off the N52. You can see Lough Owel from 499-foot (152m) Shanemore (Slanemore) Hill, 4 miles (6km) northwest of town.

Thirteen miles (21km) north of Mullingar via the R394, Tullynally Castle and Gardens, in Castlepollard, are one of County Westmeath's chief attractions. Seat of the Earls of Longford since the 17th century, the turreted and towered Gothic-revival manor house is only open to pre-booked groups, but the gardens are open to all. Extending to some 30 acres (12 hectares), they are truly magnificent, and include walled gardens, ornamental lakes, oriental gardens, woods and parkland.

The village of Fore, about 3 miles (5km) east of Castlepollard, is the setting for an interesting group of antiquities and the legend of the

'Seven Wonders of Fore'. In summer the Fore Abbey Coffee Shop provides information as well as refreshment, including a 'Seven Wonders' video shown at weekends. At the Seven Wonders pub, you can pick up the key to Fore Abbey, the ancient ruins of St Feichin's Monastery which date back to the 7th century.

ℹ️ *Dublin Road (seasonal)*

▶ *Continue south for 22 miles (35km) on the N52/N6 for Tullamore.*

2 Tullamore, Co Offaly
On the drive from Mullingar, stop off at the village of Kilbeggan, 7 miles (11km) north of Tullamore, where a museum, antiques shop and café now occupy the restored 18th-century Locke's Distillery, once one of Europe's largest.

The chief town of County Offaly, Tullamore owes its development to the Grand Canal laid out in 1798 to connect Dublin to the Shannon. The canal carried

huge cargoes of yellow brick made in the town to Dublin during its expansion in the 19th century.

Tullamore is the home of Irish Mist liquer and Tullamore

BACK TO NATURE

About 7 miles (11km) northwest of Tullamore, Clara Bog is one of the largest intact bogs of its type in Ireland. Its well-developed 'soak' system is considered to be the best in western Europe. Increased water flow from surface run-off or underground springs allows the growth of many more plant species than are normally found in a bog environment. Among those that thrive here are bog mosses, sundews, heathers, cotton grass, and bog rosemary. There are hummock/hollow complexes, bog pools and moss lawns. The bog is easily seen from the road, but is considered unsafe for exploration on foot.

Dew whiskey, and the Tullamore Dew Heritage Centre offers an excellent insight into the distillery and town history.

ℹ️ *Bury Quay*

▶ *Follow the N52 for 23 miles (37km) southwest to Birr.*

3 Birr, Co Offaly
Plan a stop in the village of Kilcormac, about 12 miles (19km) south of Tullamore on the N52, for a look at the beautifully carved wooden pietà in the Catholic church, which is thought to be the work of a 16th-century artist.

Georgian buildings and a world-famous castle and garden are the main attractions in the small town of Birr, just above the confluence of the Little Bronsa and Camcor Rivers.

Birr Castle is an impressive fortified manor house set in extensive grounds, but the building is not open to the

The restored 18th-century Locke's Distillery, Kilbeggan

public, since it has, for several centuries, been the residence of the Parsons family, Earls of Rosse. The 3rd Earl was a noted astronomer, whose giant 72-inch (180cm) reflecting telescope was the largest in the world for an astounding 70 years. The telescope has been restored to full working order and the scientific museum at Birr Castle has become Ireland's Historic Science Centre. It covers the pioneering achievements of the Parsons family and other Irish scientists, covering astronomy, engineering, photography and horticulture. The castle gardens cover 100 acres (40 hectares),

laid out on the banks of the two rivers and around a lake, with over 1,000 species of plants and trees.

> [i] Brendon Street

▶ *Take the **N62** north to Cloghan, and turn west on to the **R357** to Shannonbridge. Turn right on the **R444** for 4 miles (6km) to Clonmacnoise.*

4 Clonmacnoise,
Co Offaly

Set beside the River Shannon, this is one of Ireland's holiest places. St Ciaran's monastery, founded here in AD548, became the most famous of Ireland's monastic cities and was one of Europe's leading centres of learning for nearly 1,000 years. It enjoyed the patronage of many Irish Kings, and Rory O'Conor, the last High King, lies buried here. Its great fame and wealth attracted plunderers from home and abroad, and the final indignity came in 1552

History and science combine at Birr Castle to provide a fascinating day out

when the English garrison at Athlone carried off the spoils. Even the glass from the windows was taken, and the site was finally abandoned. Restoration began in 1647, but Cromwellian forces carried out yet another raid that put paid to the revival of its former glory. Today, there is a cathedral on the site, one of eight church ruins, two round towers, three sculptured high crosses (and parts of two others), over 200 monumental slabs and a ruined

---

FOR CHILDREN

At Shannonbridge, north of Birr on the N62, is a narrow-gauge railway trip across a stretch of bogland, with a guide giving a commentary. A slide show precedes the tour.

SPECIAL TO...

Each year on 9 September and the following Sunday, great throngs, drawn from around the world, make the pilgrimage to Clonmacnoise to commemorate St Ciaran's feast day.

castle. St Ciaran's grave is said to be in the east end of 'The Little Church', a small 9th-century cell.

i Monastic site (seasonal)

▶ Return to Shannonbridge and turn northwest on to the **R357** for the 8-mile (13km) drive to Ballinasloe.

5 Ballinasloe, Co Galway
In a strategic position of military importance in the past, Ballinasloe once centred around its castle, but today it is a thriving market town. Seven miles (11km) from town on the Athenry road is the Abbey of Kilconnell, founded in 1400. Its nave, choir, side aisles, south transept, and some of the cloisters are in perfect condition.

Clonfert, 13 miles (21km) southeast of Ballinasloe, was chosen by St Brendan in the 6th century for a monastic settlement, of which nothing remains today. The cathedral has superb

Romanesque decoration, with various motifs, including animal and human heads and intricate carvings of foliage.

i Bridge Street (seasonal)

▶ *Take the **N6** northeast to return to Athlone, a distance of 16 miles (26km).*

SPECIAL TO...

Ballinasloe's International October Fair and Festival features eight days of fierce horse trading, street entertainment, and non-stop revelry. It is one of the few such fairs still held in Ireland.

FOR CHILDREN

West of Athlone off the N6, Glendeer Open Farm has friendly farm animals, ostrich, emu and deer, a play area and nature trail. In December it becomes 'Lapland', with Christmas displays.

FOR HISTORY BUFFS

Following their defeat at the battle of the Boyne in 1690, Irish forces who supported King James withdrew to the town of Athlone to establish the Shannon as their last line of defence against the English. Their leader, Colonel Grace, held the castle for King James and withstood a week's siege from the pursuing Williamite army.
In 1691, however, the English commander laid siege to the town. The Irish, retreating across the Shannon, destroyed the bridge, but the English started rebuilding it immediately. A heroic Irish Sergeant, Custume, then called for volunteers and with a handful of men managed to break down the hastily thrown-up structure. As a result, the town held out for another ten days, after which Irish Jacobite forces withdrew.

One of the three intact carved high crosses of Clonmacnoise

The Boyne
Valley

The great grassy mound of Millmount, which gives a panoramic view over Drogheda, was first a passage grave, then a Viking meeting place, a Norman motte, and an important military barracks in the 18th century, its history mirroring that of the town. Some of Millmount's buildings have been converted into a small museum. A view from any point of the town will show that Drogheda is a town of churches, including St Peter's which contains the head of martyred Oliver Plunkett.

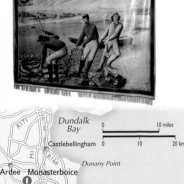

2 DAYS • 84 MILES • 134KM

ITINERARY

DROGHEDA	▶	**Monasterboice** (6m-10km)
MONASTERBOICE	▶	**Mellifont** (4m-6km)
MELLIFONT	▶	**Newgrange** (9m-14km)
NEWGRANGE	▶	**Slane** (6m-10km)
SLANE	▶	**Kells** (15m-24km)
KELLS	▶	**Navan** (10m-16km)
NAVAN	▶	**Hill of Tara** (7m-11km)
HILL OF TARA	▶	**Battle of the Boyne Site** (23m-37km)
BATTLE OF THE BOYNE SITE	▶	**Drogheda** (4m-6km)

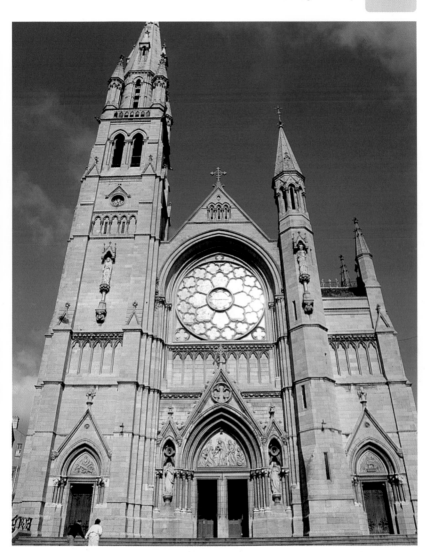

⊞ Mayoralty Street, Drogheda

BACK TO NATURE

Visit Mornington sand dunes, which lie close to Drogheda on the coast. The dunes range from newly formed areas, colonised by marram grass close to the sea, to mature 'slacks' inland. The latter support a rich variety of plants including many orchids in the spring.

SCENIC ROUTES

This part of the eastern coast of Ireland may lack the grandeur of the north and west, but there is pleasant, gentle scenery with sandy beaches and shingle shores on the road from Drogheda to Mornington, Bettsytown, Laytown and Julianstown. The road follows the estuary of the Boyne, close to the great railway viaduct.

The superb frontage of St Peter's church in Drogheda

▶ *Take the R132 north. After 5 miles (8km) turn left, passing under the motorway and following signposts for Boyne Drive, Monasterboice. In ½ mile (1km) turn left again.*

❶ Monasterboice, Co Louth Pick your way between ancient and modern graves to see two of the finest high crosses. These free-standing carvings in stone are of a quality unparalleled anywhere in Europe at the time they were erected, yet the very high round tower is a reminder that these remarkable works of art were executed in the midst of Viking plunder. The West Cross stands close to the round tower, while the Cross of Muiredach – so called because of the inscription on the base, which says 'A prayer for Muiredach by whom this cross was made' – is smaller and more perfect in appearance. The messages on these crosses follow coherent themes of God's grace to man and the parallels between Old and New Testaments. On Muiredach's Cross look for the stories of Adam and Eve, Cain and Abel, the Last Judgement and the Crucifixion of Christ.

Pope John Paul II visited in 1979, and the point where he celebrated Mass is marked on the main Belfast–Dublin road.

▶ *Continue past Monasterboice. After a mile (2km), turn right at a T-junction for Mellifont. A mile (2km) further turn left on to the Drogheda road, R168, and after a further mile (2km) turn right to Mellifont.*

② Mellifont, Co Louth

In a pleasant valley beside the River Mattock, Malachy, the former Archbishop of Armagh, founded the first Cistercian monastery in Ireland in 1142. A substantial square gate-house still stands, but only fragments of this great monastery now remain, including arches of a Romanesque cloister and a chapter house. An octagonal lavabo once equipped with water jets and basins is the most interesting structure.

▶ *Return to the crossroads just before Mellifont and turn right. After 2 miles (3km) turn right.*

Go straight over the cross-roads, following the signpost to King William's Glen. After 1 mile (1.5km) turn right on to the N51, then 2½ miles (4km) further on, turn left following signs for Newgrange.

③ Newgrange, Knowth and Dowth, Co Meath

Irish architecture may be said to have begun in the Boyne Valley, when, in about 3000BC, people who had only stone and wood for tools created the most impressive monuments of their kind in western Europe. Little is known of these people, or of those interred in these prehistoric tombs, but excavations have shown that they were cultivators of crops and had cleared areas of forest.

The mound at Newgrange, constructed with water-rolled pebbles, rises to a height of 36 feet (11m), its mass retained by a kerb of great stone blocks lying end to end, topped by white quartz and granite boulders. The passage is lined by huge stones, and the central cross-shaped chamber is roofed with a vault untouched in five millenia. Standing around the mound is an incomplete circle of stones.

Knowth has two passage-tombs surrounded by 18 smaller ones. It was used from the Stone Age, and in the early Christian era was a seat of the High Kings of Ireland. The Boyne Valley tombs are significant in that they combine art with the engineering feats of the passage-tombs of Ireland. Spirals, lozenges, zigzags, sunbursts – figures cut in stone with stone implements – decorate the monuments.

At Newgrange the sophisticated structure incorporates the unique phenomenon of a roof-box, which, only at the winter solstice, allows the rays of the rising sun to penetrate the chamber and flood it with light.

St Patrick's conversion of Ireland to Christianity took a leap forward at Slane in 433

Archaeological work continues, and important discoveries are still being made in the Boyne Valley which means that sites may be closed at times for excavation. Visits to Newgrange and Knowth are by guided tour only. These begin at the Brú na Boinne Visitor Centre – there is no direct access to the monuments – and in the busy summer months there will be delays; visits cannot be guaranteed. As well as issuing tickets, the centre has extensive interpretative displays and viewing areas.

i *Visitor Centre*

▷ *Return by minor roads to the N51 and turn left for Slane.*

4 **Slane,** Co Meath
Slane occupies an attractive curve on the River Boyne and is overlooked by the Hill of Slane, where, tradition has it, St Patrick lit his paschal fire in AD433 in defiance of the orders of King Laoghaire. In his persuasive speech to the King, Patrick used the shamrock as his illustration of the Trinity. He won his argument and permission to preach Christianity throughout the land. From the viewpoint on the hill, the pleasant village can be seen running steeply down to the banks of the river.

Just to the east is the cottage of the poet Francis Ledwidge, who died during World War I.

Slane Castle on the banks of the River Boyne is the home of the Mount Charles family. It

reopened to the public in 2001 following an extensive restoration project after a fire in 1991. The castle also hosts big open-air rock concerts.

▷ *Take the N51 for Navan, and after 1 mile (2km) turn right on to the R163 for Kells.*

5 **Kells,** Co Meath
Kells, or Ceanannus Mór, was one of the great religious centres of western Europe. You can pick out the circular ditch in the lie of the town, and see the round tower, an early church and the impressive Celtic crosses with their scriptural messages.

The town is famous for the *Book of Kells*, the celebrated illuminated medieval manuscript, now on view in the library at Trinity College, Dublin. The restored courthouse now contains the Kells Heritage Centre, with a multimedia insight into the crafts and culture of the area.

▷ *Take the N3 to Navan.*

6 **Navan,** Co Meath
Once a walled town, Navan marks the meeting of the powerful waters of the Boyne and the Blackwater. Keep a look out for the stocks outside the town hall, and also look for a very modern interesting blue sculpture, which is dedicated to 'the Fifth Province, the ideal of the cultural integration of all the people of Ireland.'

Tara, just a simple mound today, evokes a glorious past

FOR HISTORY BUFFS

Trim, south of Navan, is worth visiting for Trim Castle alone, the largest Norman castle in Ireland. It also has the Yellow Steeple, which was once part of an Augustinian monastery, a statue of the Duke of Wellington, who was educated here, and a small cathedral with a 15th-century tower. Richard, Duke of York, father of Edward IV, made Trim his Irish headquarters and initiated building projects in the town. Still magnificent, the castle has undergone extensive restoration work.

▷ *Take the N3 for Dublin, and after 6 miles (10km) turn right at the signpost for Hill of Tara.*

7 **Hill of Tara,** Co Meath
The seat of the High Kings of Ireland, the Hill of Tara commands majestic views over the fertile plains of Meath and beyond. This was the centre of Ireland's heroic age, a civilisation that had contact with the Roman Empire and was ruled by a king who was concerned with sacred rites and rituals as well as political matters. A *feis* at royal Tara was a renowned festivity, held at harvest, or for the crowning of a king, of which the dynastic O'Neills were the strongest.

Five chariot roads led here from all parts of Ireland. The Rath of the Synods is an elaborate trivallate earthwork. The Mound of the Hostages is an Iron-Age hillfort and encloses the Royal Seat, a ringfort. On Cormac's House is the Stone of Destiny, said to be the inauguration stone of the kings. Also here are the Banquet Hall, the Enclosure of King Laoghaire, the Sloping Trenches and Grainne's Enclosure.

A statue of St Patrick recalls his profound influence, but it was the coming of Christianity that led to the eventual decline of Tara. There's a good audio-visual presentation, and guided tours.

▷ *Return to the **N3** and turn right. After 2 miles (3km) turn left following signs to Skreen Church and Cross, go straight over two sets of crossroads and follow a narrow, uneven road for 2 miles (3km) to a crossroads, then turn left towards Drogheda. After another 2 miles (3km) turn left towards Slane on the **N2***

FOR CHILDREN

If your children are suffering from historical overload in the Boyne Valley, you can take them along to Newgrange Farm, beside the famous mound, where they cannot only see but also hold and feed the animals.

SPECIAL TO...

The pastures of Meath are among the richest in Ireland. Much of the land has not been ploughed for generations and provides excellent grassland for cattle and horses. In summer the pride of the country can be seen at many agricultural shows. As well as the show classes, you will find pony and horse jumping, home industries competitions, and get a real feel of the farming life at the heart of Ireland. The country's agricultural heritage is also reflected in the Steam Threshing Festival at Moynalty in August, which recalls past harvesting methods.

A cottage wall mural depicts Ireland's most famous battle

RECOMMENDED WALKS

At Townley Hall, the Forest and Wildlife Service has developed a waymarked trail that takes the walker close to the site of the Battle of the Boyne, and gives views over the valley. The walk up the wooded banks of the river is steep in places. A trail leaflet is available from the battle site.

and follow the marked route for the Battle of the Boyne Site.

🎱 **Battle of the Boyne Site,** Co Louth and Meath

It does not take a great effort of the imagination to picture the field of battle in 1690, when the armies of William of Orange and James II met each other in a conflict that was significant for Ireland, Britain and Europe. A huge orange and green sign beside the deep waters of the Boyne marks the main site of the conflict, while helpful signs along the way show where the opposing armies camped, where battle was joined and where the river was crossed. The route passes along the Boyne Navigation Canal, once a link in Ireland's waterways system.

▷ *Take the **N51** to Drogheda.*

Dublin

1/2 DAYS • 89 MILES • 143KM

& Wicklow

Dublin is a lively and attractive city with a unique brand of Irishness. Easy to explore on foot, it has superb museums, galleries and shopping, elegant Georgian streets and the historic Temple Bar area, with its narrow lanes, pubs and restaurants. The River Liffey cuts the city in two, and the lovely Wicklow Mountains rise to the south.

[i] *Suffolk Street, Dublin*

▶ *Take the R118/N31 to Dun Laoghaire.*

❶ Dun Laoghaire, Co Dublin
This is a place to promenade, along the extensive harbour piers, past the villas on the front, or through the parks. Savour the Victorian features of the place which was called Kingstown from the visit of George IV in 1821 until the establishment of the Irish Free State. When the granite piers were completed in 1859, the harbour was the biggest artificial haven in the world. Ships and ferries to England use the port and it is home to several yacht clubs, of which the Royal St George and the Royal Irish are the oldest. The town also boasts Ireland's National Maritime Museum, housed in the Mariners' Church.

Near by, at Sandycove, is a Martello tower, one of the distinctive squat round coastal defences erected in Napoleonic times. This one is of particular note as it houses a James Joyce museum (the writer stayed in this area briefly).

The Martello tower and the nearby 'Forty foot' gentlemen's bathing place are vividly described in Joyce's renowned novel *Ulysses*.

Elegant Georgian houses add an air of distinction to the resort and port of Dun Laoghaire

▶ *Take the R119 coastal road to Dalkey and Killiney.*

❷ Killiney, Co Dublin
With the broad sweep of a steeply dropping bay, elegant villas among tree-filled gardens and the two Sugar Loaf mountains to complete the vista, Killiney has been likened to the Bay of Naples. A good place to take in the full extent of the panorama is Sorrento Point.

Another good viewpoint is Killiney Hill, some distance inland from the beach, where an attractive park on the summit gives superb views of the hills and sea. Its 18th-century stone obelisk was built as a famine relief project.

▶ *Continue on the R119, then join the R761 to Bray.*

❸ Bray, Co Wicklow
This is a popular resort that retains much of its Victorian attraction. Bray's beautiful long beach stretches below the strong line of Bray Head, an extension of the Wicklow dome. From the promenade you can walk the outstanding cliff path for 3 miles (5km) to Greystones. Below the Head, fan-like fossils of the oldest known Irish animals have been found.

In the town you will find an attractive Heritage Centre. The National Sea Life Centre in the town has 70 species of sea and freshwater creatures, including a Tropical Shark Lagoon exhibit.

Kilruddery, by contrast, was one of the great set-piece landscape gardens of the 17th century. Very few of these early formal gardens, designed on a large scale with geometric patterns of water, avenues and plants, now survive.

▶ *Return to and take the*
M11/N11 for Wicklow, then
turn right for Enniskerry.

4 Enniskerry, Co Wicklow
The first Irish Roman Catholic
Gothic revival church was built
in this pretty village in 1843. Its
spire is an attractive feature in
the lovely glen of Glencullen.

The superb mountain
setting enhances Powerscourt,
one of Ireland's great gardens,
extravagantly created by the 6th
and 7th Viscounts Powerscourt,
and extensively altered
between 1843 and 1875. A
formal landscape of water,
terraces, statues, ironwork,
plants, flowers and ancient trees
is stunningly contrasted with
the natural beauty of Sugar Loaf
Mountain, combining to form
one of the most photographed
vistas in the country. The
house, a magnificent Palladian
mansion, was destroyed by fire
in 1974, but has been partly
restored. Also in the estate is
Powerscourt Waterfall where
the Dargle River plunges over a
400 feet (120m) high rockface.

▶ *Take the **R760** south,*
*turning left to join the **R755***
for 8 miles (13km) south to
Roundwood.

5 Roundwood, Co Wicklow
The highest village in Ireland,
Roundwood sits amid lovely
scenery. The Vartry Reservoir,
which helps to serve Dublin,
lies close to the village. To the
northeast is the Glen of the
Downs, a dry rocky gorge
formed in the Ice Age, with an
oak wood. The landscape gives
an idea of what Ireland would
have looked like in prehistoric
times, before the clearance of
the forests. Lough Dan and
Lough Tay are dark loughs
shadowed by granite.

Six miles (10km) southeast
of Roundwood at Ashford is
Mount Usher, one of the finest
examples of the 'Wild Garden',
an idea particularly suited to
Irish gardens. In a sheltered
valley, plants, which include
many exotic species, grow

naturally, in harmony with the
landscape. They spread along
the banks of a winding stream
with cascades spanned by
unusual suspension bridges.

▶ *Take the **R755** to Laragh,*
*then turn right on the **R756**.*
*Fork left on the **R757** to*
Glendalough.

Within the beautiful Powerscourt
Demesne is this lovely waterfall,
with woodland walks and picnic
places near by

6 Glendalough, Co Wicklow

Glendalough, the glen of two loughs, is the loveliest and most historic of all its Wicklow rivals. Two beautiful loughs lie deep in a valley of granite escarpments and rocky outcrops. On its green slopes are the gentle contours of native trees, on its ridges the jagged outline of pines. Add to this picturesque scene a soaring round tower and ruined stone churches spreading through the valley, and you have a combination which makes Glendalough one of the most beautiful and historic places in Ireland.

St Kevin came to Glendalough in the 6th century to escape worldly pleasures. He lived as a hermit, in a cell on a little shelf above the lake, but the settlement he founded flourished and grew to become a monastic city whose influence spread throughout Europe. The round tower was built when Viking raids troubled the serenity of Glendalough. Some of the little churches have fine stone carvings, and one has a good pitched stone roof. Guides will explain the full story of

Glendalough's round tower is a prominent landmark in this very special valley

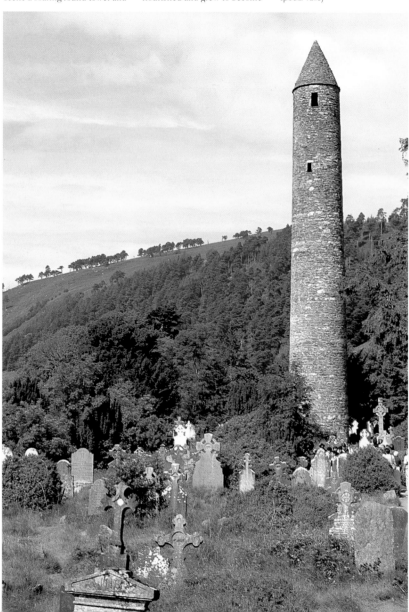

Glendalough, and a visitor centre skilfully illustrates the life of a monastery.

To the south near Rathdrum is Avondale, the home of the great Irish leader Charles Stewart Parnell. The 18th-century house, now a museum, is set in a large beautiful forest park on the banks of the Avonmore River.

BACK TO NATURE

The wide open spaces of the Wicklow Mountains offer opportunities for seeing a variety of upland birds, including peregrines, merlins, hen harriers, ring ousels and red grouse. In the glens, wood warblers and the occasional redstart may be seen.

▶ *Return to the **R756** to go through the Wicklow Gap, then turn right on to the **R758** heading for Pollaphuca.*

FOR HISTORY BUFFS

Patrick Pearse, one of the leaders of the uprising in 1916, kept a school in St Enda's Park. The building has now been converted into a museum dedicated to his memory.

---

7 **Pollaphuca,** Co Wicklow
At Pollaphuca there are large lakes, now dammed to supply Dublin's water system and also forming part of the Liffey hydroelectric scheme. The proximity to the city and the abundance of lakeside roads make it a popular venue for Dubliners.

▶ *Follow the lakeside road by Lackan to Blessington.*

8 **Blessington,** Co Wicklow
An attractive village with a long main street, Blessington was an important coaching stop on the main road south from Dublin.

Just south is Russborough House, serenely placed in a beautiful landscape before a fine lake. It was built in the middle of the 18th century, the work of architect Richard Castle, for Joseph Leeson, the Earl of Milltown. A Palladian house constructed of granite, it sweeps out elegantly along curving colonnades to flanking wings and pavilions. Features include superb plasterwork by the Francini brothers. Owing to a series of thefts, the famous Beit Art Collection may not be on show.

▶ *Take the **N81** for Dublin. After 4½ miles (7km) turn right on to the **R759** to the Sally Gap.*

FOR HISTORY BUFFS

Wicklow men played a large part in the 1798 rebellion, and in order to finally suppress the uprising and clear the mountains, the 'Military Road' was forged from Rathfarnham in the north through the Sally Gap to Aghavannagh in the south. Former barracks can be seen at Drumgoff and Aghavannagh.

---

9 **The Sally Gap,** Co Wicklow
The most complete stretch of blanket bog on the east of the country is the beautiful Sally Gap. There are many pools and

---

SCENIC ROUTES

The road from Sally Gap to Laragh rises and falls wonderfully, with views across the Cloghoge Valley to War Hill. The road goes south through rugged mountain land, into forest plantations and passes Glenmacnass, a deep glen formed by glaciers, with a magnificent waterfall.

---

streams here, as well as the characteristic bog rosemary.

▶ *Turn sharp left on to the **R115** to Killakee.*

10 **Killakee,** Co Dublin
The view from Killakee gives an outstanding picture of Dublin, as George Moore put it, 'wandering between the hills and the sea'. It takes in the crescent of Dublin Bay, bounded by the twin bastions of Howth Head to the north and Killiney Head to the south. The River Liffey is clearly defined, and you can identify the green landmark of Phoenix Park.

South of Killakee is a sinister hilltop ruin, once a retreat of the Hell Fire Club which was formed by a group of rakes in 1735. There are colourful tales of their terrible wickedness, the worst involving a game of cards with the devil.

North of Killakee, towards Dublin, is Marlay Park, with recreational amenities, miniature railway, gardens and craft centre. In the same area is Rathfarnham Castle, which dates back to 1583. A national monument, it is presented to the public as a building undergoing active conservation.

▶ *Follow the **R115** for 7 miles (11km) back to Dublin.*

RECOMMENDED WALKS

The Wicklow Way is a long-distance walk that follows a course from Marlay Park in the north to Shillelagh and then through into County Kilkenny, on high ground to the east of the Dublin and Wicklow Mountains. The route is mostly waymarked through forests, along old bog roads and up steep mountain tracks. It is best to come equipped for wet weather and wear strong walking shoes. In addition, there are dozens of forest walks through Wicklow.

Witches, Castles
& Horses

2/3 DAYS • 201 MILES • 324KM

Kilkenny is an ancient town that once rivalled Dublin in importance, and many of its historic buildings have been preserved, including the splendid 14th-century castle, perched above the river. Kilkenny is also the home of the Kilkenny Design Centre, promoting the best in Irish design and craftsmanship. The centre has craft workshops as well as a showroom.

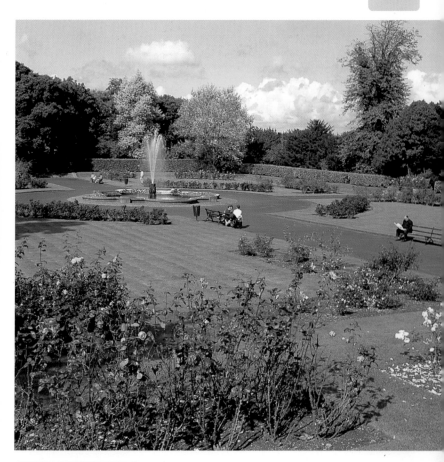

SPECIAL TO...

Kilkenny was the home of Ireland's most famous witches. In 1324 Dame Alice Kyteler was the owner of Kyteler's Inn in St Kieran's Street. A beautiful woman who had become wealthy following the successive deaths of her four husbands, she was accused of witchcraft and condemned to a public whipping, followed by burning at the stake. She escaped, leaving her maid to be burnt in her place, and was never seen again. She is said to haunt the house still. Each August, Kilkenny Arts Festival takes place, when the town is host to world-class musicians and performers.

i *Shee Alms House, Rose Inn Street*

▶ *Take the **R700** southeast for 11 miles (18km) to Thomastown.*

❶ **Thomastown,** Co Kilkenny

This prosperous little market town on the banks of the River Nore is named after Thomas Fitz Anthony Walsh, Seneschal of Leinster, who built a castle and walled the town in the early 13th century. Grennan Castle, about 1½ miles (2km) to the southwest, is now in ruins. The most impressive remains of ancient buildings in the town are those of a large church dating from the 13th century.

Jerpoint Cistercian Abbey, some 2 miles (3km) southwest

Delightful formal gardens contrast with the forbidding stone walls of Kilkenny Castle

of Thomastown on the N9, is one of Ireland's finest monastic ruins. Founded in the 12th century, it was dissolved and its lands given to the Ormonde family in 1540. The extensive remains are awe-inspiring, with the original Romanesque pillars, a fine chancel and the most decorative cloister arcade of any Irish church. The detailed secular and religious carved figures are an accurate portrayal of the armour and clothing of 15th- and 16th-century Ireland. A visitor centre provides information on the abbey's long history. Mount Juliet, signposted from the town centre, was once one of Ireland's largest private

estates, covering 1,411 acres (570 hectares) of woodlands, pastures and landscaped lawns. Now a luxury hotel, the grounds provide an exceptionally beautiful drive off the main roads, and its public rooms are open to non-residents.

Though worn by time, this decoration on a tomb shows Jerpoint's artistic heritage

RECOMMENDED WALKS

From Thomastown walk along the banks of the River Nore for 1½ miles (2km) to the southwest to reach the remains of 13th-century Grennan Castle. The river walk is through woodland, with patches of rich pasture, and the lawn between the castle ruins and the river is covered with daffodils in spring.

SCENIC ROUTES

Leaving Thomastown by the R703 east, the 8-mile (13km) drive to Graiguenamanagh provides tremendous views of the River Barrow and the long ridge of the Blackstairs Mountains and 1,694-foot (516m) Brandon Hill which lies to the south.

▶ *Take the **R700** southeast for 14 miles (23m) to Mountgarret Bridge, where it joins the **N30** for the short drive to New Ross.*

2 New Ross, Co Wexford
There is much evidence of its medieval origins in the narrow streets of New Ross, climbing the steep hill on which the town is built, overlooking the River Barrow. The town invites exploration on foot, as many of the streets are stepped and inaccessible to vehicles. The long bridge in the town centre connects New Ross to County

Jerpoint Abbey, once at the centre of its own small town, remains an impressive sight

Kilkenny. The original bridge was built around 1200 and the town was soon walled. In 1643, it held off a siege by the Duke of Ormonde, but fell to Cromwell just six years later.

The Tholsel (Town Hall), rebuilt in 1806, has a fine clock tower and holds the maces of Edward III and Charles II and ancient volumes of the minutes of the old town corporation. The 1798 memorial at the Tholsel depicts a 'croppy boy', typical of the insurgents who assaulted the town.

On the quay you can board the *Dunbrody*, a seaworthy replica of one of the emigrant ships that carried so many Irish to the New World in the mid-19th century. River cruises depart from the quay during the summer. (See also Tour 15.)

ℹ *Dunbrody Heritage Centre, The Quay*

▶ *Head north on the **N30**, turn left on to the **R700**, then right after a short distance on to the **R705** for 23 miles (37km) to join the **N9** at Leighlinbridge for the 7-mile (11km) drive into Carlow.*

BACK TO NATURE

About 6 miles (10km) south of New Ross, signposted from the N25 east, is the 480-acre (195-hectare) John F Kennedy Park and Arboretum, the Irish government's tribute to the American president (1961–3) whose ancestral home is in nearby Dunganstown. Nearly 300 acres (120 hectares) are given over to an arboretum that holds more than 5,000 shrubs and trees from all over the world. Follow the signposts to the top of Slieve Coillte for a panoramic view of south Wexford and the splendid estuary of the rivers Barrow, Nore and Suir.

3 Carlow, Co Carlow
The village of Graiguenamanagh ('the Granary of the Monks'), between New Ross and Carlow, was once a place of great ecclesiastical importance. Occupying the site was the

Abbey of Duiske, built between 1207 and 1240. It was suppressed in 1536, but determined monks stayed on for many years afterwards before abandoning the extensive settlement. By 1774 it stood in ruins and the tower collapsed. A large part of the church was roofed in 1813 and Catholic services were resumed. In the 1970s, a group of dedicated locals undertook a major restoration, and today the completely restored abbey serves as the parish church.

The county town of Ireland's second smallest county, Carlow was an Anglo-Norman stronghold, strategically placed on the border of the English 'Pale', a protected area around Dublin and its environs. The 640 insurgents who fell here during their 1798 attack on the town are remembered by a fine Celtic cross.

The west wall and the two flanking towers of 13th-century Carlow Castle can be seen near the bridge across the Barrow. This Norman castle was destroyed not by Cromwell, who captured it in 1650, but by one Dr Middleton in 1814. In his zeal to convert it into an asylum, he tried to reduce the thickness of the walls with explosives, rendering it no more than a dangerous shell, most of which had to be demolished.

The Cathedral of the Assumption, in Tullow Street, is a fine Gothic-style building erected between 1828 and 1833. Of special interest are its 151-foot (46m) high lantern tower and the marble monument by the sculptor John Hogan, of the 19th-century political writer Bishop Doyle. The Carlow Museum covers domestic and commercial life in the town, including some of the shop layouts, and Celtic finds. The museum is closed during its relocation to new premises on College Street.

RECOMMENDED WALKS

On the outskirts of Carlow town, Oak Park Forest Park has a number of circular, colour-coded and waymarked walks. Of varying lengths, they explore woodland and lakesides, and include one suitable for wheelchairs.

⟦i⟧ *Tullow Street*

▶ *Follow the **R417** north to Athy. Turn northeast on to the **N78** for Kilcullen, then northwest on the **R413**, which takes you west to Kildare.*

4 **Kildare,** Co Kildare
En route to Kildare, stop in Athy to view the Dominican church, a striking example of modern

Ireland is dotted with prehistoric remains. This ancient dolmen is at Brown's Hill, near Carlow

Collins was travelling when he was ambushed in 1922.

The Hill of Allen, legendary home of Irish folk hero Fionn MacCumhail and the site of three royal residences in ancient Leinster, is northeast of town and is crowned by a 19th-century battlemented stone tower.

i Market House

▶ Take the **M7** southwest to reach Portlaoise.

5 Portlaoise, Co Laois
Set at the junction of the Dublin/Limerick and

A climb up the round tower beside the cathedral gives a wonderful view over Kildare

Dublin/Cork main roads, Portlaoise is also the site of Ireland's national prison.

There is a well-preserved 12th-century round tower in the little village of Timahoe, about 7 miles (11km) southeast of Portlaoise via the R426. Four miles (6km) east of town, the Rock of Dunamase rises 200 feet (60m) above the plain, with the ruined 12th-century castle of Dermot MacMurrough, one time King of Leinster.

Emo Court, about 8 miles (13km) northeast of Portlaoise off the N7, is probably the premier attraction of County Laois. The grand house was designed by the celebrated architect James Gandon, and is open to the public. The gardens

church architecture. Inside are George Campbell's outstanding Stations of the Cross. To the southeast of Athy Castledermot's ecclesiastical ruins include a round tower, two high crosses and the remains of a Franciscan friary church.

Kildare's beautiful 18th-century Church of Ireland St Brigid's Cathedral incorporates part of a 13th-century church.

In the heart of Ireland's horse-breeding and training country, Kildare sits on the edge of the vast Curragh plain, and the National Stud is near by. In addition to its equine interest (see For Children panel above), the stud features a superb Japanese garden and St Fiachra's Garden, with monastic cells, crystal garden and woodland walks.

East of town, horse racing has reigned supreme for centuries at The Curragh, where all the Irish Classics are run. The Curragh Camp, handed over to the Irish army in 1922, has been an important military station for a century, and there you can see the famous 1920 armoured car in which Michael

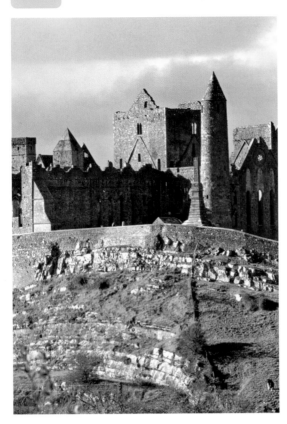

A tight cluster of majestic ruins atop the Rock of Cashel

protect the crossing. Today it is a busy, well-laid-out marketing centre for the surrounding agricultural area. It is also the cathedral town of the archdiocese of Cashel and Emly.

▶ Take the **R660** south for 13 miles (21km) to reach Cashel.

8   Cashel, Co Tipperary
Look above the ground floor of the shop opposite the city hall to see the crenellated battlements and gargoyles of what was 15th-century Quirke's Castle, named after a family who lived there in the 19th century. At the southwest end

are famous for their sweeping formal lawns, statuary and avenue of giant sequoia trees. The landscape of woodland and lake is undergoing restoration.

To the west of town the many roads crossing the Slieve Bloom Mountains offer interesting and scenic drives.

ℹ️ *James Fintan Lawlor Avenue*

▶ Take the **N8** for 9 miles (14km) south to Abbeyleix.

6   Abbeyleix, Co Laois
This attractive Georgian town, with its wide tree-lined streets and handsome buildings, is noted for the de Vesci Demesne, known as Abbeyleix House. The great house, which dates back to 1773, is not open to the public, but the splendid grounds are. They include formal terrace gardens to the west of the house, and a 'wild garden' that is

carpeted with bluebells in spring. In the walled garden of the old Brigidine Convent is the Abbey Sense Garden, created by and for people with disabilities.

The Heritage House in Abbeyleix is designed to be a focus for visitors to this historic town. Interactive multi-media displays tell the story of Abbeyleix and the surounding area.

▶ Take the **N8** southwest to the **N75** turnoff to Thurles.

7   Thurles, Co Tipperary
In ancient times, the O'Fogartys fortified this site on the River Suir, and although the Norman Strongbow's army was soundly defeated here in 1174, Anglo-Normans returned later to build a castle that would

of Main Street, the ornamental fountain is in memory of Dean Kinane and his efforts in bringing an extension of the railway to Cashel in 1904. Cashel is best known for the Rock of Cashel, Folk Museum and Heritage Centre (see Tours 3 and 10.)

ℹ️ *Heritage Centre (seasonal)*

▶ *Take the R692 southeast to Fethard.*

�“❾” **Fethard,** Co Tipperary
Fethard was an important Anglo-Norman settlement in medieval times. Remnants of the old town walls and their towers can still be seen. In the town centre, there are keeps of three 15th-century castles, including that of Fethard Castle. Well-preserved remains of a priory contain several 16th- and 17th-century tombs. More than a thousand exhibits of rural life in this area are on display at the Folk, Farm and Transport Museum.

▶ *Take the R692 northeast to Mullinahone. Turn right, staying on the R692 until the N76. Turn left, through Callan, for the 11-mile (18km) drive back to Kilkenny.*

Perfectly proportioned 18th-century Abbeyleix House

By Hook or
By Crooke

Founded in the mid-9th century on the River Slaney, Wexford retains much of its old Viking layout, with tiny lanes leading down to the river. The narrow main street, lined with traditional shopfronts and pubs, is the heart of this lively and prosperous little agricultural and tourist town.

3 DAYS • 163 MILES • 262KM

ITINERARY		
WEXFORD	▶	**Courtown (25m–40km)**
COURTOWN	▶	**Gorey (4m–6km)**
GOREY	▶	**Enniscorthy (19m–31km)**
ENNISCORTHY	▶	**New Ross (21m–34km)**
NEW ROSS	▶	**Waterford (15m–24km)**
WATERFORD	▶	**Passage East (7m–11km)**
PASSAGE EAST	▶	**Ballyhack (ferry)**
BALLYHACK	▶	**Hook Head (11m–18km)**
HOOK HEAD	▶	**Fethard (7m–11km)**
FETHARD	▶	**Kilmore Quay**
		(24m–39km)
KILMORE QUAY	▶	**Lady's Island (13m–21km)**
LADY'S ISLAND	▶	**Rosslare (7m–11km)**
ROSSLARE	▶	**Wexford (10m–16km)**

i *Crescent Quay, Wexford*

▶ *Take the **R741** north, then turn right on to the **R742** for Courtown.*

❶ Courtown, Co Wexford
This pleasant harbour town set in the wide sweep of Courtown Bay is a popular family resort, with a fine, 2-mile (3km) long sandy beach, amusements and a picturesque golf course. Its harbour piers were a part of famine relief work sponsored by the Earl of Courtown in 1847.

Ballymoney is a small resort with an excellent beach north of Courtown, and to the south, Ardamine and Pollshone are secluded coves with good swimming. At Ardamine, look for the little church by George Edmund Street, designer of the London Law Courts and restorer of Christ Church Cathedral in Dublin.

The wide sweep of Courtown Bay and its sandy beach make this one of the most popular resorts on the southeast coast

▶ *Follow the **R742** for 4 miles (6km) northwest to Gorey.*

❷ Gorey, Co Wexford
Against a backdrop of the Wicklow Mountains to the north, Gorey dates back to the 13th century. The wide Main Street and neat street plan give it a pleasant appearance. It figured prominently in the 1798 conflict, and insurgents camped at the western end of town at 418-foot (127m) high Gorey Hill before they marched on Arklow. A granite Celtic cross stands near the hill as a memorial to those who fell in battle. The Loreto convent, designed by Pugin, dates from 1839 to 1842.

i *Main Street*

▶ *Take the **N11** southwest to Enniscorthy.*

❸ Enniscorthy, Co Wexford
Set on the steeply sloping banks of the River Slaney, Enniscorthy suffered several attacks following the arrival of

the Normans, and it was a veritable storm centre of the 1798 rebellion, when insurgents led by the revered Father John Murphy held the town for four weeks before being overthrown by Crown forces under General Lake. A bronze statue of Father Murphy and a pikeman stands in Market Square.

Wexford County Museum is housed in a Norman castle built in the 13th century by the Prendergast family, recalling the town's earliest history, while spectacular displays at the National 1798 Rebellion Centre interpret the momentous events of the 1798 Rebellion and place them in an international context. Lively presentation techniques are used to illustrate the rebellion and the subsequent journey to modern democracy in Ireland.

The 390-foot (120m) high Vinegar Hill at the eastern edge of town is where the Wexford pikemen made their last stand in June 1798. Their defeat marked the end of any effective resistance in the county. Today, it is a peaceful vantage point from which to view the town and surrounding countryside. The battles of 1916 are commemorated by a memorial to Commandant Seamus Rafter that stands in Abbey Square.

St Aidan's Cathedral is an impressive Gothic-revival structure designed by Pugin.

☐ *Castle Museum (seasonal)*

▶ *Follow the N30 to New Ross.*

4   **New Ross,** Co Wexford
The busy port town of New Ross is on the River Barrow, which links up with Ireland's inland waterway system. On the quayside is the *Dunbrody*, a full-scale replica of a 19th-century three-masted famine ship, of the kind that took emigrants to the New World. You can explore above and below decks, and there are fascinating interactive displays.

Eight miles (13km) south of New Ross via the R733, the extensive ruins of Dunbrody Abbey, founded in 1182, are near the village of Campile. They are among the finest in Ireland, with a well-preserved nave, aisles, choir and transepts.

Each transept is joined by three vaulted and groined chapels. (See also Tour 14.)

FOR HISTORY BUFFS

South of New Ross at Dunganstown is the ancestral home of the Kennedys. Still owned and farmed by members of the family, it relates the departure of JFK's grandfather to America, and follows the fortunes of the famous Irish-American family, with plenty of memorabilia of the former president.

☐ *Dunbrody Heritage Centre, The Quay*

▶ *Take the N25 southwest for 15 miles (24km) to Waterford.*

5   **Waterford,** Co Waterford
The most important seaport in the southeast, Waterford's face is lined with traces of its past.

The massacre at nearby Vinegar Hill is among the displays in the museum at Enniscorthy Castle

The French Church in Greyfriars Street was built in 1240 for the Franciscan order, but was later used by Huguenot refugees who fled religious persecution in France in the 17th century. Near the City Hall, St Olaf's Church dates from the 11th century. The impressive Church of Ireland Christ Church Cathedral sits on the elevated site, one street off the quay. The original structure was replaced in 1773, and the present building has been enlarged and renovated.

Waterford Treasures combines an extensive collection of rare and beautiful objects with the latest technology. A Viking Show, with music, song, dance and storytelling is staged on certain evenings in summer.

Waterford's lively cultural scene includes the Waterford Arts Centre in O'Connell Street, which has permanent and visiting exhibitions, and the Garter Lane Arts Centre, also in O'Connell Street, is the venue for special events and exhibitions. (See also Tour 10.)

i 41 The Quay

▶ *From Waterford take the R683 east to Passage East.*

❻ **Passage East,** Co Waterford

This picturesque village at the foot of the steep hill overlooking the Waterford harbour estuary was fortified in years gone by to control shipping on the river. These days, it is the County Waterford terminal for the car ferry across to County Wexford. (See also Tour 10.)

▶ *Take the passenger ferry from Passage East across the estuary to Ballyhack.*

❼ **Ballyhack,** Co Wexford

The ruined castle overlooking the estuary was part of the Preceptory of the Knights of St John, founded in the 11th century. To the south, 16th-century Duncannon Fort sits on a

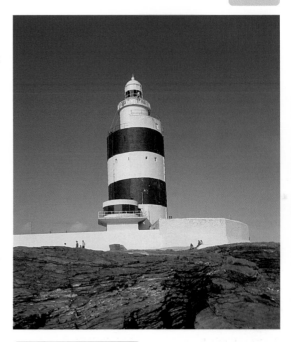

The Hook Head lighthouse is a distinctive landmark, night or day, for passing ships

SCENIC ROUTES

The road leading southeast out of Ballyhack gives extensive and beautiful views of Waterford harbour estuary as far as Hook Head on the Wexford side and the bulk of Creadan Head on the Waterford side.

promontory. It preserves a number of major buildings within star-shaped ramparts.

▶ *Turn southeast from Ballyhack on to the R733. Just past Arthurstown turn right for Duncannon. Shortly turn on to an unclassified signposted road south to Hook Head.*

❽ **Hook Head,** Co Wexford

Perched on a craggy sea-carved peninsula, the striking black-and-white lighthouse called the Tower of Hook is thought to date from the 13th century. The tradition of a light to guide ships through the treacherous waters of this dangerous point began long before then. Legend has it that it was the Welsh monk, St Dubhann, who first tended a cauldron of burning pitch, which he hoisted to the top of a high platform each night. The practice continued right through the 10th to 12th centuries as first the Vikings and then the Normans occupied the Hook area. Raymond le Gros, an important Norman leader, is believed to have built the tower some 700 years ago on the site of of St Dubhann's beacon, and it was this structure that was renovated in 1677, when an oil lamp was installed. Guided tours climb 115 steps to the parapet for superb views, passing through chambers with an audio show and displays about the history of the lighthouse. The former keeper's house has visitor facilities and a craft shop.

▶ *Return north on the unclassified road to the point where it branches right on to another unclassified road and take this road to Fethard.*

FOR HISTORY BUFFS

Hook Head gave to the English language one of its most frequently used expressions when the Norman leader Strongbow, Earl of Pembroke, declared in 1170 that 'I will take Waterford by Hook or by Crooke'. He was referring to the Tower of Hook on the Wexford side and to Crooke Castle on the Waterford shore near Passage East, both of which were heavily fortified. Strongbow made good his vow and thus changed the course of Irish history.

⑨ Fethard, Co Wexford

This pleasant little resort on the eastern shore of the Hook Peninsula has a fine sandy beach. In ancient times, there was woodland here, and traces of fossilised tree trunks have been found buried in the sands. The monument in the village centre is in memory of nine members of the Fethard lifeboat crew who drowned in 1914 as they made a gallant attempt to save the crew of a Norwegian vessel that had gone aground.

Fethard Castle, now in ruins but with its round tower still intact, was built in the mid-14th century. Tintern Abbey, 3½ miles (6km) north of Fethard between Wellington Bridge and Duncannon, dates from about 1200 and was built by the Earl of Pembroke in thanks for surviving a fierce storm at sea. The long drive into the wooded estate is signposted at the gate. In 1540, following the dissolution of the monasteries, the land and buildings passed into private hands, and parts of the church and tower were used as a residence until 1963. The domestic alterations have now been removed.

▶ *Take the R734 north for about 4 miles (6km), then turn east on the R733 to Wellington Bridge. Turn right on to the R736 to Duncormick, then right again via unclassified roads to Kilmore Quay.*

⑩ Kilmore Quay, Co Wexford

The charming little fishing village of Kilmore Quay is noted for its lobsters and deep-sea fishing, and is also the port of departure for the Saltee Islands to the south. There is also a small maritime museum on board a former lightship.

Between the Quay and the village of Kilmore, look for Brandy Close and the mound of wooden crosses at the roadside – tradition decrees that mourners place a small cross on the resident pile each time a funeral passes.

The outstanding feature of the village of Kilmore, further along, is its concentration of fine thatched cottages.

BACK TO NATURE

The Saltee Islands, 4 miles (6km) offshore from Kilmore Quay, harbour huge seabird colonies including razorbills, kittiwakes, puffins and thousands of gulls. Negotiate with local boatmen for a trip out, or arrange for one of the fishing trawlers to drop you on their way out to sea and pick you up on their return.

BACK TO NATURE

Northeast of Wexford stretch the Wexford Slobs, which are a world-famous wintering ground for wild geese, including greylags, snow, bean and Brent geese. Most remarkably, about a third of the world's population of white-fronted geese – some 10,000 of them – spend the winter here. Other birds that come here include whooper and Bewick's swans, and you might also see birds of prey. The Wexford Wildfowl Reserve has a visitor centre here, with an audio-visual presentation and interesting displays.

road north, then turn northeast on to the **R736** to its junction with the **N25**. Turn right to reach Rosslare Harbour, and drive straight across to reach Rosslare.

⏶ **Rosslare,** Co Wexford
Rosslare is a popular seaside resort with a fine 6-mile (10km) curving beach and good restaurants and accommodation. Car and passenger ferries from Wales and northern France arrive daily at Rosslare Harbour, 5 miles (8km) to the south.

▶ *From Rosslare take the R740 to the N25 and turn right to return to Wexford.*

SPECIAL TO...

Johnstown Castle, 4 miles (6km) south of Wexford, is the home of the Irish Agricultural Museum. It offers a comprehensive insight into farming through the ages, and features replica farmhouse kitchens from 1800, 1900 and 1950, rural crafts, tools, machines, transport and a dairying exhibit. Another major exhibition here covers the history of the potato and the Great Famine.

Fethard, now a quiet little resort, is close to the place where the first Anglo-Normans landed

▶ *Take the R739 northeast, through Kilmore, to the junction with the R736. Turn right on to this road and proceed to its junction with a signposted, unclassified road south (at Twelveacre Cross Roads) to Lady's Island.*

⏶ **Lady's Island,** Co Wexford
Lady's Island is at the head of a saltwater lagoon, Lady's Island Lake, which is an important bird habitat. The two islands in the lake are home to breeding colonies of all five species of tern. With the coming of Christianity, it became one of the first shrines of the Blessed Virgin and an important place of pilgrimage. The church was destroyed and the holy men were savagely butchered by Cromwellian forces in 1649, but pilgrimages began again at the end of the Cromwellian era and continue to this day.

▶ *Return to Twelveacre Cross Roads via the unclassified*

Kilmore Quay is at the heart of an area where traditional thatched roofs are still maintained

CONNACHT

The counties that make up the province of Connacht seem to fit the popular image of Ireland more than any other region. It is a land of stony fields, brooding mountains, windswept cliffs along a rugged coastline dotted with offshore islands, and wide skies alive with the shifting light and shadow of clouds moving inland from the Atlantic.

County Galway's eastern landscape stretches along flat, fertile plains from Lough Derg and the Shannon Valley north to Roscommon. The streets and lanes of Galway town are filled with medieval architecture and a lively creative arts-and-crafts culture. Poet William Butler Yeats drew inspiration from the surroundings of his beloved Thoor Ballylee tower home near Gort, and Lady Gregory, the moving force behind Dublin's Abbey Theatre, gathered some of Ireland's most distinguished writers around her hearth at nearby Coole Park. In western Galway, peaks of the Twelve Pins (Bens) face the misty heights of the Maumturk range across a lake-filled valley in rock-strewn Connemara, whose jagged coastline has a stark, silent beauty punctuated with rocky fields and tiny hamlets. The three Aran Islands, some 30 miles (48km) offshore, are a repository of antiquities left by prehistoric peoples and the language, customs and dress of a Celtic Twilight heritage.

County Mayo holds reminders of a great prehistoric battle on the plain of Southern Moytura near Cong. Christianity came with St Patrick, and pilgrims still follow his footsteps to the summit of Croagh Patrick on the shores of island-studded Clew Bay. Achill Island, connected to the mainland by a bridge, is ringed by mighty cliffs and tiny coves, with a flat, boggy interior.

Boyhood visits to his uncle's home in Sligo nurtured W B Yeats's deep love for the west, and some of his best works celebrate Sligo landmarks. Lough Ree was the haunt of early Christians, who had churches and monasteries on many of its islands. Lough Key lies in a luxurious forest park, with the remains of a great abbey at Boyle.

A long, narrow inlet, Killary Harbour, cuts into the hills of Connemara at Leenane (Tour 19)

Dominated by inland lakes and the River Shannon, County Leitrim has its fair share of mountains and hills. Carrick-on-Shannon, which grew up at one of the traditional fords of the Shannon, is home to a vast flotilla of cruisers for exploring the river and lakes.

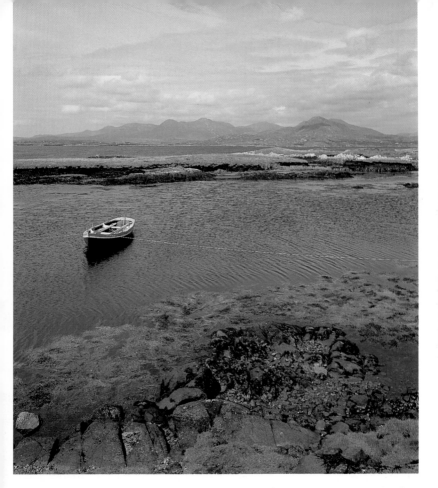

Tour 16

This tour, which starts in the bright town of Sligo, is steeped in echoes of Ireland's greatest poet, William Butler Yeats, passing his grave beneath the majestic profile of the mountain, Benbulben, and visiting places which inspired some of his finest lyric poetry. This corner of Ireland is a happy unison of wooded lakes, bare mountaintops and Atlantic seascapes, and abounds in history from prehistoric times.

Tour 17

The majestic ruins of its 12th-century abbey and the beauties of its riverside setting and nearby Lough Key Forest Park make Boyle an attractive touring base. The Shannon, with its cruiser-filled marina at Carrick-on-Shannon, lures you onward, with perhaps a stop or two along the way for fishing in the trout-filled waters of this region. Roscommon's ruined castle speaks of the town's turbulent history, while Clonalis, the 'great house' of Castlerea, is a relic of more gracious times.

Tour 18

The ghost of Grace O'Malley will follow you on this tour after a visit to magnificent Westport House, with its museum and zoo. After a side trip to her Clare Island home, the route travels to Newport and one of her numerous strongholds before heading for Achill Island, Ireland's largest and most scenic, with yet another castle of the sea queen. At Knock, a huge basilica honouring a miraculous vision of the Blessed Virgin dominates the town. Monastic ruins and impressive Ashford Castle lie

Typical Connemara landscape near Roundstone (Tour 19)

along the route as you make your way back to Westport through the county town of Castlebar.

Tour 19

Galway town's many historic and cultural attractions may tempt you to tarry before setting out on this tour. A trip out to the very special Aran Islands beckons before embarking on the swing through Connemara's starkly beautiful landscape. This Gaeltacht (Irish-speaking) region is one of rocky, untillable fields, where the Twelve Bens mountain range faces the Maumturk range across a lake–filled valley. The jagged coastline is a solitary place of rocks and tiny hamlets and stark, silent beauty.

Sligo &
Yeats Country

The busy town of Sligo has good shops, traditional public houses, thriving art galleries and a theatre. There are fine 18th- and 19th-century buildings and 13th-century abbey ruins, all set against the distinctive backdrop of Benbulbin, an extraordinary flat-topped and rugged-faced mountain profile.

1/2 DAYS • 98 MILES • 157KM

ITINERARY	
SLIGO	▶ **Drumcliff** (5m-8km)
DRUMCLIFF	▶ **Lissadell** (4m-6km)
LISSADELL	▶ **Bundoran** (19m-31km)
BUNDORAN	▶ **Kinlough** (3m-5km)
KINLOUGH	▶ **Manorhamilton** (16m-26km)
MANORHAMILTON	▶ **Glencar** (9m-14km)
GLENCAR	▶ **Lough Gill** (15m-24km)
LOUGH GILL	▶ **Dromahair** (4m-6km)
DROMAHAIR	▶ **Dooney** (10m-16km)
DOONEY	▶ **Strandhill** (8m-13km)
STRANDHILL	▶ **Sligo** (5m-8km)

i Temple Street, Sligo

SCENIC ROUTES

From the main Sligo–Donegal road, the Gleniff Horseshoe is a signposted loop that passes the dramatic and jagged summits of Benwisken and Truskmore.

▶ Take the **N15** for 5 miles (8km) to Drumcliff.

❶ Drumcliff, Co Sligo
'Under bare Ben Bulben's head
In Drumcliff churchyard Yeats is laid
An ancestor was rector there

Long years ago; a church stands near,
By the road an ancient cross,
No marble, no conventional phrase;
On limestone quarried near the spot,
By his command these words are cut:
Cast a cold eye
On life, on death,
Horseman, pass by!'

Yeats's poem "Under ben Bulben", describes Drumcliff completely, and his grave can be found easily in the Protestant churchyard. The visitor centre at the church includes an audiovisual presentation on Yeats and Early Christianity.

▶ Continue on the **N15** and almost immediately take a left turn for 4 miles (6km) to Lissadell.

❷ Lissadell, Co Sligo
The slightly forbidding classical façade of Lissadell hides the romantic background of the Gore-Booths. Yeats was a regular visitor here and his poem in memory of the two sisters, Eva and Constance, begins:
'The light of evening, Lissadell,
Great windows open to the south,
Two girls in silk kimonos, both
Beautiful, one a gazelle.'

Lissadell House would ring to the romanticism of poetry and patriotic fervour

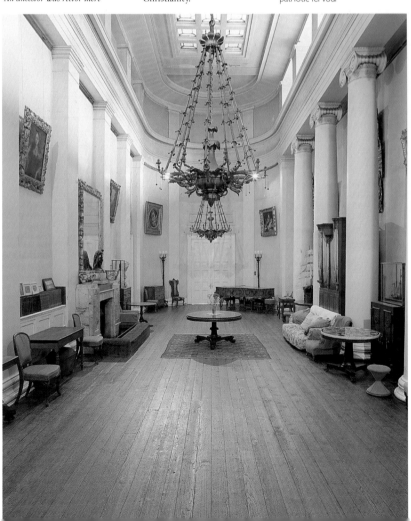

Constance became the Countess Markievicz, a leader in the Easter Rising of 1916, and the first woman elected to Westminster, although she never took her seat.

The fine 1830s mansion, built of Ballisodare limestone, has been undergoing restoration since 2004, after becoming the family home of Edward Walsh, his wife Constance Cassidy and their seven young children. Their enthusiasm for the project and devotion to the history of Lissadell is already shining through, with many rooms now reflecting their former glory, and in 2007 Prime Minister Bertie Ahern opened the Countess Markievicz Exhibition in the coach house.

The gardens here are also being restored, and in the extensive grounds traditional breeds of Irish livestock are being reintroduced.

BACK TO NATURE

At Streedagh, there is a dune system based on a shingle ridge, which is of international importance and which supports the plant, insect and bird life associated with dunes. The limestone rocks are laced with varieties of fossil coral. Bunduff Lake, near Creevykeel, is a salt-water marsh, where whooper and Bewick swans, Greenland white-fronted geese and many species of duck spend the winter.

SCENIC ROUTES

The Knocknarea scenic drive gives spectacular views to the south, and to the Ox mountains and Croagh Patrick in the north.

FOR HISTORY BUFFS

Creevykeel Court Tomb, southwest of Bundoran, is regarded as the finest example of a classic court tomb in Ireland. The cairn has a kerb of large stones surrounding a ritual court, with a boundary of upright stones. In the two burial chambers, which were originally roofed, a Harvard archaeological expedition found four cremated burials, as well as decorated neolithic pottery and stone weapons. These are now held in the National Museum in Dublin.

▶ *Drive through the parkland to rejoin the road and turn left, then right at the fork. Shortly turn right and continue to Grange. Turn left, to rejoin the N15 for Bundoran.*

8 Bundoran, Co Donegal

Glencar Waterfall plunges 30 feet (10m) through a ferny chasm into Glencar Lough

Bundoran is a busy seaside resort, and presents quite a contrast to the placid towns and coastal villages of the northwest, offering a wide variety of attractions, as well as a 'blue flag' beach and cliff walks.

To the southwest of Bundoran, at Streedagh, is a small park that commemorates the place where three vessels of the Spanish Armada foundered in 1588. Members of the crew who struggled ashore from the overladen ships found little succour on land.

ℹ️ *The Bridge*

▶ *Take the R280 for 3 miles (5km) to Kinlough.*

4 Kinlough, Co Leitrim

At the north end of Lough Melvin, this village is a good place for coarse and salmon fishing. The ruins of Rossclogher Abbey stand on the shore, and on an artificial island are the remains of the MacClancy Castle (known as Rossclogher Castle), where nine survivors of the Armada were given refuge.

▶ *Follow the R281 along the shore of Lough Melvin for 8 miles (13km), then turn right on to the R282 for Manorhamilton.*

5 Manorhamilton, Co Leitrim

This unassuming village stands in an area of untouched mountain valleys and grey cliff walls. Lush fertile slopes, steep clefts and lofty peaks characterise this part of Leitrim. Glenade Lough and the valley where the River Bonet rises have a special quality. The ruined castle that overlooks the town was built at the meeting of four mountain valleys by the Scottish

---

SPECIAL TO...

Sligo and the surrounding district is famous for its music and dancing. Visit the Michael Coleman Heritage Centre off the Manorhamilton to Glencar road, named after one of Ireland's greatest fiddlers.

Parke's Castle, built in 1609, looks out over the tranquil waters of Lough Gill

17th-century planter Sir Frederick Hamilton, who gave his name to the village.

▶ *Take the N16 west for Sligo. After 7 miles (11km) turn right on to an unclassified road for Glencar Lough.*

RECOMMENDED WALKS

Two good town trails can be found in Sligo and Dromahair. There are fine walks from the picnic site beside the village of Kinlough through Kinlough Forest, by Lough Melvin. A spectacular walk takes you from the Glencar Lake up a mountain road into Swiss Valley, a steep-sided cleft surrounded by peaks. The route then returns to the point where the waterfall cascades into the lake below.

7 **Lough Gill,** Co Leitrim

From Parkes Castle there is a superb view of Lough Gill, one of Ireland's loveliest loughs, dotted with islands and wooded with native trees like yew, arbutus, white beam, oak and birch. The bare mountain reaches down deep ferny glens to the lake below.

Parkes Castle is an impressively reconstructed fortified manor house, originally a stronghold of the O'Rourkes, but owing its present name to the English family who were 'planted' here. An audiovisual show and tea-room will enhance a visit. At the lake you will find a sweat-house, medieval Ireland's answer to the sauna.

▶ *Continue on the **R286**, then turn right on to the **R288** for Dromahair.*

8 **Dromahair,** Co Leitrim

This area is O'Rourke country, overlooked by a rock plateau called O'Rourke's Table. Dromahair hosts gatherings of the O'Rourke family, as well as a Wild Rose Festival, but it was an English family, the Lane-Foxes, who laid out the pretty village around the River Bonet based on a plan of a Somerset village. In Thomas Moore's song *The Valley Lay Smiling Before Me*, the tale is told of the elopement from Dromahair in 1152 of Dervorgilla O'Rourke and the King of Leinster (her husband was away on a pilgrimage of penitence for beating her).

To the west is the Isle of Innisfree. You can take a cruise from Parkes Castle aboard the Wild Rose Water Bus, with an entertaining commentary of poetry, folklore and history.

▶ *Take the **R288** for Carrick-on-Shannon, then turn right on to the **R287** for Sligo. After 2½ miles (4km) turn right again on the **R287**, and follow the road past the sign for Innisfree to Dooney Rock Forest, before rejoining the **N4**.*

6 **Glencar,** Co Leitrim

Glencar is a beautiful lake; the steep slopes of the valley are generously clothed with mixed woodland and topped with cliffs. Plants grow here in profusion, including rare species, while the mountaintops are luxuriantly covered with heather. Glencar waterfall cascades down from a rocky headland to a deep pool, white with spray. Yeats immortalised the waterfall in his poem *The Stolen Child*.

▶ *Follow the lakeside road to rejoin the **N16** and turn right towards Sligo, then turn left on the **R286** to Parkes Castle Visitor Centre.*

Echoes of England are still in evidence in the purpose-built village of Dromahair

---

FOR CHILDREN

Although they were not conceived with children in mind, the Hazelwood Park wooden sculptures have proved to be a delight to young visitors. Along paths in the woods by Lough Gill are huge works of art, hewn, constructed and carved in wood. More obvious children's fun is on offer at Bundoran's Adventure Park, Waterworld and Glowbowl and Macks Amusement Complex, or at Waterpoint in Sligo.

---

9 Dooney, Co Sligo
This beautiful corner of Lough
Gill has forests and paths to
satisfy any enthusiastic walker,
offering great views of the
lough. Dooney Rock Forest
bears the vestiges of a once
important oak forest. You can
see the 'twining branches', two
linked oaks. Yeats wrote of 'the
Fiddler of Dooney', who made
folk 'dance like the waves of the
sea'. The poem has inspired a
Fiddler of Dooney competition
for the champion fiddler of
Ireland, held in Sligo in July.

Slish Wood, or Sleuth Wood
as Yeats knew it, has a lovely
stream. Cairns Hill Forest Park
marks the two cairns on Belvoir
and Cairns peaks. A legend tells
of two warriors, Romra and
Omra. Romra had a daughter,
Gille, and Omra fell in love with
her. When a mortal battle
ensued after the lovers were
discovered by Romra, Gille
drowned herself, and Lough
Gill was formed from the tears
of her nursemaid. The legend
holds that the two cairns are the
burial places of the warriors.

Cashelore stone fort is a
large oval stone enclosure, once
the settlement of an important
Celt. The tranquil Tobernalt is
a holy well where Mass was said
in penal times. A stone altar was
erected in thanksgiving when
the town was spared the worst
ravages of a fever at the turn of
the century.

▶ *Travel south on the N4, then
turn right on to the R292 for
Rathcarrick and Strandhill.*

10 Strandhill, Co Sligo
Great Atlantic breakers crash on
to the beach at Strandhill,
making the small seaside village
a favoured place for surfing
championships. Lifeguards
watch bathers, but if you prefer
calmer waters, drive round to
the beach at Culleenamore,
which is safer and quiet.
Culleenamore nestles under the
mountain of Knocknarea, which
is capped by a cairn visible for
miles round. It is known locally
as the grave of Queen Maeve,
the warrior queen of Connacht.
If you climb to the summit of

Knocknarea, Sligo tradition
suggests that you add a stone to
the cairn, as a protection against
the fairies.

Among the fields below
Knocknarea at Carrowmore is
Ireland's largest group of megalithic tombs; more than 60 can
be found here, mostly passage
graves and dolmens. The best
place to start to discover
Carrowmore is from the
Interpretive Centre, where a
map is on display.

▶ *Take the R292 for 5 miles
(8km) back to Sligo.*

SPECIAL TO...

The Yeats Memorial Building
(tel: 071 9142693) in Sligo features an exhibition and films
relating to the poet and his
family, together with special
events and activities.

Firm sand and rolling waves attract
bathers and surfers to the resort
of Strandhill

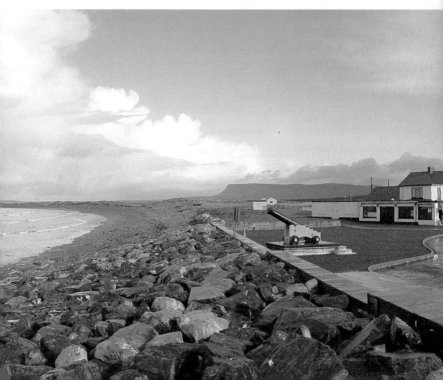

Boyle &
The Lake Country

Lakes dotted with small wooded islands are the main characteristic of County Roscommon. Beautifully situated on the
bank of the River Boyle at the foot of the Curlew Hills, the town
of Boyle offers excellent fishing. Close to the river at the north
end of town are impressive ruins of the Cistercian abbey, and
the King House has excellent displays and presentations.

1 DAY • 87 MILES • 140KM

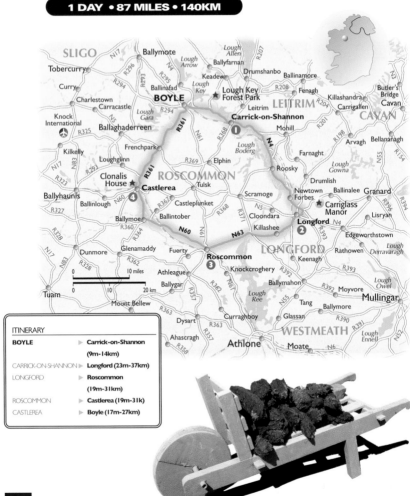

ITINERARY		
BOYLE	▸	**Carrick-on-Shannon**
		(9m-14km)
CARRICK-ON-SHANNON	▸	**Longford (23m-37km)**
LONGFORD	▸	**Roscommon**
		(19m-31km)
ROSCOMMON	▸	**Castlerea (19m-31k)**
CASTLEREA	▸	**Boyle (17m-27km)**

[i] *King House, Boyle (seasonal)*

▶ *Take the N4 for 9 miles (14km) southeast to Carrick-on-Shannon.*

❶ **Carrick-on-Shannon,**
Co Leitrim
Chief town of Ireland's most sparsely populated county,

Carrick-on-Shannon is also the smallest county town in the country, and was first given its charter by James I. When river traffic was superseded by road and rail, it hit the town hard, but the growing demand for pleasure boating gave it a reprieve. Its situation on Shannon's navigational system makes this attractive town a major river-cruising and fishing centre.

Among the best preserved buildings in the town are the 19th-century Court House and the Protestant church.

[i] *The Marina*

▶ *Follow the N4 southeast for 23 miles (37km) to Longford.*

❷ **Longford,** Co Longford
Set on the south bank of the River Camlin, the market town of Longford dates back to 1400, when a Dominican priory was founded here. Nothing remains of that ancient establishment, but the slight ruins of a castle built in 1627 are incorporated into the old military barracks. In the town centre is the grey limestone, Renaissance-style St Mel's Cathedral, a classical building of the 19th century by J B Keane. Near by is Carriglass Manor, a romantic Gothic revival house, still occupied by the Lefroy family. A Palladian stable yard, a costume museum and some delightful woodland walks add to the charm of Carriglas.

Longford was a terminal of a branch of the Royal Canal, called the 'Shoemaker's Canal'.

The riverside abbey ruins are a peaceful haven right in the centre of Boyle

SCENIC ROUTES

Heading south from Carrick-on-Shannon on the N4, leave the main road to divert to Jamestown on the Shannon and visit Drumsna, a small town in an exceptionally scenic setting. As you continue southeast to Longford, the landscape is dotted with many small lakes that are part of the Shannon system. Two miles (3km) beyond Aghamore, an unclassified road to the right leads to the wooded Derrycarne promontory, which projects into Lough Boderg.

i Dublin Street (seasonal)

FOR HISTORY BUFFS

About 13 miles (22km) west of Longford, the National Irish Famine Museum is located at Strokestown Park. It offers an excellent insight into the causes and effects of the Great Irish Famine of the 1840s, and shows the links that exist with famine in the world today. Strokestown Park is a superb Georgian mansion with glorious gardens. If you take this detour, there is no need to return to Longford to continue the route; simply head south via the R368 and N61 to Roscommon, the next point on the tour.

▶ Take the **N63** southwest to Roscommon.

❸ Roscommon, Co Roscommon

Situated at an important road junction, Roscommon is the county's chief town, named after St Coman, founder of an early 8th-century Christian monastery here. The ruin of the Dominican friary is mainly 15th-century and includes the 137-foot (42m) long, 23-foot (7m) wide church. A tomb in a burial niche in the north wall of the chancel is thought to be that of Felim O'Conor, King of Connacht, who founded the abbey in 1253. His effigy is perhaps the most interesting figure within the ruins. The eight gallowglasses (figures of mail-clad warriors) who support the tomb belonged originally to a much later tomb dating from around 1500.

Built in 1269 by Robert d'Ufford, the English Justiciar, but much altered since, Roscommon Castle was captured by the Irish four years later and razed to the ground. It was rebuilt in about 1280 and was besieged many times until the English Civil War, when it was held for the King by Sir Michael Earnley. It was surrendered to Cromwellian forces in 1652, who promptly dismantled it. The ruins form a large quadrangular area, with a round bastion tower at each corner. The gateway is protected by two similar towers that project from the eastern wall. Roscommon County Museum has a facinating collection, including early Christian relics, folk items, crafts, farm machinery and a display on the Old Jail and Lady Betty, Ireland's last hangwoman.

i Harrison Hall (seasonal)

▶ Take the **N60** to Castlerea.

❹ Castlerea, Co Roscommon

This pretty little town was the birthplace, in 1815, of Oscar Wilde's father, Sir William Wilde, who was an antiquarian and oculist. Just west of town the fine 'great house' of Clonalis, rebuilt in the 19th century, was the seat of the O'Conor Don, a direct descendant of the last High King of Ireland, who abdicated after the Anglo-Norman invasion of 1169. Ownership of such a manor house by a Gaelic family is unique, and Clonalis's furnishings reflect a more informal elegance than many other houses. The drawing room, for example, although beautifully furnished with Victoriana, is also a warm, comfortable room. Nineteenth-century portraits hang in the library, which also holds many fine books. There is a private chapel, and the highlight of the museum is the harp of Ireland's last great bard, Turlough O'Carolan (1670–1738), whose portrait is displayed. Among his many compositions was the tune to which the Star Spangled Banner is now sung.

Priceless Gaelic manuscripts, Victorian costumes, Sheraton furniture, porcelain and glass are also featured in the museum.

▶ Take the **R361** back to Boyle.

FOR CHILDREN

Apart from Lough Key Forest and Leisure Park (see Back to Nature, page 107), there's fun for young children at Tullyboy Farm Visitor Centre (tel: 071 9668031), off the N61 just south of Boyle. Rosbowl (tel: 090 6634372), in the Cluan Fraoigh Retail Park on the edge of Roscommon, caters for all ages, and includes ten-pin bowling and an adventure playground for under 12s.

SPECIAL TO...

In early August, the little town of Keadew (northeast of Boyle) buzzes with musical and sports events during the ten-day O'Carolan Harp adn International Traditional Music Festival, in memory of the last of the Irish bards, Turlough O'Carolan, who is buried in Kilronan Church cemetery, just northwest of the village.

The modest proportions of Clonalis House give no hint of the fascinating items within

Achill Island &
County Mayo

Port an Chlóidh (Portacloy) · Béal Deirg (Belderg) · Ballycastle · Easky

Béal an Mhuirthead (Belmullet) · R314 · Céide Fields · Killala Bay · Inishcrone · Dromore West

Gleann na Muaidhe (Glenamoy) · R314 · Killala · R297 · N59 · M15

Bun na hAbhna (Bunnahowen) · Carrowmore Lake · R315

R313 · Bangor Erris · **MAYO** · Rosserk Friary

Cuan an Fhóid Dhuibh (Blacksod Bay) · N59 · **Ballina** · ❸ · Bunnyconnellan · Ox

719 · Crossmolina · R294

671 · Doogort · Ballycroy · 806 · Lough Conn · Nephin · R310 · N26

Slievemore · Keel · R319 · N59 · Nephin Beg Mountains · Foxford · Curry

Achill Island ❷ · Lough Feeagh · R315 · Lough Cullin · Charlestown

Mallaranny · R317 · R312 · Swinford · Knock International ✈

Newport ❶ · R311 · Turlough · N5 · R320 · Kilkelly

Clew Bay · N59 · **Castlebar** · Kiltamagh · R322

WESTPORT · N5 · Balla · R324 · **Knock** ❹ · N83

Louisburgh · 762 · Croagh Patrick · R335 · Ballyhean · Ballintober Abbey · N60 · R323 · Ballyhaunis

Claremorris · R327

Partry · Lough Carra · R331 · R328

0 | 10 miles · 0 | 10 | 20 km

Leenane · N59 · 673 · R300 · Lough Mask · **Ballinrobe** ❼ · Ballindine · Dunmore

R335 · Kilmaine · N17 · N83

Neale · R345 · Shrule · R332 · **Tuam** ❺ · R322

Cong · R334 · R333

Lough Corrib · **Headford** ❻ · Knockmoy Abbey

Westport nestles in a hollow, and its tree-lined Mall along each side of the Carrowbeg river is an attractive main artery. The town has splendid Georgian houses, a fine Heritage Centre, and lovely Westport House, a castle of the O'Malley clan, which dates back to the 1730s and is a major attraction.

2 DAYS • 207 MILES • 333KM

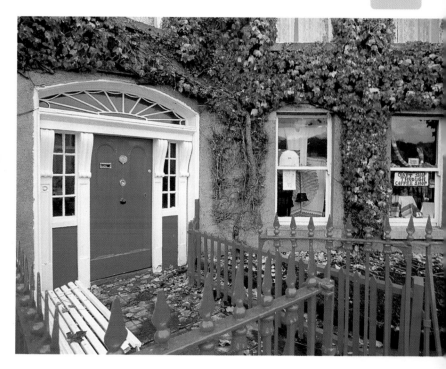

i | *James Street, Westport*

RECOMMENDED WALKS

Croagh Patrick, 5 miles (8km) west of Westport via the R335, rises some 2,500 feet (762m) above the shore of Clew Bay near the little town of Murrisk. This is Ireland's Holy Mountain, on which St Patrick is said to have spent the 40 days of Lent in 441. It is an easy climb that takes only about an hour by way of a path from Murrisk. Alternatively, informative guided walks of Westport (twice weekly, Jul–Aug; tel: 098 26852 for details) start out from the Clock at the junction of Bridge Street and Shop Street.

► *Take the **N59** north for 8 miles (13km) to Newport.*

❶ Newport, Co Mayo

This picturesque little town, which dates from the 17th century, faces Clew Bay and is sheltered by mountains. It is a noted angling centre, with fishing on loughs Furnace, Beltra and Feeagh as well as in the rivers Burrishoole and Newport. Its neo-Romanesque Catholic church was built in 1914 and features a superb stained-glass window of the Last Judgement designed by Harry Clarke.

Four miles (6km) west of town, off the N59, Rockfleet Castle, sometimes called Carrigahowley Castle, is another of Grace O'Malley's strongholds. Dating from the 15th and 16th centuries, the tower dwelling has four storeys with a corner turret. The indomitable pirate queen came to live here permanently after her second husband died in 1583.

► *Follow the **N59** west to Mallaranny, then the **R319** to Achill Island, a distance of 28 miles (45km).*

❷ Achill Island, Co Mayo

The largest of Ireland's islands, Achill Island is connected to the mainland by a bridge. Only 15 miles (24km) long and 12 miles (19km) wide, its landscape is one of dramatic cliffs and seascapes, with a boggy, heather-covered interior. Fishing for shark and other big-game fish is excellent, with boats and guides for hire. There are also very good bathing beaches, and the beautiful Atlantic Drive around the island climbs from gently rolling mountain foothills, past stretches of sandy beaches, and through tiny picturesque villages with excellent views of the sea, Clew Bay and the mainland. At Kildownet, another Grace O'Malley castle is well preserved, and ruins of a small 12th-century church are near by. At the centre of holiday activities is Keel, which has a fine sandy beach and a small harbour with fishing and sightseeing boats for hire.

Seen from a boat, the sea-carved rocks below the Menawn

Westport is a lively and attractive town, with some splendid Georgian houses and colourful gardens cliffs at the eastern end of the beach take on fanciful shapes. At Doogort, nestled at the foot of Slievemore, boatmen take visitors to the fascinating Seal Caves cut far into the cliffs of Slievemore.

☐ *Cashel (seasonal)*

▶ *Take the **R319** back to Mallaranny, then turn north on the **N59** for the drive to Ballina, passing through Ballycroy and Bangor (where the **N59** turns sharply east).*

3 **Ballina,** Co Mayo

An important angling centre on the River Moy near Lough Conn, Ballina is County Mayo's largest town. Founded in 1730, it is also a cathedral town, and near its 19th-century Cathedral of St Muiredach, which has a fine stained-glass window, are ruins of a 15th-century Augustinian friary.

About 3 miles (5km) north of Ballina, the 15th-century Rosserk Friary sits peacefully on the shore of Killala Bay. The ruins include a tower, a small cloister, nave, chancel, a fine arched doorway and east window.

Eight miles (13km) north of Ballina via the R314, Killala, the small harbour where General Humbert and his French forces landed in 1798, has a wealth of antiquities in the immediate vicinity, as well as one of the finest round towers in the country. Nearby Franciscan Moyne Abbey was founded in the mid-15th century. Although burned in 1590, the well-preserved

Beautiful Achill Island is remote yet easily accessible

A tangible representation of the vision that made Knock famous over 100 years ago

ruins include a six-storey square tower, vaulted chapter room, and a partially vaulted sacristy.

ℹ️ *Cathedral Road (seasonal)*

▶ *Take the N26 south, then southeast through Foxford to Swinford. Follow the R320 south to Kiltimagh, then turn southeast on the R323 for 5 miles (8km) to reach Knock.*

4 **Knock,** Co Mayo

This small town was the scene of an apparition in 1879, the central figure of which was the Blessed Virgin. After intensive investigation by Catholic authorities, it was declared authentic and named a Marian shrine. A large, circular church was built to accommodate the huge number of pilgrims, with 32 pillars in the ambulatory contributed by all counties in the country, and four windows in medieval style that represent the four provinces of Ireland. In 1979 Knock was visited by Pope John Paul II.

The Knock Folk Museum exhibits relics of rural and small-town life in this part of Ireland.

ℹ️ *Village centre (seasonal)*

▶ *Take the N17 south to Tuam.*

5 **Tuam,** Co Galway

A thriving commercial and agricultural centre under James I's charter of 1613, the layout of Tuam was altered to include a diamond-shaped town 'square' on which all roads converged. St Mary's Cathedral, founded in 1130 and rebuilt largely in the 19th century, is a fine example of Gothic-revival architecture and incorporates a 12th-century chancel with magnificent windows. The town's 12th-century High Cross, well adorned but incomplete, now stands in its grounds. A slightly earlier Roman Catholic Cathedral of the Assumption is a marvellous neo-Gothic building with fine window and tower carvings.

Tuam can claim Ireland's first industrial museum, the Mill Museum, an operational corn mill with millwheel and other interesting industrial exhibits.

Just outside the town, on the Ryehill road, there is an interesting medieval lake dwelling, known as Loughpark Crannóg. Seven miles (11km) to the southeast, on the shores of a small lake, is the 12th-century Knockmoy Abbey. The tomb of its founder, Cathal O'Connor, King of Connacht, can be found within the ruins, as well as traces of ancient murals.

ℹ️ *Mill Museum (seasonal)*

▶ *Leave Tuam on the N17 southwest, and about 3 miles (5km) from town turn west on the R333 for 9 miles (14km) to reach Headford.*

6 **Headford,** Co Galway

This popular angling and market centre is very close to Lough Corrib, and there are boats for hire at nearby Greenfield. Two miles (3km) northwest of town, Ross Errilly Friary is a large 1498 Franciscan friary that fell victim to Cromwellian forces in 1656. Its original size can be judged by

FOR HISTORY BUFFS

About 10 miles (16km) north of Ballinrobe, on the N84, Ballintober Abbey is unique in the English-speaking world in that Mass has been celebrated continuously since its foundation in 1216. It was suppressed by Henry VIII in 1542, the roof was removed by Cromwellians in 1653 and the central tower collapsed. Then there were the Penal Laws in the 18th century, but despite all this, celebrants continued to worship here.

An excavated 5,000-year-old, 12 sq mile (31 sq km) rural landscape, the Ceide Fields, lies 22 miles (35km) northwest of Ballina.

its two courtyards, around which are the domestic buildings, including a refectory, dormitories, and a kitchen with a surprising forerunner of modern fish tanks.

At the heart of Castlebar, the courthouse overlooks this delightful leafy green

▶ *Take the R334 northwest for just over 6 miles (10km), then turn left to Cong via the R346. From Cong take the R345 northeast to rejoin the R334 and turn left to reach Ballinrobe.*

7 Ballinrobe, Co Mayo
In a beautiful spot, near three good fishing lakes (loughs Corrib, Mask and Carra), this small town is surrounded by mountains and woodlands. At the north end of town are the ruins of a 1313 Augustinian friary, and about 3 miles (5km) to the southwest is Killower Cairn, one of the most impressive in Connacht.

Just 7 miles (11km) south of Ballinrobe (take the R334 and turn west on the R345), the little town of Cong was the setting for most of the popular film *The Quiet Man*. That, however, is the least of its claims to fame. More notable are the ruins of the Royal Abbey of Cong, built by Turlough Mor O'Conor, High King of Ireland in the 12th century, on the site of a 7th-century monastic community, and burial place of

Ireland's last High King, Rory O'Conor, who died in 1198. The impressive Ashford Castle is now a luxury hotel. Its rather eccentric architecture incorporates several styles and periods.

i *Cornmarket (seasonal)*

▶ *Follow the N84 to Castlebar.*

8 Castlebar, Co Mayo
The county town of Mayo, Castlebar has figured in several major Irish insurrections, most notable in 1798, when Irish–French forces routed British cavalry, causing such a hasty retreat to Hollymount, Tuam and Athlone that the campaign gained the nickname 'The Race of Castlebar'.

Four miles (6km) east of Castlebar in the village of Turlough, is Ireland's only National Museum outside Dublin, the National Museum of Country Life. The national folklife collection, set in the grounds of Turlough Park House, portrays all aspects of rural life – hunting, religion, education and leisure pursuits – between 1850 and 1950.

i *Town centre*

▶ *Take the N5 southwest back to Westport.*

SPECIAL TO...

Westport's Street Festival in July features street performers and folk singers from all over Ireland.

BACK TO NATURE

Ten miles (16km) west of Westport, 2 miles (3km) east of Louisburgh and ½ mile (1km) on a signposted road off the R335, the National Forest Old Head Wood is a welcome stop. There is a car park and also picnic grounds, with well-marked pathways through the small reserve. Oak is the dominant species, but shares the territory with native birch, willow and rowan. Beech and sycamore trees, not native to the area, have also been introduced. There are fine views over Clew Bay.

Ashford Castle at Cong is now a sumptuous hotel

Region of
Stony Beauty

Galway is a thriving commercial and university city with a particularly lively cultural scene. The heart of the city is a maze of colourful medieval streets and the famous Spanish Arch is a relic of the old city walls. Attractions include the impressive modern cathedral, and, on a much smaller scale, Nora Barnacle's House.

2/3 DAYS • 136 MILES • 218KM

i *Forster Street, Galway*

FOR HISTORY BUFFS

Take a look at the Lynch Memorial Window in Galway's Market Street, and the inscription above the doorway. The story goes that Lord Mayor James Lynch FitzStephen's popular 19-year-old son murdered one of his closest friends, who he thought paid undue attention to a young lady they both admired. Overcome with remorse, the son turned himself in, and his father sat as magistrate in the case, returning a death-by-hanging sentence. The executioner refused to perform his duty, so the father carried out the sentence himself.

▷ *Take the coast road, the R336, west to An Spidéal.*

❶ An Spidéal (Spiddal),
Co Galway

This charming little resort town has a marvellous beach, the Silver Strand, and shore

---

FOR CHILDREN

West of Galway, Salthill is a children's paradise. In addition to a good beach and pedal buggies for riding along the promenade, attractions at Leisureland Amusement Park are guaranteed to please. The town is also home to Atlantiquaria, the National Aquarium of Ireland, including touch tanks and a model sub.

---

fishing is especially good here. Roman Catholic St Eanna's Church, completed in 1904 in Celtic Romanesque style by William A Scott, is an architectural delight. A popular pastime in summer are races between local curraghs (lightweight wood and canvas boats). The Spiddle Craft Centre, a complex of craft workshops and showrooms, is well worth a visit.

▷ *Continue west on the R336 for 12 miles (19km) to Rossaveel Ros an Mhíl), which lies just off this road.*

The lovely Eyre Square in the centre of Galway has many interesting monuments

❷ Rossaveel, Co Galway

There are still thatched cottages scattered about this small harbour village, from which peat for fuel is shipped by barge to the Aran Islands. The passenger boat trip out to the islands takes just 40 minutes from Rossaveel, rather than the 1½-hour voyage from Galway.

The Aran Islands group consists of three inhabited islands: Inishmore, with the only safe harbour for steamers; Inishmaan and Inisheer, where curraghs meet incoming boats to take passengers or freight to the docks.

Prehistory has left its mark on the faces of all three islands – promontory forts, ringforts and beehive huts speak of the 'Celtic Twilight' era – while lofty round towers, oratories and tiny churches are reminders of the early days of Christianity in Ireland.

A visit to Aran is an easy, delightful day-trip from Rossaveel, and accommodation

can be arranged in advance for those who want to stay longer. Steamers to Inishmore, the largest of the islands, dock at the main port of Kilronan, and jaunting cars are waiting to take visitors exploring. Rented bicycles are also available, and walkers will delight in following the one main road around the island, with an occasional stop to chat with its local inhabitants.

Dún Aonghasa is an 11-acre (4.5-hectare) stone fort perched on a cliff some 300 feet (91m) above the sea, one of the finest prehistoric monuments in western Europe. Its three concentric enclosures are surrounded by drystone walls, and from the innermost rampart there are outstanding views of the islands and across the sea to the Connemara coast.

Near the village of Cowrugh, the grounds of a small 15th-century church hold four great flagstones marking the graves of saints, and south of the church there is a holy well. The area surrounding this village is littered with ancient monuments. But, then, it is literally impossible to go very far on this large island or the two smaller ones without encountering a vivid reminder of centuries past in one form or another.

Among the remains on Inisheer are the medieval tower of O'Brien's Castle which is situated on a prominent rocky hill, St Gobnet's Church and the Church of St Cavan.

The oval fort of Dun Conor rises from a steep-sided hill on Inishmaan; there is also a fine dolmen. Visits to Inishmaan and Inisheer can be arranged with boatmen in Kilronan.

▶ Turn north on the **R336** for 9 miles (14km) to Scrib.

3 Scrib (Screeb), Co Galway
There is excellent game fishing from the small town of Scrib,

The Twelve Pins (or Bens) are rarely out of view on the Connemara horizon

and one of Ireland's peat-burning electricity generating stations is also in the vicinity.

▶ Turn west on to the **R340** to An Gort Mór (Gortmore).

4 An Gort Mór (Gortmore), Co Galway
From this village, a left turn will take you to Ros Muc, site of Padraig Pearse's cottage. It was here that the great Irish leader, who was executed in 1916, spent his holidays and wrote his most important works.

▶ Follow the **R340** southwest to Carna.

5 Carna, Co Galway
Lobster fishing is still the main occupation in this picturesque village. Three miles (5km) to the south, a bridge connects Mweenish Island to the mainland. The beautiful beaches and interesting University College Galway marine biology station make this a worthwhile detour from the route.

A boat trip is available from Carna to St Macdara's Island, named after the 6th-century saint who lived here.

▶ Take the **R340** north for about 7 miles (11km), then turn west on to the **R342** (signposted Cashel) and at Toombeola turn south on to the **R341** for the 4-mile (6km) drive to Roundstone.

6 Roundstone, Co Galway
This pretty village on the west side of Roundstone Bay is a quiet holiday resort that in recent years has attracted a host of artists and craftspeople as permanent residents, with workshops and showrooms. The settlement here was originally established in the early 19th century for Scottish fishermen.

About 2 miles (3km) out on the Ballyconneely road is a fine sandy beach at Dog's Bay (Port-na-Feadog).

▶ Continue on the **R341** northwest to Clifden.

RECOMMENDED WALKS

About 2 miles (3km) from Roundstone on the Ballyconneely road (R341), leave the car at Dog's Bay and walk its beautiful sandy beach around the coast to Gorteen Bay, which also has a lovely sandy beach. Errisbeg Mountain, which hovers over this part of Connemara, is an easy climb, with magnificent views of the lakes and stony landscape to the north, and fine seascapes that reach as far as Clifden to the northwest and the Twelve Pins to the northeast.

7 Clifden, Co Galway
Nestled between the mountains and the Atlantic, with the Twelve Pins (or Bens) rising to the east, Clifden is often called 'The Capital of Connemara'. It lies at the head of Clifden Bay. Built in the 19th century, the town has managed to keep its Georgian character. Its two churches dominate the skyline, and the 1830 Catholic church is built on the site of an ancient monastic beehive stone hut, a clochan, which gave the town its name. The 1820 Protestant church is also a fine structure and holds a silver copy of the Cross of Cong. Clifden Castle was built by John d'Arcy in 1815. Its grounds give a fine marine view.

About 4 miles (6km) south of Clifden (1½ miles/2.5km north of Ballyconneely), look for signposts to the Alcock and Brown Memorial, the spot in Derrygimlagh Bog where intrepid aviators Alcock and Brown crash-landed at the end of the first non-stop flight across the Atlantic from St John's, Newfoundland, in 1919. About 1½ miles (2.5km) away a limestone aeroplane commemorates the event.

Near by are masts and foundations of the first transatlantic wireless transmitting station, set up here by Marconi, the Italian pioneer of radio.

The Connemara Heritage and History Centre, on the N59 about 5 miles (8km) from Clifden, tells the story of life in the area. Reconstructed buildings include a ring fort, a crannog, a clochaun and the homestead of Dan O'Hara, immortalised in a popular ballad. There's also an audiovisual presentation, craft and agricultural demonstrations and other entertaining activities.

i *Galway Road (seasonal)*

▶ *Take the N59 northeast for 11 miles (18km) to Kylemore Abbey.*

8 **Kylemore Abbey,** Co Galway

Situated in the scenic Pass of Kylemore, palatial Kylemore Abbey looks less like an ecclesiastical institution than any other in Ireland. Not surprising, since this magnificent gleaming white castellated mansion was built in the late 1800s as a private residence for millionaire MP Mitchell Henry. Its setting is enhanced by the castle's shimmering image reflected in the waters of one of the three Kylemore lakes. Now a convent of the Benedictine nuns of Ypres, it also houses a pottery and a restaurant run by the nuns. Visitors are welcomed to

The gleaming fairy-tale towers of Kylemore Abbey are reflected in the lake

both, as well as to the lovely grounds and the Gothic chapel.

En route to Leenane, the Maamturk mountain range comes into view, with loughs Fee and Nacarrigeen on your left. Further on, the road follows the southern shore of Killary harbour, a 10-mile (16km) long fiord-like inlet from the sea that runs between steep mountains.

▶ *Continue northeast on the* ***N59*** *for 9 miles (14km) to Leenane.*

9 Leenane, Co Galway
Set near the head of Killary harbour, Leenane is a popular angling centre and mountain-climbing base. This is the western end of the Partry Mountains, and the 2,131-foot (650m) Devil's Mother is the most striking feature of the landscape around this lovely village, location of the film, *The Field*. Close to Leenane (on the road to Louisburgh) is the beautiful

The ruins of Aughnanure Castle

Aasleagh waterfall, which is well worth a short detour.

▶ *Turn southeast on to the* ***R336*** *to Maam Cross (An Teach Dóite).*

10 Maam Cross, Co Galway
This crossroads between north and south Connemara lies amid beautiful scenery.

Mountain peaks are relatively easy to climb and provide marvellous views. For good views of Lough Corrib and its fabled Castlekirk (the Hen's Castle), a 13th-century keep built by Rory O'Connor, take the road north signposted Maum and turn right at the T-junction. According to legend, Castlekirk was built overnight by a witch and her hen.

▶ *Continue southeast on the* ***N59*** *to Oughterard.*

11 Oughterard, Co Galway
This lively town on the upper shores of Lough Corrib is also a

popular salmon- and trout-angling resort. Views along the loughside road are impressive, and local boatmen take visitors on excursions to the islands. You can see the Hill of Doon by following the loughside road north. Aughnanure Castle, built by the O'Flahertys in about 1500, is a six-storey tower house by the shores of Lough Corrib.

Out on the Clifden road, Glengowla Mines offers guided tours into marble and quartz caverns where silver and lead were once mined.

ℹ *Main Street*

▶ *Follow the* ***N59*** *southeast for 17 miles (27km) to Galway.*

SCENIC ROUTES

The 10-mile (16km) drive from Maam Cross to Oughterard passes through a landscape of amazing variety, encompassing lakes, moorland, mountain scenery and bogland.

SPECIAL TO...

Galway town seems always to be celebrating one thing or another with a festival. Among the most important are the Race Week in late July or early August, six days of horse racing, music and feasting; and the International Oyster Festival in late September, which attracts people from around the world to participate in oyster-opening competitions and non-stop feasting on these bivalves.

ULSTER

Ulster is a beautiful place, rich in history, rare in scenery, a province of mountains, loughs, coast and countryside, with tranquil villages and friendly people. The ancient province of Ulster had nine counties: Antrim, Down, Londonderry, Fermanagh, Tyrone and Armagh, which now form Northern Ireland; and Donegal, Cavan and Monaghan, which are part of the Republic of Ireland.

When Patrick came to Celtic Ireland, he chose Armagh for his ecclesiastical capital, because of the strength of Emain Macha, the Palace of the Red Branch Knights. Ulster made a contribution to Ireland's claim to be a land of saints and scholars. Great monasteries and educational establishments were founded, like that at Bangor, in County Down, which sent out missionaries to light up the Dark Age of Europe.

Since Patrick's time the province, like the rest of Ireland, has had successive waves of invaders. Vikings, Normans, English, Scots, Huguenots and refugees have settled here. However, in Ulster it was the number of Scots and Celts, but mostly Presbyterians, that created the special blend of Planter and Gael in Ulster. The hardy race of Scots-Ulster had a temperament tough enough to cope with the frontiers of the New World of America, and enterprising enough to leave a land where nonconformists were at a disadvantage. A dozen American presidents came from this stock. These were the men who defended Derry in the siege, fought with William at the Boyne, won glory for their bravery at the Somme and rejected an independent Ireland in the 1920s.

The lovely Mourne Mountains include great forests, remote lakes and scenic coast (Tour 25)

There is evidence of the two distinctive traditions in Ulster – fife and drum, uillean pipes and bodhran, paintings of King Billy or Mother Ireland on gable walls (most likely drawn by the same man). However, you may be surprised at how little difference there is between the two. Ulster people are delighted to see visitors and very anxious to show them the best of their province. Local councils have worked hard to provide fine amenities in even the most out-of-the-way places. Small villages are festooned with hanging baskets, and window boxes and flower-filled carts give the best impression. When Ulster people are really enjoying themselves – and they do, often – they say 'It's a great craic'. 'Craic' is fun, music, laughter and story-telling, often washed down with a drink or two, and they will be happy to share 'the craic' with visitors.

Tour 20

From historic walled Derry, a proud city rich in song and humour, the tour enters Donegal, whose incomparable scenery is world-renowned – empty beaches stretching for miles are commonplace, amid a landscape of rugged hills, stone walls and white cottages crouching against the Atlantic. The tour passes through fishing and farming communities where the Irish language and traditions are cherished, and ends with Donegal's treasure, Glenveagh National Park.

Tour 21

The Antrim Coast road, which clings to the shore between glens and mountains, headlands and villages, begins a drive of stunning variety. The Giant's Causeway is an essential destination, but the tour takes in lesser-known delights, as well as dramatic castles and historic landscapes, returning to Larne through pleasant countryside.

Tour 22

Belfast, a city of character, is the starting point for a tour that is full of interest for those who love history and wildlife or who simply enjoy discovering quiet villages in beautiful settings. The route takes in the Ulster Folk and Transport Museum, the two fine country houses of Mount Stewart and Castle Ward, and important early Christian sites. The tour focuses on Strangford Lough, rich in marine biology and no less important to ornithologists.

Tour 23

Fermanagh is a very distinctive Ulster county, more water than land it seems, and the land is sparsely populated. The combination of water, woodland and ancient buildings is nowhere so varied as in Fermanagh. The tranquil waters of Lough Erne are a fisherman's paradise. The route begins in the historic town of Enniskillen and includes the haunting beauty of the monastic round tower at Devenish and the neoclassical splendour of Castle Coole. Belleek pottery and Marble Arch caves provide additional interest.

Tour 24

Armagh, the ecclesiastical capital of Ireland, is the starting point for a tour that climbs from the gentle pastures and orchards of County Armagh to the rugged mountains of County Tyrone. This is a journey through Ulster's history, from the heroic era of the Red Branch Knights and the coming of Saint Patrick to the Irish emigrants' new world of America. Country houses, glens and forests, peatlands and parkland come together to form a picture of mid-Ulster.

Tour 25

County Down's distinctive landscape is that of the drumlins, small rounded hills that roll and roll, sheltering quiet green valleys and offering sudden views of sea or lough. The route leaves Newry and goes by way of the charming village of Hillsborough, and then winds through hills again until they give way to the Mountains of Mourne. The Kingdom of Mourne has its own identity, from the small fishing harbours of the rocky coast, through farmland crisscrossed by stone walls to the heights of the mountains. The end of the journey takes in beautiful Carlingford Lough, abundant in forests, castles and pleasant resorts.

The magnificent Palm House of Belfast's famous Botanic Garden, near the city centre (Tour 22)

Seascapes &
Mountain Passes

History is in evidence all around Londonderry (or Derry), not least in the famous Walls of Derry, which form the most complete network of walls, gates and bastons in the British Isles. This town on the River Foyle is also a lively centre for the performing arts, and has craft shops, an art gallery and a museum.

2/3 DAYS • 172 MILES • 276KM

ITINERARY	
LONDONDERRY	▷ **Grianán of Aileach** (7m–11km)
GRIANÁN OF AILEACH	▷ **Letterkenny** (18m–29km)
LETTERKENNY	▷ **Rathmelton** (8m–13km)
RATHMELTON	▷ **Rathmullan** (7m–11km)
RATHMULLAN	▷ **Millford** (31m–50km)
MILLFORD	▷ **Carraig Airt** (10m–16km)
ATLANTIC DRIVE	▷ **(10m–16km)**
CARRAIG AIRT	▷ **Creeslough** (7m–11km)
CREESLOUGH	▷ **Dunfanaghy** (7m–11km)
DUNFANAGHY	▷ **Errigal** (16m–26km)
ERRIGAL	▷ **Glenveagh** (13m–21km)
GLENVEAGH	▷ **Londonderry** (38m–61km)

ⓘ *Foyle Street, Londonderry*

▶ *Take the **A2** for Buncrana, then the **N13** Letterkenny road to the sign for Grianán of Aileach.*

❶ The Grianán of Aileach, Co Donegal

This massive stone fort can be seen for miles around, and the climb to Grianán Mountain gives majestic views over Lough Foyle and Lough Swilly. It is easy to see why this commanding site should have been chosen for the royal residence of the O'Neills, Kings of Ulster. It was enthusiastically restored by Dr Bernard of Derry in 1870, and his work has left us with a complete picture of walls 17 feet (5.25m) high and 13 feet (4m) thick, with steps rising to four levels. The fine modern church at Burt has architectural echoes of Grianan.

▶ *Return to the **N13** and turn left to follow it to Letterkenny.*

❷ Letterkenny, Co Donegal

An administrative and commercial centre in the northwest, Letterkenny sits at the south-west end of Lough Swilly on a fertile plain. In the 19th century it was spoken of as 'fast becoming a place of importance and wealth' and had a steamer communication with Glasgow. It gained the richly Gothic St Eunan's Cathedral at the end of the last century.

About 3 miles (5km) outside town, Newmills Corn and Flax Mills preserve a complex of old mill buildings and Ireland's largest waterwheel. Harnessing the powerful flow of the River Swilly, it is an impressive sight when in action powering the corn mill.

ⓘ *Neil T Blaney Road*

▶ *Take the **R245** for 8 miles (13km) to Rathmelton.*

❸ Rathmelton, Co Donegal

The long curve of the River Leannan, steep hills, tree-lined streets and handsome warehouses on the riverfront all combine to make Rathmelton a place of great charm. It was a Planters' town ('planters' were Presbyterian Scots and Anglican English settlers loyal to the English crown who were encouraged to settle in Ireland and replace the rebellious Catholic Irish landowners). Prosperity gained by the easy navigation from the river mouth brought fine Georgian houses, as well as corn mills, a brewery, bleach greens and linenworks in the early 19th century. The first Presbyterian church in America was formed in 1706 by Reverend Francis Makemie, who emigrated from Rathmelton. Anglers come here to fish, and 'The Pool', near by, is a well-known salmon beat.

Killydonnell Friary, founded by the Franciscans in the 16th century, is 2½ miles (4km) to the south in the grounds of Fort Stewart. There are excellent views of the surrounding countryside from Cam Hill.

> The purpose of Grianán of Aileach may lie in its name – 'stone palace of the sun'

▶ *Take the **R247** for 7 miles (11km) to Rathmullan.*

❹ Rathmullan, Co Donegal

Rathmullan is a pretty village, fringed with trees, on a beautiful beach on Lough Swilly, looking over to the hills of the Inishowen peninsula, with the ruin of a 16th-century priory at the water's edge. Large fishing ships come into its pier, without upsetting the tranquillity. Despite its present peacefulness, Rathmullan has witnessed two major historical events. In 1587, Red Hugh O'Donnell was treacherously lured on board a disguised merchant ship and carried as prisoner to Dublin Castle; and that evocative moment in Irish history, the

Flight of the Earls, took place from here in 1607. The O'Neill, Earl of Tyrone, and the O'Donnell, Earl of Tyrconnell, with about 100 lesser chieftains, finally gave up their resistance to English law and authority in Ulster, and went into exile in Europe, leaving their estates to be forfeited and colonised by English and Scottish settlers. A Heritage Centre in Rathmullan tells the story.

Rathmullan is at the start of the Fanad Drive, with its beaches, streams, lakes and mountain ridges.

▶ Follow the signposts for the Fanad Drive by Portsalon and Carrowkeel to Millford.

5 Millford, Co Donegal

Millford is a leafy contrast to the grand headlands and magnificent bays of Donegal. It stands at the end of the narrow, islanded inlet of Mulroy Bay, and among its wooded hills are two lovely glens with waterfalls, named Golan Loop and Grey Mare's Tail.

▶ Take the R245 to Carraig Airt.

6 Carraig Airt (Carrickart), Co Donegal

This busy little town is tucked in an inlet of Mulroy Bay. To the north is Rosapenna, which boasts a championship golf course that is as scenic as it is challenging.

Nature challenged man and won in the 18th century, when a massive sandstorm engulfed houses and gradually overtook Rosapenna House, finally forcing the occupant, the Reverend Porter, from the top floor in 1808. From Rosapenna beach you can see the Muslac caves, cut by the sea into quartzite folds.

The Downings is a small resort, particularly popular with families with small children, and has an important tweed factory and shop.

▶ Follow the signs for the Atlantic Drive.

7 The Atlantic Drive, Co Donegal

It is believed that the feast of scenery along the road around the Rosguill Peninsula, called the Atlantic Drive, is Donegal's best. The spectacular circuit passes both Sheep Haven and Mulroy bays; Horn Head and Melmore Head are in focus, with Muckish and Errigal mountains more distant to the south. The road passes little shingly bays, and hillsides dotted with white cottages, then opens out to the incomparable sight of Tranarossan Strand. Here the Youth Hostel is in a slightly idiosyncratic building designed by the English architect Edwin Lutyens.

▶ Return to Carraig Airt and follow the R245 to turn right for Creeslough.

8 Creeslough, Co Donegal

Overlooking Sheep Haven Bay is the little village of Creeslough. Doe Castle stands on a low, narrow promontory, bounded by the sea on three sides and a rock-cut ditch on the fourth. It is fortified with corbelled bartizans or turrets, firing platforms and musket loops, a round tower and a great square keep. It has had a colourful and turbulent history. It became the stronghold of the MacSweeneys, who were 'gallowglasses' (foreign warriors), a professional fighting force invited by the O'Donnells from Scotland. It was a refuge for Spanish Armada sailors, taken by the Cromwellians and

comandeered as a garrison for William of Orange. Finally it came into the hands of an English family, the Harts. The initials of General George Vaughan Hart are over the door.

▶ Follow the signs for Dunglow, then take the N56 for 7 miles (11km) to Dunfanaghy.

FOR CHILDREN

Marble Hill, 4 miles (6km) to the east of Dunfanaghy, is a safe and beautiful strand, where windsurfing and canoeing have been tailored for children, with special lessons and the right size of wetsuits and equipment. Over-10-year-olds, even those with no experience, can join a canoe expedition. Basic instruction is given, and the expeditions, under qualified supervision, are an ideal introduction to the joys of canoeing in magnificent surroundings.

---

9 Dunfanaghy, Co Donegal

This is a good point from which to explore Horn Head. Thought by many to be the finest of all Irish headlands, this wall of quartzite rises from the sea, its ledges alive with gulls, puffins, guillemots and razorbills. You

---

SCENIC ROUTES

In this rugged part of Donegal it would be easier to mention those roads that are not scenic. Try the circuit around Bloody Foreland and its sheltered beaches, small fishing inlets, stone-walled fields and white cottages. Look for islands – Gabhla (Gola) to the west, Inishbofin, Inishdooey, Inishbeg and Toraigh (Tory) to the north – and learn that Bloody Foreland, the northwest tip of Ireland, gets its name, not from a grisly past, but from the granite boulders that glow red in the rays of the setting sun.

RECOMMENDED WALKS

At Ards Forest Park, near Creeslough, Lough Lilly is rich with flowering water-lillies in high summer and an enclosed park contains deer. At this most northerly forest park, the trees go right down to the sea, and there are places to bathe as well as walk.

---

can appreciate the full majesty of Horn from Traghlisk Point to the east.

To the northwest is Toraigh (Tory) Island, still inhabited by people who make their living from the sea. The art world has considerable respect for the naïve paintings of the island's artists. To the southwest is An Fál Carrach (Falcarragh), the best point from which to climb the flat-topped mountain, Muckish.

▶ *Continue on the N56 to An Fál Carrach, then to Gort an Choirce (Gortahork). Turn left for Errigal Mountain.*

Dunfanaghy and its superb beach lie sheltered behind Horn Head

10 Errigal Mountain, Co Donegal

Errigal Mountain is a distinctive peak, and once recognised you will see it from many parts of Donegal. Its cone-shaped summit rises 2,466 feet (752m) with silver-grey scree spilling around the slopes. Avoid the scree and, if you can, climb to the top for a panorama that can stretch from Scotland to Knocklayd in County Antrim, wide over the Donegal coastline and south to Sligo's Benbulben – on a clear day, of course. Below lies Dunlewy Lough, and the Poisoned Glen, a sinister name for so pretty a place, but probably deriving from the toxic Irish spurge which used to grow there.

▶ *Take a sharp left onto the R251, and follow the signs for Glenveagh*

⓫ Glenveagh, Co Donegal
Glenveagh is a beautiful place, and unusually for Donegal, the beauty here owes something to human hands. Henry McIlhenny, an American who acquired Glenveagh after it had been owned by several other Americans, developed a garden landscape of outstanding planting that never jars with the superb natural setting of water, mountain and bogland. He then gave the property to the nation to become a National Park. His 'garden rooms' are sensitively enclosed, and a walk through the garden follows the route he enjoyed showing to his visitors.

The castle is redolent of the house parties for which Glenveagh became famous, when film stars mixed with aristocracy. It bears witness throughout to Mr McIlhenny's fascination with deer.

Glenveagh's origins lie in its use as a hunting lodge, and Ireland's largest herd of red deer still roams the hills in a very important wilderness area.

Close by at Church Hill is the Regency Glebe House and Gallery, which has been exquisitely furnished and decorated by Derek Hill, the painter. The art gallery displays selections from the Derek

Glenveagh Castle and its lovely gardens are at the heart of a spectacular national park

Hill collection and beautiful gardens run down to the lakeside. The Columcille Heritage Centre at nearby Gartan celebrates the life and influence of the saint who is also known as St Columba.

FOR HISTORY BUFFS

Eviction and emigration are recurrent nightmares that stalked the troubled history of land tenure in Ireland. At Derryveagh, one of the most notorious mass evictions took place and was the cause of contemporary outrage. In 1861, John George Adair, landlord of Glenveagh, evicted 244 people from their homes to face the workhouse or emigration after a bitter feud with his tenants and the murder of his land steward. The eviction cottage is marked by a plaque put up by An Taisce, the National Trust, at a spot 1 mile (1.5km) from the Glebe Gallery.

BACK TO NATURE

The peat bog, a familiar feature of the Irish landscape, is a natural habitat not to be taken for granted and is now increasingly protected. A lowland blanket bog lies at Lough Barra in a broad valley below Slieve Snaght, and contains pools and rivers. It is an important site for Greenland white-fronted geese, a protected species. There is a raised peat bog in the glacial valley of Glenveagh National Park. Here, a rich variety of ferns and mosses grow in the woodland, while red grouse and red deer can be seen on the moorland.

▶ *From Glenveagh, turn right on to the R251 for Glebe Gallery, then follow this road before returning left on to the R250 for Letterkenny. Take the N13 back to Londonderry.*

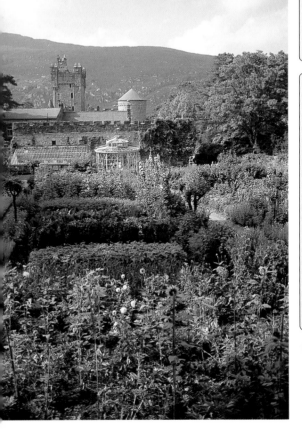

The Causeway
Coast

2/3 DAYS • 163 MILES • 263KM

Larne is a busy port, the terminus for the shortest sea-crossing between Ireland and Britain. To the north is Carnfunnock Park, which has a maze in the shape of Northern Ireland. Larne marks the start of the scenic Antrim Coast Road, which was constructed in the 1830s to link the remote Glens of Antrim to the rest of Ulster.

ITINERARY		
LARNE	▸	**Glenarm** (12m–19km)
GLENARM	▸	**Carnlough** (3m–5km)
CARNLOUGH	▸	**Glenariff** (14m–22km)
GLENARIFF	▸	**Cushendall** (7m–11km)
CUSHENDALL	▸	**Cushendun** (6m–10km)
CUSHENDUN	▸	**Fair Head** (10m–16km)
FAIR HEAD	▸	**Ballycastle** (6m–10km)
BALLYCASTLE	▸	**Carrick-a-Rede** (6m–10km)
CARRICK-A-REDE	▸	**Giant's Causeway** (8m–13km)
GIANT'S CAUSEWAY	▸	**Bushmills** (2m–3km)
BUSHMILLS	▸	**Portrush** (6m––10km)
PORTRUSH	▸	**Downhill** (12m–19km)
DOWNHILL	▸	**Limavady** (11m–18km)
LIMAVADY	▸	**Ballymoney** (20m–32km)
BALLYMONEY	▸	**Ballymena** (19m–31km)
BALLYMENA	▸	**Larne** (21m–34km)

ℹ️ Narrow Gauge Road, Larne

▶ *Take the **A2** coastal road north for 12 miles (19km) to Glenarm.*

❶ Glenarm, Co Antrim

The Antrim Coast Road is so attractive that it is difficult to resist its magnetic lure, but leave it for a moment to sample the charm of Glenarm, a village that clings to the glen rather than to the coast. The neo-Tudor Glenarm Castle is the seat of the Earls of Antrim; its barbican and battlemented, buttressed walls of 1825 rise above the river just as it approaches the sea. The village has twisting streets (Thackeray apparently enjoyed their names), pavements patterned in limestone and basalt, a market house with an Italianate campanile and good, modest Georgian houses and shops.

The forest, through the gateway at the top of the village, gives the first opportunity to walk up an Antrim glen. This one is narrow, leafy and dense with pathways and waterfalls.

▶ *Take the **A2** to Carnlough.*

❷ Carnlough, Co Antrim

Carnlough, at the foot of Glencloy, the least dramatic of the glens, has a good, safe beach. A railway used to carry lime from the kilns above the village to the harbour, over the bridge that spans the coast road. The bridge, the clock tower and the former town hall are made from great chunks of limestone. Frances Anne Vane Tempest Stewart, Countess of Antrim and Marchioness of Londonderry, was responsible for many major works, including Garron Tower, built in 1848, once a family home, now a boarding school. She is remembered in the town's main hotel, the Londonderry Arms, which was built in 1854 and has the feel of a coaching inn.

▶ *Take the **A2**, following sign-posts for Cushendall for 9 miles (14km) to Waterfoot. Turn left on to the **A43** for 5 miles (8km) to Glenariff Forest Park.*

❸ Glenariff, Co Antrim

The road obligingly provides a perfect route along this magnificent glen. The bay at its foot is 1 mile (1.5km) long and the chiselled sides draw in the fertile valley symmetrically to the head of the glen. There, the Forest Park allows easy exploration of the deep, wooded gorge with its cascades, 'Ess-na-crub' (Fall of the Hoof), 'Ess-na-laragh' (Fall of the Mare) and Tears of the Mountain.

Waterfoot, the little village at the foot of the glen, hosts The Glens of Antrim Feis (pronounced 'fesh') in July, a major festival of traditional music and dancing.

All along the Antrim Coast Road, wonderful views unfold

Between Red Bay and the pier are three caves. Nanny's Cave was inhabited by Ann Murray until her death, aged 100, in 1847. She supported herself by knitting and by selling poteen (an illicit distillation, pronounced potcheen), or 'the natural' as she called it.

▶ *Turn right to follow the **B14** to Cushendall.*

4 Cushendall, Co Antrim
'The Capital of the Glens', Cushendall sits on a pleasant, sandy bay below Glenballyemon, Glenaan and Glencorp and in the curve of the River Dall. The rugged peak of Lurigethan broods over the village, while the softer Tieveragh Hill is supposedly the capital of the fairies. Cushendall owes much to an East Indian nabob, Francis Turnley, who built the Curfew Tower in the centre as a 'place for the confinement of idlers and rioters'.

In a tranquil valley by the sea just north of the village is the 13th-century church of Layde. The MacDonnells of Antrim are buried here, as are Englishmen stationed in these lonely posts as coastguards, and one memorial stone mourns an emigré killed in the American Civil War in 1865 when he was only 18.

▶ *Continue on the **A2** for 3 miles (5km), then turn right on to the **B92** for Cushendun.*

5 Cushendun, Co Antrim
The very decided character of Cushendun is a surprise. This is a black-and-white village, with an orderly square and terraces of houses that were designed to look Cornish. Lord Cushendun married a Cornish wife, Maud, and commissioned the distinguished architect Clough Williams-Ellis to create a streetscape with style.

A little salmon fishery stands at the mouth of the River Dun, the 'dark brown water'. To the south is Cave House, locked in cliffs and approachable only through a long, natural cave. Castle Carra is to the north, the place where the clan quarrel between the O'Neills and the MacDonnells caused the treacherous murder of the great Shane O'Neill during a banquet in 1567.

▶ *At the north end of the village turn on to the road sign-*

Cushendun is famous for its unusual architecture

posted 'scenic route' for Ballycastle by Torr Head. After 9 miles (14km) turn right to Murlough Bay.

6 Fair Head and Murlough Bay, Co Antrim
Paths from the cluster of houses known as Coolanlough cross the barren headland broken by three dark lakes – Lough Doo, Lough Fadden and Lough na Cranagh, which has a crannóg or lake dwelling. Fair Head itself is exposed and barren, a place inhabited by wild goats and choughs (red-legged crows). The careful walker can descend the cliff using the Grey Man's Path, which follows a dramatic plunging fissure.

By contrast, Murlough Bay is green and fertile, generous in contours and abundantly wooded. Tradition has it that the Children of Lir were transformed into swans to spend 300 years here. At the top of the road is a monument to the Republican leader Sir Roger Casement, and a row of lime kilns, which would have burned the stone for use in fertiliser, whitewash or mortar.

▶ After 1 mile (2km) turn right for Ballycastle, then right again on to the **A2** to Ballycastle.

BACK TO NATURE

For bird-lovers, a trip on the boat to Rathlin Island is not to be missed. Up to 20,000 guillemots, razorbills, fulmars, kittiwakes and puffins can be seen on the sheer rock stacks close to the West Lighthouse. Shearwaters can sometimes be seen offshore. Early summer is the best time to see them.

❼ Ballycastle, Co Antrim

There are two parts to Ballycastle – the winding main street which carries you up to the heart of the town, and Ballycastle by the sea, with its fine beach and tennis courts.

At the foot of the Margy River is Bonamargy Friary, founded by the Franciscans as late as 1500. The notorious Sorley Boy MacDonald is buried here. Elizabeth I found that he eluded all her attempts at capture, but in 1575, when he had sent his children to Rathlin Island for safety, he had to stand on the mainland helpless while they were murdered.

Ballycastle's museum illustrates the folk and social history of the Glens of Antrim.

At the harbour is a memorial to Gugliemo Marconi, who carried out the first practical test on radio signals between White Lodge, on the clifftop at Ballycastle, and Rathlin Island in 1898. You can travel by boat to Rathlin and savour the life of the 30 or so families who live and farm here. The island is a mecca for divers and birdwatchers. Robert the Bruce hid in a cave on Rathlin after his defeat in 1306. Watching a spider repeatedly trying to climb a thread to the roof, he was encouraged to 'try, and try again'. He returned to Scotland to fight on, and was successful at the Battle of Bannockburn.

ⓘ *Sheskburn House, Mary Street*

SPECIAL TO...

The Oul' Lammas Fair in Ballycastle, held every August Bank Holiday, is a real horse fair with a lot more besides. The streets of Ballycastle are crammed with stalls, including traditional games of chance, and the town is alive with music and fun. Horse-trading lives up to its reputation, and you are likely to hear the refrain:
*Did you take your Mary Ann
For some dulse and yellow man.
At the oul' Lammas Fair in
Ballycastle-O.*
Dulse is edible dried seaweed and yellow man is a chewy sweet confection.

▶ From the shore follow the **B15** coastal route west for Ballintoy, then turn right, following the signpost to Carrick-a-Rede and Larry Bane.

❽ Carrick-a-Rede, Co Antrim

A swinging rope bridge spans the deep chasm between the mainland and the rocky island of Carrick-a-Rede, and if you have a very strong heart and a good head, you can cross it. The bridge is put up each year by salmon fishermen, who use Carrick-a-Rede, 'the Rock in the Road', as a good place to net the fish in their path to the Bush and Bann rivers. The rope bridge is approached from Larry Bane, a limestone head which had once been quarried. Some of the quarry workings remain, and the quarry access to the magnificent seascape provides some guaranteed birdwatching. It is possible to sit in your car and spot kittiwakes, cormorants, guillemots, fulmars and razorbills, though you might have to use binoculars to catch sight of the puffins on Sheep Island further out to sea.

Just to the west is Ballintoy,

a very pretty little limestone harbour, at the foot of a corkscrew road. A little further west is the breathtaking sandy sweep of White Park Bay, accessible only on foot, and worth every step. Among the few houses that fringe the west end of the beach, tucked into the cliff, is Ireland's smallest church, dedicated to St Gobhan, patron saint of builders.

▶ Take the **B15** to join the **A2** for Portrush, then turn right on to the **B146** for the Giant's Causeway.

❾ Giant's Causeway, Co Antrim

Sixty million years ago, or thereabouts, intensely hot volcanic lava erupted through narrow vents and, in cooling rapidly over the white chalk, formed into about 37,000 extraordinary geometric columns and shapes – mostly hexagonal, but also with four, five, seven or eight sides. That is one story. The other is that the giant, Finn MacCool, fashioned it so that he could cross dry-shod to Scotland.

Generations of fanciful guides have embroidered stories and created names for the remarkable formations – the Giant's Organ, the Giant's Harp, the Wishing Chair, and Lord Antrim's Parlour. The Visitor Centre tells the full story of the fact and fiction, the folklore and traditions, and provides a bus service down the steep road to the Causeway.

One story absolutely based on fact is of the *Girona*, a fleeing Spanish Armada galleon, wrecked in a storm on the night of 26 October 1588. A diving team retrieved a treasure hoard from the wreck in 1967, now on display in the Ulster Museum in Belfast. The wreck still lies under cliffs in Port na Spaniagh, one of a magnificent march of bays and headlands on the Causeway.

The most famous sight in Ireland, the Giant's Causeway never fails to amaze and delight

FOR CHILDREN

Portrush has all the fun of a traditional seaside holiday town for children, from donkey rides to candy floss. It also has a countryside centre, with animals to pet, and there are regular firework displays on Ranmore Head. Should it rain, Portrush also has indoor activities, including Waterworld, with swimming and other facilities, the Dunluce Centre and an indoor funfair.

Near the Visitor Centre is the Causeway School Museum, a reconstructed 1920s schoolroom, complete with learning aids and toys of the era.

RECOMMENDED WALKS

There can be few more spectacular walks than the 10-mile (16km) coastal path between the Giant's Causeway and White Park Bay. Magnificent amphitheatres of rocky cliffs, dramatic clefted inlets, basalt sea stacks, an abundance of wild flowers and the company of seabirds add to the pleasure of this walk. A guide will help identify the evocative names for each bay and the historic features, including the remains of tiny Dunseverick Castle.

[i] Visitor Centre, 44 Causeway Road, Bushmills

▶ Take the **A2** to Bushmills.

⑩ Bushmills, Co Antrim
This neat village is the home of the world's oldest legal distillery, which was granted its licence in 1608. The water from St Columb's rill, or stream, is said to give the whiskey its special quality, and visitors can discover something of its flavour on tours of the distillery.

The 'water of life', patiently maturing in oak barrels at the Bushmills Distillery

The River Bush is rich in trout and salmon, and its fast-flowing waters not only supported the mills that gave the town its name, but generated electricity for the world's first hydroelectric tramway, which carried passengers to the Giant's Causeway between 1893 and 1949.

▶ Follow the **A2** west to Portrush.

⑪ Portrush, Co Antrim
Portrush is a typical seaside resort, which flourished with the rise of the railways. It has three good bays, with broad stretches of sand, ranges of dunes, rock pools, white cliffs and a busy harbour.

Nearby Dunluce is one of the most romantic of castles, where a sprawling ruin clings perilously to the clifftop, presenting a splendid profile. The castle was a MacDonnell stronghold until half the kitchen fell into the sea on a stormy night in 1639. The Dunluce Centre is a high-tech entertainment complex.

[i] Dunluce Centre

▶ Take the **A29** for Coleraine, then follow the **A2** for Castlerock, then on to

BACK TO NATURE

Ballymena's ECOS Centre deals with environmental issues in a way that is both thought provoking and fun, appealing to adults and children alike. Displays explain how each of us can make a difference in the world, and the country park setting provides the opportunity to see local wildlife along scenic walks. Kids particularly love the pond-dipping, and there's a playground next to the coffee shop.

Downhill, a distance of 12 miles (19km).

⑫ Downhill, Co Londonderry
The feast of magnificent coastal scenery is given a different face at Downhill. Here Frederick Hervey, who was Earl of Bristol and Bishop of Derry, decided to adorn nature with man's art, by creating a landscape with eyecatching buildings, artificial ponds and cascades, in keeping with the taste of the time. He was a great 18th-century eccentric, collector and traveller, who gave his name to the Bristol hotels throughout Europe. Although nature has won back much of the Earl Bishop's ambitious scheme, the spirit of the place is strongly felt. Mussenden Temple, a perfect classical rotunda, stands high on a clifftop above a wonderful headland.

Near by is Benone Tourist Complex, beside the 7 mile (11km) Benone Strand, reputedly one of the cleanest beaches in Europe, backed by a duneland park.

SCENIC ROUTES

The Bishop's Road runs over Eagle Hill and Binevanagh Mountain, rising steeply from Downhill. The Earl Bishop had it built to provide local employment in the 18th century. From Gortmore viewpoint the panorama stretches from Donegal to Fair Head, above the fertile shores of Lough Foyle and beyond to Scotland. The AA has placed a chart here showing directions and distances of the views, and another plaque recalls that this was the site chosen in 1824 by surveyors for the most accurate measurement ever then achieved between two places.

▶ *From the **A2** turn left on Bishop's Road for Gortmore, then after 8 miles (13km) turn right on to the **B201**, then left on to the **A2** for Limavady.*

13 Limavady, Co Londonderry

The Roe Valley was the territory of the O'Cahans, and O'Cahan's Rock is one of the landmarks of the nearby Roe Valley Country Park. One story says that it was here a dog made a mighty leap with a message to help relieve a besieged castle, giving this pleasant market town its name, 'The Leap of the Dog'.

The *Londonderry Air* was first written down here by Jane Ross, when she heard it being played by a street fiddler. Limavady was the birthplace of William Massey (1856–1925), Prime Minister of New Zealand from 1912 to 1925.

i *7 Connell Street*

▶ *Take the **A37** for Coleraine, then turn right on to the **B66**; follow signs for the **B66** to Ballymoney.*

14 Ballymoney, Co Antrim

A bustling town, Ballymoney recalls its farming past at Leslie Hill Open Farm, where visitors can travel through the park by horse and trap. Drumaheglis Marina provides access to the River Bann, elsewhere a fairly secluded river, and offers water-

bus cruises. Three miles (5km) northeast, in Conagher, off the road to Dervock, is the birthplace of the 25th President of the US, William McKinley.

▶ *Take the **A26** to Ballymena.*

15 Ballymena, Co Antrim

Ballymena, the county town of Antrim, boasts as one of its sons Timothy Eaton, who founded the now defunct Eaton's Stores in Canada. To the east the hump of Slemish Mountain rises abruptly from the ground. It was here that St Patrick worked when he was first brought to Ireland as a slave. In the southen suburbs is the 40-foot (12m) high Harryville motte and bailey – one of the finest surviving Anglo-Norman earthworks in Ulster.

Just to the west is 17th-century Galgorm Castle, a Plantation castle built by Sir Faithful Fortescue in 1618. Beyond is the charming village of Gracehill, founded by the Moravians in the 18th century.

▶ *Take the **A36** for 21 miles (34km) and return to Larne.*

Farming the old-fashioned way at the Leslie Hill Open Farm in northern County Antrim

Strangford
Lough

From the centre of Belfast, the rolling hills which cradle the city catch the eye at the end of many streets. Belfast is an industrial city with a strong ship-building tradition and the skyline is dominated by two huge cranes in the dockyard. Near by the Waterfront Concert Hall is a splendid venue for international events. The city is rich in Victorian and Edwardian architecture, from the magnificent City Hall to the atmospheric Crown Liquor Saloon. The peaceful Botanic Gardens, closed until 2009, also contain the superb Ulster Museum.

2 DAYS • 87 MILES • 138KM

ITINERARY

BELFAST	▶ **Cultra (7m-11km)**
CULTRA	▶ **Newtownards (7m-11km)**
NEWTOWNARDS	▶ **Mount Stewart (7m-11km)**
MOUNT STEWART	▶ **Portavogie (9m-14km)**
PORTAVOGIE	▶ **Kearney (6m-10km)**
KEARNEY	▶ **Portaferry (8m-13km)**
PORTAFERRY	▶ **Strangford (ferry)**
STRANGFORD	▶ **Downpatrick (9m-14km)**
DOWNPATRICK	▶ **Killyleagh (5m-8km)**
KILLYLEAGH	▶ **Nendrum (14m-22km)**
NENDRUM	▶ **Belfast (15m-24km)**

FOR CHILDREN

A visit to the Odyssey on Belfast's Queens Quay is sure to create excitement. Lots of indoor sports, entertainment, food outlets, and W5 – a science exploratory experience – will keep children amused for hours.

▶ *Leave Belfast via the **A2**, following signposts for Bangor, and after 7 miles (11km) turn off for the Ulster Folk and Transport Museum.*

❶ Cultra, Co Down

The Ulster Folk and Transport Museum, in the grounds of Cultra Manor (also open), tells the story of the province's past through buildings that have been saved and meticulously reconstructed at this site.

Visitors can wander through former Ulster homes, which include a thatched cottage, a rectory and a terraced house, and watch demonstrations of traditional crafts. A church, schoolhouse, water-powered mills and many other buildings give a vivid picture of the past.

In the transport section, the collection spans the history of transport, from creels used by a donkey carrying turf, through the grand ocean-going liners built in Belfast, to ultra-modern aircraft from the Belfast firm Short Brothers and Harland.

This is undoubtedly one of the best museums in Ireland.

▶ *Turn left and follow the **A2** for 4 miles (6km). Turn right following the signpost for Newtownards.*

❷ Newtownards, Co Down

This thriving town lies among some of the richest arable land in Ulster. St Finnian founded Movilla Abbey in AD540, and the Dominican priory was

---

SPECIAL TO...

The area around Newtownards is home to some of the world's most famous roses. The Dickson family first opened a nursery here in 1836 and have been international prize-winning rose breeders since 1887, bringing much-loved favourites like 'Grandpa Dickson' and 'Iceberg' to a worldwide market. The dynastic chain has continued unbroken, and Dickson's are still perfecting new varieties at their nurseries at Newtownards.

---

established by the Normans in the 13th century. The hollow, octagonal, 17th-century market cross also served as the town watch and gaol. The impressive town hall was built around 1770, by the Londonderry family who also built Scrabo Tower, on the hill overlooking the town.

This dominant landmark, standing 135 feet (41m) high, was erected in memory of the

The rectory and village church, part of the display at the Ulster Folk and Transport Museum

third Marquess of Londonderry. It now houses an audio-visual presentation about Strangford Lough. The surrounding country park has woodland walks, sandstone quarries and panoramic views.

i *31 Regent Street*

▶ *Take the **A20**, following signs for Portaferry, to Mount Stewart.*

❸ Mount Stewart, Co Down

Mount Stewart is a magnificent garden where many exotic plants flourish in formal terraces and parterres or in natural settings, enjoying the mild climate of the peninsula.

Lady Londonderry, the renowned hostess and leader of London society, created it after World War I, and this unique garden is considered one of the finest in these islands. It was designated European Garden of

Inspiration in 2003. Each garden is given a name – 'Tir n'an Og' (the Land of Eternal Youth), the Mairi Garden, Peace Garden, the Dodo Terrace and the Italian Garden. The lake is particularly beautiful.

The house, the early home of Lord Castlereagh, contains the 22 chairs used at the Congress of Vienna and a masterpiece by the painter

The Mount Stewart estate is one of the finest National Trust properties in Ireland

George Stubbs among its treasures. Designed as a banqueting house, the Temple of the Winds is an exquisite piece of 18th-century landscape architecture.

The shoreline is an excellent place for viewing birds, including thousands of Brent geese that winter on the lough.

▶ *Follow the **A20** for 7 miles (11km) to Kircubbin. Take a left turn on to the **B173** for 3 miles (5km), then turn left for Portavogie.*

4 **Portavogie,** Co Down
Up to 40 boats fill the attractive harbour of Portavogie when the fleet is in. Shellfish are plentiful and hotels serve a good variety of fresh fish. Seals regularly follow the boats into the harbour to scavenge for food while the catch is being unloaded, and auctioned in the harbour.

▶ *Take the **A2** south for 2 miles (3km). At Cloughey turn left and follow signposts to Kearney. After 1 mile (1.5km) turn left for Kearney and*

The Mount Stewart estate is one of the finest National Trust properties in Ireland

follow signposts at two left turns for Kearney, about 3 miles (5km).

5 Kearney, Co Down

Kearney is a tiny village of whitewashed houses in the care of the National Trust. Once a fishing village, it now offers fine walks along a rocky shoreline that looks out across the Irish Sea to the Isle of Man, Scotland and the north of England. Close by is the sandy beach of Knockinelder, and south is Millin Bay cairn, a neolithic burial site with ancient decorated stones.

At Temple Cowey and St Cowey's Wells, on a remote and peaceful shore, are a penance stone and holy well at a site founded in the 7th century, and later used for worship in penal times. Mass is still held here from time to time.

▶ *Turn left and left again to follow the road around the tip of the peninsula by Barr Hall and Quintin Bay to Portaferry.*

6 Portaferry, Co Down

One of Ulster's most beautifully sited villages, Portaferry's attractive waterfront of colourful terraced cottages, pubs and shops is framed by green meadows and wooded slopes. No fewer than five defensive tower houses guard the narrow neck of the lough. The Marine Biology Station, part of Queen's University, Belfast, is situated opposite the ferry jetty. Close to the tower house is the Northern Ireland Aquarium, Exploris, set beside a pleasant park, which explains the unique nature of the marine life of Strangford Lough. Over 2,000 species of marine animal thrive in the waters of Strangford, including large colonies of corals and sponges in the fast-flowing tides of the Narrows, and sea anemones, sea cucumbers and brittle stars in the quieter waters. The lough is home to large fish, including tope and skate. A regular, 5-minute car-ferry service to Strangford, gives stunning views of the lough.

▶ *Take the car ferry to Strangford. Boats leave at half-hourly intervals.*

7 Strangford, Co Down

Strangford is a small village with two bays, pretty houses and a castle. Close by is Castle Ward, set in fine parkland with excellent views over the lough. The 18th-century house is exactly divided into Gothic and classical architectural styles, the result of disputed tastes between Lord and Lady Bangor. Restored estate buildings demonstrate the elaborate organisation which once supported a country house. A small theatre is used for many events, including a midsummer opera festival.

One mile (1.5km) south, on the A2 to Ardglass, a lay-by at Cloughy Rocks is a great place for viewing seals when the tide is right. Further south is Kilclief Castle and Killard Point, at the narrowest point of the neck to the lough. This lovely grassland area with its low cliffs and a pretty, small beach is rich in wild flowers.

▶ *Take the A25 to Downpatrick.*

8 Downpatrick, Co Down

Down Cathedral stands on the hill above the town, while English Street, Irish Street and Scotch Street jostle together below. There has been a church on the site of the cathedral since AD520, but the present building dates largely from the 18th century. Ireland's patron saint is reputed to be buried in the churchyard with the bones of St Brigid and St Columba. The Norman John de Courcy ordered their reinterment:
In Down three saints one grave do fill
Brigid, Patrick and Columcille.
The supposed grave is marked by a granite stone erected in 1900. Down County Museum has recently extended

SCENIC ROUTES

The roads around Strangford are a delight for drivers, as they are generally quiet, with accessible picnic sites. Many small roads hug the water's edge, as does the road just north of Portaferry. The views across the lough are breathtaking, as the scenery changes from noble parkland with ancient towers, to a tree-lined bay filled with yachts at mooring, then pleasant farmland dotted with cottages. Sunsets on Strangford can be spectacular, and often a change of light will reveal the profile of the Mourne Mountains in the distant southwest.

FOR CHILDREN

Castle Ward, west of Strangford, has a Victorian playroom with toys, rocking horse, books and dressing-up clothes, which can all be enjoyed. Children can experiment with hoops, or stilts, or tops and whips. The Strangford Lough Barn on the estate provides another 'hands-on' display about the wildlife of the area, plus regular video shows.

RECOMMENDED WALKS

St Patrick's Way passes many of the sites associated with St Patrick around Downpatrick. The saint is said to have landed at the mouth of the River Slaney in AD432, and to have returned there to die. At Saul, a small church with a distinctive round tower in traditional style marks the spot where he preached his first sermon. The Way is a network of marked paths, lanes and quiet roads, and is designed to be as long or as short as the walker wishes, from 1 to 7 miles (1.5km to 11km).

into the refurbished Governor's Residence, where 'Down Through Time' is a fascinating interactive display.

The Saint Patrick Centre is a cutting-edge exhibition about Ireland's saint and his legacy, including the impact of Irish missionaries in the Dark Ages.

i *The St Patrick Centre, 53A Market Street*

▶ *Follow the A22 to Killyleagh.*

9 Killyleagh, Co Down

A fairy-tale castle with towers and battlements overlooks this quiet loughside village. The Hamilton family has lived there for 300 years, and although the original castle was built by the Normans, its present appearance owes more to the 19th century. Sir Hans Sloane, the physician and naturalist whose collection formed the nucleus of the British Museum, was born in Killyleagh in 1660 and educated in the castle. It is said that the famous Emigrant's Lament – 'I'm sitting on the stile, Mary', written by Lady Dufferin, a guest at the castle during the Famine – was inspired by the stile at Killowen Old Churchyard.

▶ *Follow the A22 for 5 miles (8km) to Balloo crossroads. Turn right at the sign for*

FOR HISTORY BUFFS

Driving through the centre of Comber, you cannot fail to see the statue of Major General Rollo Gillespie. Born in this square in 1766, he became a cavalryman at 17, eloped, fought a duel, was acquitted of murder, shipwrecked off Jamaica and attacked by pirates, of whom he killed six. He then settled down to an army life, and the list of his battles in Java, Bengal and elsewhere is recorded at the foot of the column, together with his famous last words – 'One shot more for the honour of Down' – uttered after he had been shot through the heart attacking the fort of Kalunga.

Killinchy, and continue for 4 miles (6km), turning right three times for Comber. After 2½ miles (4km) turn right, following the sign for Nendrum Monastic Site.

10 Nendrum Monastic Site, Co Down

A place of great tranquillity, Nendrum monastic site was established on one of the many islands that are sprinkled along Strangford's calm middle waters, and is now reached by a causeway. The site is one of the

---

The graveyard of Downpatrick's cathedral is said to contain the burial place of St Patrick

most complete examples of a very early monastery in Ireland, and the ruins, in three concentric rings, include the stump of a round tower, monks' cells and a church with a stone sundial.

BACK TO NATURE

A short distance from Nendrum is Castle Espie Wildfowl and Wetlands Centre. When disused clay pits began to fill with water, a sensitive owner quickly realised that this was an important habitat for wildfowl. The careful management that followed has made Castle Espie a haven for birds and an attractive place to visit. Birds which use Strangford Lough can be seen here, as well as endangered species from exotic places. In particular, look for Brent geese, wigeon, sanderling, knot and grey plovers. There is also an art gallery, and the tea-room has views over the lough.

▶ *Return across the causeway and after 3 miles (5km) turn right for 3 miles (5km) to join the A22 to Comber, and on to Belfast.*

Fermanagh
Lakeland

At Enniskillen, 'the Island Town', water greets you at every turn – from Lower and Upper Lough Erne and the River Erne, which flows through the town. Places of interest include the museums housed in Enniskillen Castle, and the fine, neo-classical Castle Coole.

1/2 DAYS • 84 MILES • 133KM

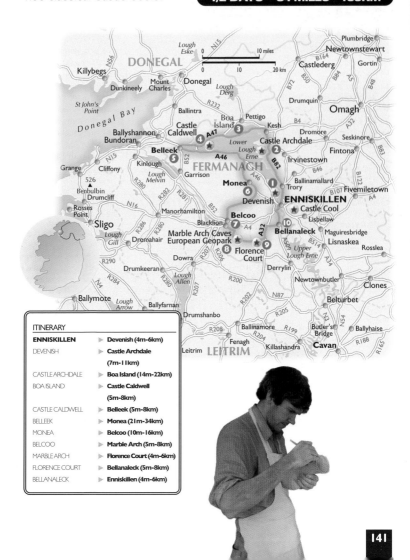

ITINERARY

i *Fermanagh Information Centre, Wellington Road, Enniskillen*

RECOMMENDED WALKS

There are 114 miles (183km) of the Ulster Way, the province's network of paths, in County Fermanagh. A helpful booklet is available from tourist information centres.

▶ *Take the A32 towards Omagh for 2 miles (3km) until you reach the signpost for the ferries to Devenish.*

1 Devenish, Co Fermanagh

Take a ferry from Trory to get to Devenish Island. Across the silvery water is one of the most important monastic sites in Ulster, founded by St Molaise in the 6th century, although the remarkable group of buildings dates mostly from the 12th century. The round tower was repaired in the 19th century, and is regarded as one of the finest in Ireland, beautifully proportioned, with finely cut stone and precision of line. The towers, famous symbols of Christianity in Ireland, acted as signposts, bell towers and places of refuge and retreat in attack, and a safe storage place for treasures during Viking raids. The great treasure of Devenish, the book shrine of Molaise, which is a masterpiece of early Christian art, is kept at the National Museum in Dublin.

On a hill, with uninterrupted views over both loughs, Devenish was such a favoured place for parleys in disputes between Ulster and Connacht that it was sometimes called 'Devenish of the Assemblies'.

▶ *Take the B82 for 7 miles (11km) for Kesh and Castle Archdale.*

2 Castle Archdale, Co Fermanagh

With a marina, caravan sites, a youth hostel and recreational activities, Castle Archdale is one of the busiest places around Lough Erne, but it is still very easy to find a quiet place in this country park. In the old estate of the Archdale family is an arboretum, butterfly park and farm with rare breeds. The ruins of the old castle, burnt in the Williamite wars of 1689, can be seen in the forest, and the stable block of the 18th-century house is an important part of the park. The focus of Castle Archdale is the marina, where concrete jetties and slipways, built for flying boats taking off for the Battle of the Atlantic in 1941, have been turned to more peaceful use. You can hire a boat with a 'gillie' (a man to help you with the fishing). It is possible to reach White Island from here to see the enigmatic carved

Round towers are an evocative symbol of ecclesiastical sites. This one is on Devenish Island

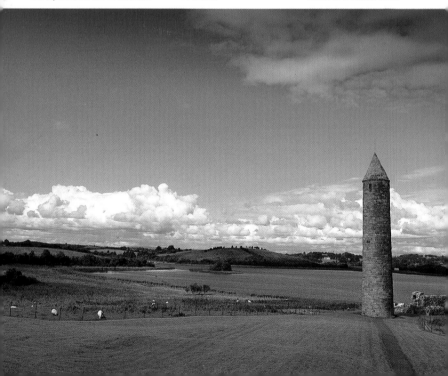

stones that for centuries have puzzled experts and fascinated visitors. Set in the little 12th-century church, they seem to represent biblical figures, with the exception of 'Sheil-na-gig', a female fertility figure, a strange meeting of Celtic pagan art and Christianity.

▶ *Turn left on to the B82. After 2 miles (3km), turn left for Kesh via the scenic route for 4 miles (6km). At Kesh turn left for Belleek, on to the A35, then after 1 mile (1.5km) turn on to the A47 and drive for 8 miles (13km) to Boa Island (pronounced Bo).*

The carved stone Janus figure on Boa Island is a mysterious relic of pre-Christian times

---

BACK TO NATURE

If you are extremely fortunate, you may hear the distinctive call of the corncrake or land rail. Fermanagh is one of the last refuges of this bird, whose population has diminished rapidly in Britain and the rest of Europe, as it has become increasingly disturbed by mechanical methods of hay-making. Some experts feel that the complete extinction of this attractive bird is inevitable, but it can still be found here. You are, however, more likely to hear its grating 'crex-crex' call than see this secretive bird.

---

❸ Boa Island, Co Fermanagh

Two bridges connect Boa Island to the mainland. Just before the bridge at the west end is a track on the left to Caldragh cemetery, where there are two pagan idols in stone. One is called a Janus figure because it is double-faced; the other, a small, hunched figure, was moved here from Lusty Beg Island. Boa Island, with its echoes of pre-Christian Ireland, is said to be named after Badhbh, the Irish goddess of war.

▶ *Continue on the A47 for 5 miles (8km) to Castle Caldwell.*

❹ Castle Caldwell, Co Fermanagh

The Fiddler's Stone at the entrance to Castle Caldwell, is a memorial to fiddler Dennis McCabe, who fell out of Sir James Caldwell's family barge on 13 August, 1770, and was drowned. The obituary ends:
On firm land only exercise your skill
That you may play and safely drink your fill.

The castle, now in ruins, had the reputation of enjoying one of the most beautiful situations of all Irish houses. The fine views are still the same, across water rich in wildlife, with bird hides that allow visitors to catch sight of many ducks, geese and grebes.

FOR CHILDREN

Located beside Upper Lough Erne, just outside Belcoo, Corralea Activity Centre (tel: 028 66386668) offers organised outdoor activities, plus canoe, windsurfer and bicycle hire by the half-day.

▶ *Continue on the A47 to Belleek.*

❺ Belleek, Co Fermanagh

This border village is famed for its fine parian china, best known for its delicate basketwork, shamrock decoration and lustre-finish. The range of goods produced by the Belleek Pottery has expanded to include designer items alongside the classic patterns, and visitors can tour the 1857 factory, see the best examples of the china and watch exquisite craftsmanship – the result of skills handed down from generation to generation. To this, Belleek adds the lure of a restaurant where the food is served on Belleek tableware.

Visitors can witness the art of the craftspeople at Belleek

route for 2 miles (3km). Rejoin the **A46** and after 6 miles (10km) turn right, and follow signs to Monea.

6 Monea, Co Fermanagh
Monea (pronounced Mon-ay) is the ruin of a Plantation castle, remote among marshy ground on a rocky outcrop. Built by 'undertakers', or Planters, arriving from the lowlands of Scotland in the early 17th century, it has a Scottish look about it, particularly in the corbelling. The castle was captured by the Irish in 1641 and finally abandoned in 1750. There are still remnants of the bawn wall that surrounded the castle, and an ancient crannóg, or artificial island dwelling, can be picked out in the marsh in front of Monea. In the parish church is a 15th-century window, removed from Devenish.

▶ *Turn left leaving Monea, then left for Enniskillen. Turn right, following signs to Boho for 5 miles (8km), then right again for Belcoo.*

7 Belcoo, Co Fermanagh
Belcoo sits neatly between the two Lough Macneans, surrounded by mountains and adjacent to its neighbouring County Leitrim village, Blacklion. The two loughs are large and very beautiful.

To the south of Lower Lough Macnean is the limestone cliff of Hanging Rock, and by the road is the Salt Man, a great lump of limestone, which, it is said, fell off the cliff and killed a man pulling a load of salt.

Just north of Belcoo is the Holywell, traditionally visited by pilgrims in search of the curative powers of St Patrick's Well.

▶ *From Belcoo, cross the border into the Republic and Blacklion for a very short distance, then cross back into Northern Ireland, taking the road along the south shore of Lower Lough Macnean. Turn right along Marlbank Scenic Loop and drive for 3 miles (5km) to Marble Arch.*

▶ *Take the **A46** for Enniskillen. After 13 miles (21km) turn right on the Slavin scenic*

8 Marble Arch Caves European Geopark, Co Fermanagh

One of the highlights of a visit to Fermanagh, the mysterious beauty of the Marble Arch Caves, is enhanced by a ride on a quiet, flat-bottomed boat through still, dark waters. Over 300 million years of history is here among a strange landscape of chasms and valleys, amid stalactites and stalagmites. The deep gorge of Marble Arch is dramatically beautiful, and it is worth taking time to walk further into the Cladagh Glen. Common wild flowers are seen in glorious abundance and variety, as well as some Irish rarities.

▶ *Turn left, then right and drive for 4 miles (6km) to Florence Court.*

9 Florence Court, Co Fermanagh

Florence Court was the home of the Enniskillen family, who moved from a castle in the county town to this wild and beautiful setting in the 18th century. The house was named after a new English wife.

The present building, which dates from the middle of the 18th century, is very Irish in character with exuberant rococo plasterwork of the highest order, fine Irish furniture, pleasant grounds and interesting estate buildings. In the gardens is the original Florence Court yew, the originator of all Irish yews.

▶ *From Florence Court, turn right. After a mile (1.5km)*

turn left on to the A32, then after 2 miles (3km) turn right for Bellanaleck.

10 Bellanaleck, Co Fermanagh

A base for cruising, with a popular marina, Bellanaleck gives a glimpse of the winding, mazy ways of Upper Lough Erne, as its waters thread through 57 islands between Enniskillen and Galloon Bridge to the southeast. Here are hidden remote treasures such as Castle Balfour and the estate at Crom, rich in history and rare in wildlife.

The village is also home to the Sheelin Irish Lace Museum, featuring exquisite garments, bedlinen, curtains and other finely crafted lace items dating from 1890 to 1920. All five styles of Irish lace are included, and the wedding dresses and christening gowns are particularly enticing. You can buy antique lacework in the shop here.

▶ *Return to Enniskillen via the A509.*

Expansive parkland surrounds lovely Florence Court

The Heart
of Ulster

2 DAYS • 123 MILES • 198KM

The ecclesiastical capital of Ireland, Armagh is a gracious and historic city richly endowed with the culture and architecture of centuries of Christianity. Two cathedrals dedicated to Saint Patrick rise above winding streets which follow the contours of ancient earth mounds. Just outside the city is the ancient site of Emain Macha.

ITINERARY	
ARMAGH	▶ **Loughgall (6m-10km)**
LOUGHGALL	▶ **Moy (15m-24km)**
MOY	▶ **Dungannon (5m-8km)**
DUNGANNON	▶ **Cookstown (11m-18km)**
COOKSTOWN	▶ **Gortin (24m-39km)**
GORTIN	▶ **Omagh (9m-14km)**
OMAGH	▶ **Fintona (11m-18km)**
FINTONA	▶ **Fivemiletown (10m-16km)**
FIVEMILETOWN	▶ **Armagh (32m-51km)**

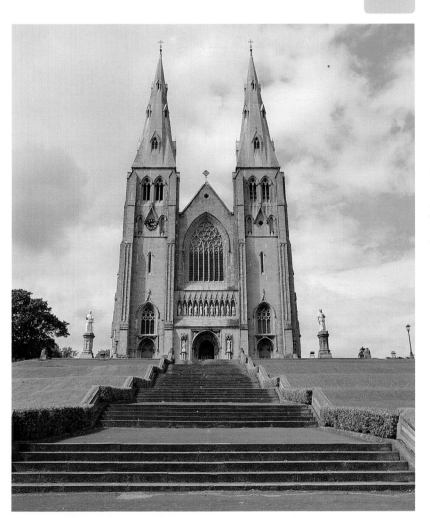

i 40, English Street, Armagh

FOR CHILDREN

Not far from Loughgall is
Benburb, a hidden valley with
adventurous walks, a castle on
a clifftop and a restored linen
mill. The Heritage Centre has a
model and talks about the
Battle of Benburb in 1646,
when Irish forces under Owen
Roe O'Neill defeated General
Monroe's Scottish and English
armies.

▶ *Take the **B77** to Loughgall.*

❶ **Loughgall,** Co Armagh
This is one of the pretty flower-
filled villages, surrounded by
orchards, in the heart of
Armagh, which is known as the
Orchard County. The Orange
Order was founded near here
after a battle in 1795.

Close by is 17th-century
Ardress House, which was given
an elegant new look in the 18th
century with exquisite plasterwork by stuccodore Michael
Stapleton, and some remarkably
fine Irish furniture. Ardress still
has the feel of a gentleman
farmer's residence, and the
restored farmyard is full of fowl,
animals and traditional farming

The impressive Roman Catholic
Cathedral of St Patrick in Armagh
was completed in 1873

equipment. A woodland playground is popular with the children and there is a pretty garden
and a woodland walk.

▶ *Follow the **B77** for 3 miles
(5km), then turn left on to the
B131. After 2 miles (3km) turn
left on to the **B28**, following
the signs for Moy. After a mile
(1.5km) pass Ardress House,
and immediately after, branch
right on to an unclassified
road. Turn right again and
follow signs for the **M1** for*

The Argory sits in over 300 acres (120ha) of woodland

BACK TO NATURE

The Peatlands Park, at the Loughgall junction of the M1, is the first of its kind in the British Isles, designed to protect bogland and to tell the story of peatlands in an enterprising way. The park is a mosaic of cutaway bogland, with small virgin bogs, low wooded hills and small lakes.

The bog is seen as a living archive covering 10,000 years. An outdoor turbary (turf-cutting) area gives an insight into the process of cutting turf, and a most attractive feature is the narrow-gauge railway, originally set up for carrying turf and now a popular way of carrying visitors out on to the bog, thus saving it from the wear and tear of human erosion.

3 miles (5km). At the roundabout, take the B131, which becomes the B34, towards Dungannon for 3 miles (5km), then turn left on to the B106 for a further 3 miles (5km) to Moy.

2 **Moy,** Co Tyrone
More commonly called 'the Moy', this is on the Tyrone side of the Blackwater River.

Charlemont lies opposite on the banks of the river in County Armagh. Once one of the most important strongholds of the English, only the impressive wrought-iron gates of Roxborough House and earthworks that were artillery bastions remain. The Moy had one of the most famous horse fairs in Ireland in the 19th century, held in a fine square, where a plaque recalls a son of the village, John King, Australian soldier and explorer.

The Argory close by is situated above the river in lovely grounds. The house will be closed for refurbishment until March 2008.

RECOMMENDED WALKS

An attractive stretch of the Ulster Way takes the walker along the banks of the Blackwater from Caledon in County Tyrone through Amagh to Lough Neagh.

▶ *Take the A29 to Dungannon.*

3 **Dungannon,** Co Tyrone
A flourishing town, this was once the chief seat of the O'Neills, kings of Ulster for 500 years. Now it is more famous for fine cut glass, and the Tyrone Crystal factory is a popular attraction. At Park Lane, a fishery offers trout for sale, an equestrian centre and walks.

Off the main Dungannon-Ballygawley road, at Dergenagh, is the ancestral home of Ulysses S Grant, President of the US from 1869 to 1877, restored to its appearance of 1880, and set on a farmstead worked by traditional methods of the time.

[i] *190 Ballygawley Road*

▶ *Continue on the A29 for 11 miles (18km) to Cookstown.*

4 **Cookstown,** Co Tyrone
The broad main street runs through a typical mid-Ulster farming town, but the area around Cookstown has plenty to interest the visitor.

Drum Manor Forest Park to the west is small but very attractive, with a butterfly garden, a shrub garden, a forest garden containing small plots of many tree species, and an arboretum. There is a heronry, and waterfowl inhabit the fish ponds.

In the same area is Wellbrook Beetling Mill, a

water-powered mill used for beetling or polishing, the final process in the manufacture of linen, dating from 1765. Not so long ago there would have been many such mills operating on the Ballinderry River.

The Beaghmore stone circles to the northwest of Cookstown are mysterious in their origin and purpose. Perhaps they were formed in the Stone Age or early Bronze Age for ceremonial purposes, with lines pointing to the midsummer sunrise.

i *Burn Road*

▶ *Take the **A505** for Omagh. After 13 miles (21km) turn right on to the **B46** to Gortin for 11 miles (18km).*

FOR HISTORY BUFFS

Northeast of Cookstown is Springhill, a lovely 17th-century house with 18th- and 19th-century additions, built at a time when strength and fortification were giving way to comfort and convenience. The Lenox-Conynghams, who built Springhall and lived there for nearly 300 years, were a family of soldiers; their story, and the house, provides a fascinating view of the history of Ireland and of events further afield. The charming house has a fine oak staircase, a good library, lovely old gardens and an interesting costume museum.

SCENIC ROUTES

Linking the Cookstown-Gortin road with the Gortin-Omagh road is Gortin Lake scenic route. The blend of loughs, evergreen and deciduous forests, heather-topped moors and the village below create a fine panorama. Features with evocative names like Curraghchosaly (Moor with the Rocky Face), the meandering Owenkillew (River of the Curlew) and Mullaghbolig (Humped Top) add richness to the picture.

A splendid way to travel, and to enjoy the sights and smells of the lovely Gortin Lake scenery

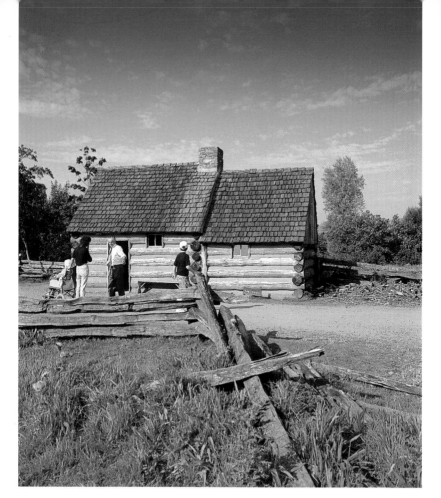

5 Gortin, Co Tyrone
This beautiful, sparsely populated area is a gateway to the Sperrin Mountains. Those who want to venture further and even pan for the gold occasionally found in these hills should go north and call at the Sperrin Heritage Centre.

Gortin has a fine forest park with a herd of Japanese sika deer, and the area is rich in some very good walks. On the Gortin side of the entrance to the forest park look out for a stone seat beside a cool stream, which has the inscription 'Rest and be thankful'.

Four miles (6km) from Gortin on the B48 look out for the place known locally as the Magnetic Hill, which gives the illusion that your car is travelling uphill, when it is really going downhill.

▶ *Take the B48 to Omagh.*

RECOMMENDED WALKS

From Gortin Glen Forest Park a number of walks radiate over ideal walking country, with panoramic views.. Children enjoy the educational Nature Trail, dotted with information boards, and the Pollan Trail, which follows the Pollan Burn to a waterfall. A longer and more energetic trail leads to Ladies View, the highest point in the park, for a great panorama. A number of walks radiate over ideal walking country, with panoramic views. Children enjoy the Burn Walk, which follows a stream all the way to the heart of Gortin village.

The Ulster-American Museum

6 Omagh, Co Tyrone
Omagh sits high on a hill, spires and the outline of the court house giving the town a distinctive profile. The outstanding attraction of the area is the Ulster-American Folk Park, on the A5 to Newtownstewart. It is designed very much in the American style, with costumed interpreters baking bread or spinning by a turf fire. In the Dockside Gallery you are invited to sail away to the New World. The park illustrates the two cultures in Ulster's tradition of emigration, from the reconstructed street of shops and the thatched cottages, representing the Old World (Ulster), to the American street and the log cabins, representing the New World. One of the most telling

exhibits is the re-creation of the brig *Union*, an emigrant ship. Here, visitors can experience the dreadful conditions, smells and sounds of a transatlantic passage. There is an extensive programme of special events throughout the year.

[i] *I Market Street*

▶ *Take the A5 signed for Belfast. After 7 miles (11km) turn right on to the B46 for Seskinore and Fintona.*

FOR CHILDREN

Omagh's Leisure Complex on Old Mountfield Road (tel: 028 82246711) includes a pool with giant water slides and a kiddies corner.

7 Fintona, Co Tyrone
Fintona is a very quiet little village, once celebrated for its horse-drawn tram. The Forest of Seskinore is extremely productive, growing high-quality crops of hard and soft woods. It harbours a rich variety of wildlife and game. Seskinore

was once dependent on using horse power to extract timber. Today's Forest Service has brought back Irish draught horses and trained them to this work once again.

▶ *Take the B122 to Fivemiletown and the Clogher Valley.*

8 The Clogher Valley, Co Tyrone
Augher, Clogher and Fivemiletown are the villages of the Clogher Valley, and the names roll off the local tongue, being the stations of the old Clogher Valley railway, much loved by Ulster people.

Visitors to the tiny village of Clogher will be surprised to learn that it has a cathedral, its importance dating from the 5th century, when St Patrick made McCartan first Bishop of Clogher. The folly on a hill to the south of Clogher was a mausoleum erected by a newly rich landlord, Brackenridge, so that 'he could look down on the neighbours who had looked down on him'.

Fivemiletown has a carriage museum and recreational

facilities around the lake. The valley has three forests with different attractions – Fardross, Knockmany and Favour Royal.

▶ *Take the A4 for Augher for 8 miles (13km), then the A28, passing through Aughnacloy and Caledon to Armagh.*

SPECIAL TO...

If you're very lucky you may catch a game of Ireland's most unusual sport, road bowls or 'bullets', now found only in a few areas. Players hurl a 28oz (794g) metal ball (it is said that the game started with cannon-balls) on a set course along winding roads. The aim is to get the ball to the end of the road in the least number of throws. Spectators beware! Watching crowds tend to be quickly dispersed by hurtling missiles, but organised championships are held annually in Armagh in April.

Rural Ireland is dotted with wayside shrines and curiosities

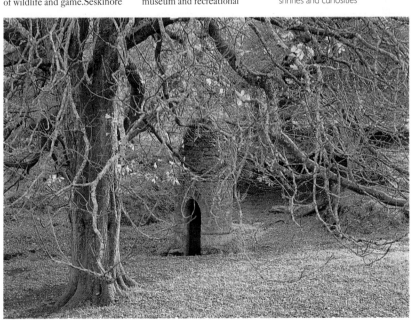

Mourne
Country

A town of great historic importance in the Gap of the North between Slieve Gullion and the Carlingford Mountains, Newry is close to the Mourne Mountains and Carlingford Lough. Its town hall, which actually spans the Clanrye River, has been converted into an arts centre.

2 DAYS • 95 MILES • 153KM

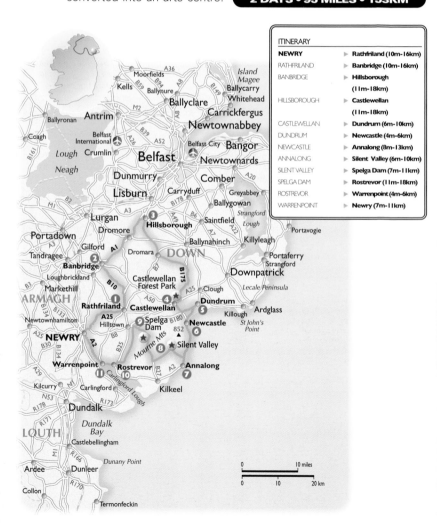

ⓘ *Town Hall, Bank Parade, Newry*

▶ *Take the **A25** following signposts for Rathfriland.*

❶ Rathfriland, Co Down
A quiet village atop a steep hill, Rathfriland commands views over a tranquil valley, where shady roads wind among small farms. This is the country of Patrick Brontë, father of the famous writers Charlotte, Emily and Anne, and it is said that his stories of County Down were a memorable part of their childhood. Little Drumballyroney school, where he taught, marks the beginning of the 10-mile (16km) signposted Brontë Homeland route. The tour also includes Patrick's birthplace, the childhood home of his mother, and the Brontë Interpretive Centre.

▶ *Take the **B25** northwards from Rathfriland, turning left on to the **B10** for Banbridge.*

❷ Banbridge, Co Down
The steep hill in the centre of Banbridge was cut through in 1834 to spare the horses on the busy Belfast–Dublin road, and now the wide thoroughfare is divided into three with an elegant underpass. At the foot of the hill, close to the River Bann, is an elaborate monument guarded by polar bears. It commemorates Captain Crozier (1796–1848), who was second-in-command of the expedition that discovered the North-West Passage.

ⓘ *Gateway Centre, Newry Road*

▶ *Take the **A1** for Belfast. After 11 miles (18km) turn right for Hillsborough.*

❸ Hillsborough, Co Down
Take time to explore this pretty and elegant Georgian village, full of interesting shops, pubs and historic buildings. Hillsborough Castle is the residence for members of the royal family when they visit Northern Ireland, and the permanent residence of the Secretary of State. It stands in a square, not typical of an Ulster village, lined with graceful Georgian terraces. In the centre is the 18th-century market house, aligned with a fine gateway and tree-lined avenue to a fort. There was a defended settlement here in early Christian times, but the present building was rebuilt as a picturesque toy-like fort in the 18th century by the Hill family, who carefully planned the village through successive generations. The Georgian parish church adds to the harmony of Hillsborough, and the forest park has a lake with pleasant walks.

▶ *Take the road for Newry, but before joining the **A1** turn left for Dromara. After 1 mile (1.5km) turn left again and drive for 8 miles (13km) to Dromara. In Dromara, turn left following signposts for Dundrum. After 8 miles (13km) turn right and follow the **B175** for 5 miles (8km) to the junction with the **A25**. Turn right for Castlewellan.*

Castlewellan Lake, overlooked by a Victorian castle, is at the heart of the superb forest park

4 Castlewellan, Co Down
Another County Down village of steep hills, broad views and quiet tree-lined squares of pleasant terraces, Castlewellan's centre is marked by a solid market house, now a library, and its boundaries enhanced by two handsome churches.

Close to the village, the forest park covers 1,500 acres (600 hectares) of hilly ground, including a small mountain, Slievenaslat, and surrounds a beautiful lake. At its heart stands a 19th-century castle, in Scottish baronial style. It is now a conference centre. The arboretum is particularly fine. The Peace Maze, planted in 2000, is the largest permanent hedge maze in the world, covering 2.7 acres (just over 1 hectare), with a 2-mile (3-km) path to the centre lined by 6,000 yew trees. Fishing, pony trekking and camping can be enjoyed here, and a Craft Centre has been set up in the handsome Grange.

▶ Take the **A50** for Newcastle. After 2 miles (3km) turn left on to the **B180**, and after 3 miles (5km) turn left again for Dundrum.

> ### SPECIAL TO...
>
> Castlewellan Forest Park's arboretum is internationally famous, and so is a variety of leylandii (cypress) that was developed here.
> The lovely yellow foliage of Castlewellan Gold is now grown in many parts of the world.

> ### FOR CHILDREN
>
> At Seaforde, a pretty village 3 miles (5km) north of Dundrum, is a butterfly house. It is an extraordinary experience to find that these beautiful creatures are attracted to visitors and will settle on arms and shoulders.

5 Dundrum, Co Down
You can just see the top of the keep of the Norman castle among the trees above Dundrum. John de Courcy chose a superb rocky site commanding strategic views over sea and countryside to build his castle in the 13th century, although the name 'the Fort of the Ridge' goes back to an early Christian defence. The sand dunes below

Above: a delightful rocky cascade in the ever-popular Tollymore Forest Park near Newcastle

Left: a mixture of pastureland and wild moorland in the lovely Mountains of Mourne

BACK TO NATURE

Murlough National Nature Reserve at Dundrum is as beautiful as it is interesting. The dune system here has been carefully managed and it merges into heathland, the whole area bounded by estuary and sea. The range of habitats nurture a wide variety of plants, insects and birds, and wardens lead guided walks through restricted areas. From the magnificent beach, sea birds and seals can be seen, while the inner bay estuary has a good variety of birds such as redshank, greenshank, Brent geese and godwits in the winter. Migrant birds often shelter among the marram grass and sea buckthorn in the dunes.

have yielded evidence of Stone-Age and Bronze-Age settlements, while at Sliddery, just south of the village, an 8-foot (2.5m) dolmen was erected, probably 4,000 years ago.

▶ Take the **A2** to Newcastle.

FOR CHILDREN

Experience warm seawater in the open air at the Tropicana in Newcastle, where water fun is provided with games and slides.

6 **Newcastle,** Co Down
When Percy French wrote of the place where 'The Mountains of Mourne sweep down to the sea', he must have had this part of County Down's

coast in mind. Newcastle itself is in the shelter of the highest of the peaks, Slieve Donard, but to the south of the town there is barely room for the road to scrape through between the mountains and the sea.

The town is a traditional seaside resort, with a promenade, parks, swimming pools and holiday recreation facilities. A magnificent beach sweeps from Dundrum to the harbour, and borders the championship golf course, Royal County Down. The staff of the Mourne Heritage Trust, who provide general information about the mountains, also organise a series of walks for the inexperienced visitor.

Two miles (3km) to the west is Tollymore, a magnificently situated and very popular forest park on the slopes of

Slievenabrock and Luke's Mountain, in the valley of the Shimna River. There are attractive walks enlivened by the picturesque cascades, bridges and numerous follies built by the Roden family.

i Central Promenade

RECOMMENDED WALKS

There are many excellent walks in the Mournes. Generally they will not be sign-posted, but walks leaflets are available locally. From Bloody Bridge, a short distance south of Newcastle on the A2, a path climbs the mountain along the Bloody River, so called because of the massacre in the 1641 rebellion. This is part of the Brandy Pad, a track that winds its way through the mountains by Hare's Gap to Hilltown, and which was used by smugglers distributing wines, spirits, tobacco, silks and spice, a thriving 18th-century trade.

The shoreline at Newcastle, a coastal resort and centre for the Mourne Mountains

▷ *Take the **A2** following signs for Kilkeel to Annalong.*

7 **Annalong,** Co Down
Two rocky clefts shelter the small fishing fleet that uses Annalong harbour, with lobster pots and fishing nets lining the stone pier. A fine corn mill right on the edge of the harbour can produce flour and oatmeal, and the Marine Park is a pleasant focal point on the shore with a play area, boat park and herb garden. A fish smokery and granite-cutting yards add activity to the narrow, winding streets and low cottages.

▷ *Return to the **A2** towards Newcastle, then turn left following signs for Silent Valley for 6 miles (10km).*

8 **The Silent Valley,** Co Down
Impressive gates admit the visitor to the vast area of the Silent Valley, which contains two reservoirs and dams that provide water for the Greater Belfast area. The Water Commissioners of the early part of this century planned the landscaping of the reservoirs, and the area has a peculiarly municipal feel with flowering shrubs and formal flowerbeds. The splendid mountain panoramas predominate, and today's guardians, the Department of the Environment, have provided walks, a visitors' centre and a shuttle bus (you cannot take a car up to the Silent Valley).

SPECIAL TO...

The drystone walls, or more properly, stone ditches, of the Mournes are an especially attractive feature, enclosing tiny fields and creating intriguing patterns below the high peaks. Some are single width, seemingly higglegy-piggledy and gaping with holes – no mortar here – others are comapct, thick and splendidly flat on top. The Mourne Wall is quite different. Solid and massive, it provided employment between 1904 and 1922. The Wall starts and ends at the Silent Valley. Travelling 22 miles (35km), it spans the summits of 15 mountains, and encloses the entire Mourne water catchment area.

▷ *Turn right and right again for Spelga Dam. After 1½ miles*

*(2km) turn right on to the **B27** for Hilltown. After 5 miles (8km) turn left, still following the **B27**.*

9 Spelga Dam, Co Down
Just above Spelga is the highest point a road reaches in Northern Ireland. To the east is a good place for access into the inner Mournes, the ring of mountains – Doan, Meelbeg, Bearnagh, Donard, Lamagan and Binnian – that shields the beautiful, deep blue Lough Shannagh, and the source of the River Bann. To the north is the pretty Fofanny dam, and the Trassey river, where a path gives an approach to the north Mournes.

> ### SCENIC ROUTES
>
> On the road from Silent Valley, past Spelga to Rostrevor, look for the red metal gates with round knobs on the posts, which mark the water pipelines. Each mountain has its own characteristics, scattered with firs and pines and rocky outcrops, or smothered with naturalised rhododendrons. As the road dips into dark forest, there is a perfect picnic site at the Yellow River, with imaginative tables in wood and stone in an idyllic setting beside a fast-running stream.

▶ *Continue west on the **B27** and after 3 miles (5km) turn left and continue for 8 miles (13km) to Rostrevor.*

10 Rostrevor, Co Down
Rostrevor is a picturesque place with a flourishing arts festival every year, and the exotic plants and lush vegetation you will see all around you prove its claim to be the most sheltered spot in Northern Ireland, tucked as it is between Slieve Martin and the temperate waters of Carlingford Lough.

As the Mournes descend to Rostrevor the forest pines and conifers give way to an area of native oak woodland, which forms a National Nature Reserve. Climb to Cloughmore, the 'Big Stone' reputedly thrown by Finn MacCool from Slieve Foye across the lough.

A real Irish giant is buried in Kilbroney churchyard. He was the tallest man in his day at over 8 feet (2.5m) tall, and died in Marseilles in 1861. Two ancient crosses stand in this churchyard, but a Celtic bronze hand-bell, which was found in a ruined church wall, is preserved in St Mary's Church.

A granite obelisk commemorates Major General Robert Ross, who captured Washington DC in 1814, and ate the dinner prepared for the fleeing President Madison. He died three weeks later in Baltimore.

Rostrevor Forest Park and Kibroney Park have various recreational facilities, including toilets, a playground, picnic sites and a forest drive.

▶ *Take the **A2** for 4 miles (6km) to Warrenpoint.*

The restored 19th-century corn mill at Annalong overlooks the pretty little harbour

11 Warrenpoint, Co Down
Warrenpoint is a traditional seaside resort, with park and bandstand, marina, beach, sports and boat trips to Omeath. It also has a growing port where Carlingford Lough narrows to become an enclosed fiord-like waterway. The Vikings gave Carlingford its name, and this steep-sided inlet must have seemed familiar to them. Carlingford gave them excellent access for their plundering of the rich pickings of Armagh. They may have been the 'foreigners of Narrow Water' who were recorded in AD841.

The English garrison built a stronghold at Narrow Water in 1560, at a cost of £361, and the three-storey tower house with battlements, murder hole and bawn wall is a stone's throw from County Louth in Leinster.

▶ *Take the **A2** for a distance of 7 miles (11km) back to Newry.*

MOTORING IN IRELAND

ACCIDENTS

In the event of an accident, the vehicle should be moved off the carriageway wherever possible. (See also **Warning Triangle/ Hazard Warning Lights** page 159.)

You must also stop immediately and exchange details with the other people involved in the accident. If this is not possible you must report the accident to a member of the Garda Siochana (in the Republic) or the Police (in Northern Ireland).

If damage or injury is caused to any other person or vehicle you must stop, give your own and the vehicle owner's name and address and the registration number of the vehicle to anyone having reasonable grounds for requiring the information.

If for some reason you do not give your name and address at the time of the accident, you must report the accident to the police as soon as reasonably practicable, at least within 24 hours.

BREAKDOWNS

If the car is rented, contact the rental company who will probably have an arrangement with a motoring organisation or other breakdown service. If it is your own car, and you are a member of the Automobile Association or one of the AIT (*Alliance International de Tourisme*) driving clubs you can call on the AA rescue service run by the Automobile Association of Ireland in the Republic and the Automobile Association in Northern Ireland. The RAC (Royal Automobile Club) operates a similar service for its members, but only in Northern Ireland.

In the event of a breakdown, the vehicle should be moved off the carriageway wherever possible. (See also **Warning Triangle/Hazard Warning Lights** page 159.)

CAR HIRE

It is always best to rent a car in advance, from home if possible. Renting a car in the Republic is expensive compared with Northern Ireland. Check the details, such as insurance, unlimited mileage, and pick-up and drop-off conditions.

Drivers must hold, and have held for one year, a valid national licence or an International Driving Permit. The minimum age for hiring a car ranges from 18 to 25, depending on the model of car. Some companies have a maximum age limit of 70.

Make sure you have personal insurance as well as Collision Damage Waiver (CDW).

Most cars use unleaded fuel; make sure you know what your car takes before filling the tank.

The Car Rental Council of Ireland's website (www.carrentalcouncil.ie) has information on car hire, although you can't actually reserve a car on this site.

CHILDREN

Children up to the age of twelve and under 53in (1.35m) tall are required to travel in a child car seat appropriate for their height or weight (baby seat, child seat, booster seat or booster cushion). The only exception is travel in the rear of a taxi.

Children from 3 to 12 years must use the correct child restraint in the front passenger seat, but may travel unrestrained in the rear seat of a vehicle if seat belts are not available. Over the age of 12/13 (or over 1.35m/4ft 5in tall) seat belts must be worn if available.

Note: under no circumstances should a rear-facing restraint be used in a seat with an active airbag.

CRASH (SAFETY) HELMETS

Visiting motorcyclists and their passengers must wear crash or safety helmets.

DOCUMENTS

You must have a valid driver's licence (with an English translation if you wish to rent a car).

If you are bringing a vehicle, you need its registration book with a letter of authorisation from the owner if they are not accompanying the vehicle.

DRINKING AND DRIVING

The laws regarding drinking and driving are strict and the penalties severe. The best advice is if you drink don't drive.

DRIVING CONDITIONS

Traffic drives on the left (it goes clockwise at roundabouts/traffic circles). Most signposts in the Republic give distances in kilometres: in the North, they give distances in miles. (See also **Warning Triangle/Hazard Warning Lights** page 159.)

FUEL

Fuel stations in villages in the Republic usually stay open till around 8pm and open after Mass on Sundays. In Northern Ireland, where fuel is more expensive, 24 hour stations are fairly common and many stations are open on Sundays.

INSURANCE

Fully comprehensive insurance, which covers you for some of the expenses incurred after a breakdown or an accident, is advisable. Ensure that you are covered for both the Republic and Northern Ireland if you intend to cross the border.

LIGHTS

You must ensure your front and rear side lights and rear registration plate lights are lit at night. You must use headlights when visibility is seriously reduced and at night on all unlit roads and those where the street lights are more than 600 feet (185m) apart.

MOBILE PHONES

The use of a mobile phone while driving is restricted to hands-free units only in both the Republic and Northern Ireland.

ROADS
Republic of Ireland

There are some stretches of motorway in the Dublin area:

The M50 encircles the east side of the city, and from it the M1 extends north beyond Dundalk. The construction of a new motorway, the M3, to run northwest from Dublin's outskirts towards Cavan, and pass close to Navan and Kells, is currently beset by delays caused by conservationist, archaeological and political concerns.

The M4 heads west and extends almost to Mullingar; the M7 (via the N7) goes southwest to Portlaoise, with an extension under construction that will divide and lead to the N7 (for Limerick) on one branch and the N8 (for Cork) on the other.

Although mostly free, some sections of motorway incur toll charges.

There are a few stretches of dual carriageway on certain major arterial routes, but elsewhere the roads vary to a lesser or greater extent, and the classification actually gives no reliable indication of the width of the road or the surface quality – some primary roads are little better than country lanes.

Potential hazards include the relaxed attitude of Dublin drivers to red traffic lights, while in country areas there may be loose chippings, livestock and occasionally a game of road bowls to contend with.

Northern Ireland

Motorways in the north are the M1, which heads south then west from Belfast to skirt the southern shore of Lough Neagh and end just short of Dungannon.

The M2 goes northwest from Belfast. All other major roads are fast, well-maintained and seldom congested.

ROAD SIGNS

In Gaeltacht areas of Ireland, where the Irish language is still spoken as a community language, road signs may be shown only in Irish, and this can be confusing unless you have planned your route in advance. There are Gaeltacht areas in counties Waterford, Cork, Kerry, Galway, Meath, Mayo and Donegal. If you need to ask for directions, bear in mind that some older people may speak Irish only.

Distances shown on signposts will be in kilometres in the Republic of Ireland and in miles in Northern Ireland.

ROUTE DIRECTIONS

Throughout the book the following abbreviations are used for roads:

M – Motorways
Republic of Ireland only
N – National primary/seconday roads
R – Regional roads
Northern Ireland only
A – Main roads
B – Local roads

SEAT BELTS

The wearing of seat belts is compulsory for drivers and their front seat passenger. Passengers travelling in the rear seats of the vehicle must wear a seat belt if one is fitted.

SHORT CUTS

These ferry routes serve as useful short-cuts:

Ballyhack–Passage East

crosses Waterford Harbour, and is a boon for travellers heading west from Rosslare harbour to Waterford.

Tarbert–Killimer is a pleasant 20-minute ride across the Shannon estuary, saving the need to loop around Limerick in order to get from west Kerry to west Clare.

Portaferry–Strangford at the top of the Ards Peninsula in Northern Ireland is a short hop

that saves a 50-mile (80km) drive by road.

SPEED LIMITS
Republic of Ireland

Speed limits are 50kph (30mph) in built-up areas and 100kph (60mph) elsewhere, unless otherwise indicated, and 120kph (74mph) on motorways; for vehicles with one trailer, the maximum is 80kph (50mph) outside built-up areas and motorways.

Northern Ireland

Speed limits are 30mph (50kph) in built-up areas, 60mph (100kph) outside built-up areas and 70mph (121kph) on dual carriageways and motorways, unless otherwise indicated; for trailers the maximum is usually 40mph (64kph).

WARNING TRIANGLE/ HAZARD WARNING LIGHTS

Hazard warning lights should be used in the event of a breakdown or an accident.

If available, a red triangle should be placed on the road at least 55 yards (50m) before the obstruction and on the same side of the road.

WORDS AND PHRASES

Her are a few basic words you may find useful:

fáilte	welcome
tá/sea	yes
níl/ní hea	no
le do thoil	please
go raibh maith aguth	
	thank you
dia dhuit	hello
slán	goodbye
oscailte	open
dúnta	closed
gardaí	police
leithreas	toilet
fir	men
mná	women
an lár	middle of town
óstán	hotel
bialann	restaurant
tábhairne	pub/bar
caife	café
oifig an phoist	
	post office
oifig malairte	
	exchange office

ACCOMMODATION AND RESTAURANTS

Wherever possible the following hotels and restaurants are on the tour route and have been selected to offer a variety of hotel styles.

The AA Hotel Booking Service is a free, fast and easy way to find a place for a short break or holiday; tel: 0870 5 05 05 05. Full listings of the Irish hotels and B&Bs available through the service can be found and booked on the AA's website: www.theAA.com/getaway

Hotel prices
The hotels listed are grouped into three price categories based on a nightly rate for a double room including breakfast:
Very expensive €€€€/££££ – over €300/£200
Expensive €€€/£££ – between €150/£100 and €300/£200
Moderate €€/££ – between €75/£60 and €150/£100
Budget €/£ – under €75/£60

Restaurant prices
The restaurants listed below are grouped into three price categories based on a two-course meal for one person, without drinks:
Expensive €€€/£££ – over €40/£30
Moderate €€/££ – between €20/£15 and €40/£30
Budget €/£ – under €20/£15

TOUR I
ENNIS, Co Clare
◇ **Cill Eoin House €–€€**
Killadysert Cross, Clare Road (tel: 065 684 1668, fax: 065 684 1669).
Closed 22 Dec–9 Jan.
14 rooms.
◉ **The Cloister €–€€**
Club Bridge, Abbey Street (tel: 065 682 9262).
Lovely old pub built into the cloister ruins, with a menu that features local produce and vegetarian options. The seafood is outstanding. Pub lunches available in the bar. Restaurant open daily 12.30–3pm, 6–9.30pm.

◉ **Cruise's Pub Restaurant €**
Abbey Street (tel: 065 684 1800).
Ancient building with a good choice of favourite pub food, including Irish stew, grills and seafood. Daily 12.30–10pm.
◇ **Fountain Court €–€€**
Lahinch Road (tel: 065 682 9845, fax: 065 684 5030).
Closed 21 Dec–7 Mar.
18 rooms.
◇ **Magowna €€**
Inch, Kilmaley (tel: 065 683 9009, fax: 065 683 9258).
Closed 24–26 Dec.
10 rooms.
◇◉ **Temple Gate €€–€€€**
The Square (tel: 065 682 3300, fax 065 682 3322).
Mainly traditional dishes with some international influences. Daily 7–9.45, Sun 12.45–2.30. Closed 25 Dec.

MILLTOWN MALBAY, Co Clare
◇ **Burkes Armada €€–€€€**
Spanish Point, 2 miles (3km) west (tel: 065 708 4110, fax: 065 708 4632).
64 rooms.

LEHINCH, Co Clare
◇ **Grovemount House €–€€**
Lehinch Road, Ennistymon, 4 miles (6km) east on the N85 (tel: 065 707 1431 or 065 707 1038, fax: 065 707 1823).
Closed late Oct–Apr.
7 rooms.
◇ **Moy House €€€–€€€€**
0.5 miles (0.8km) from Lahinch on the Milltown Malbay road (tel: 065 708 2800, fax: 065 708 2500).
9 rooms.

BALLVAGHAN, Co Clare
◇ **Cappabhaile House €€**
Newtown, 0.5 miles (1km) from town on the Aillwee Caves road (tel/fax: 065 707 7260).
Closed Jan.
8 rooms.

◇ **Drumcreehy €–€€**
1 mile (2km) north on the N67 (tel: 065 707 7377, fax: 065 707 7379).
11 rooms.
◇◉ **Gregans Castle €€€–€€€€**
3 miles (5km) south on the N67 (tel: 065 707 7005, fax: 065 707 7111). *Closed late Oct to mid-May.*
22 rooms.
Fine modern cuisine based on local produce and fresh fish; the lamb is specially recommended. Daily 7–8.30pm. Closed Nov–Feb.
◇ **Rusheen Lodge €€**
0.5 miles (1km) north on the N67 (tel: 065 707 7092, fax: 065 707 7152).
Closed mid-Nov to mid-Feb.
9 rooms.

LISDOONVARNA, Co Clare
◇ **Aran View House €**
Coast Road, Doolin, 4 miles (6km) west (tel: 065 707 4061 or 065 707 4420, fax: 065 707 4540).
Closed Nov–1 Apr.
19 rooms.
◇ **Cullinan's €–€€**
Village centre, Doolin, 4 miles (6km) west (tel: 065 707 4183, fax: 065 707 4239).
8 rooms.
◇◉ **Sheedy's €€**
Lisdoonvarna (tel: tel: 065 707 4026, fax: 065 707 4555)
The restaurant here serves traditional dishes, such as roast lamb, with a modern twist, and the seafood bar offers the same high standards. Open mid-Mar to early Oct, daily 6.45–8.45.
11 rooms.

BUNRATTY, Co Clare
◇ **Bunratty Lodge €€**
Bunratty (tel: 061 369402)
Closed early Nov to mid-Mar.
5 rooms.
◇ **Clover Hill Lodge €**
Low Road, near Castle and Folk Park (tel: 061 369039, fax: 061 360520).
Closed Nov–Feb.
3 rooms.

◊ **Shannon Shamrock Bunratty €€€**
Village centre (tel: 061 361177, fax: 061 364863).
Closed 24–26 Dec.
115 rooms.

TOUR 2
LIMERICK, Co Limerick
(See also Tour 3)
◊ ⁣◉ **Castletroy Park €€€**
Dublin Road (tel: 061 335566, fax: 061 331117).
107 rooms.
Fixed and à la carte menus offer such dishes as sea bass with seared pak choi and ginger.
Daily 12.30–2.30pm, Tue–Sat 5.30–10pm, Sun 1.30–8pm. Closed 25 and 31 Dec.
◊ **Clarion Hotel Limerick €€–€€€**
Steamboat Quay (tel: 061 444100, fax: 061 444101).
Closed 24–25 Dec.
123 rooms.
◉ **The Dish €**
O'Connell Avenue (N20), Punch's Cross (tel: 061 229588).
Popular pub-restaurant on the southern edge of the city, serving a varied menu that might include beef Wellington and vegetable lasagne.
Daily 10.30am–11.30pm.
◉ **Green Onion Caffé €–€€**
Old Town Hall Building, Rutland Street (tel: 061 400710).
Spearheading a culinary revival in Limerick, the talented chef here produces down-to-earth dishes that are bursting with natural flavours.
Tue–Sat noon–10pm.
◊ **Hotel Greenhills €€–€€€**
Caherdavin, 2 miles (3km) from city centre on the N18 (tel: 061 453033, fax: 061 453307).
18 rooms.
◊ **Old Quarter Lodge €€**
Denmark Street (tel: 061 315320, fax: 061 316995).
26 rooms.
◊ ⁣◉ **Radisson SAS €€**
Ennis Road (tel: 061 456200, fax: 061 327418).
154 rooms.
Relaxing open-plan restaurant offering seasonally interesting dishes, such as tian of crab with roquette, or roast rack of Limerick lamb.
Mon–Fri 12.30–2.30pm, 5.45–9.30pm, Sat–Sun 1–2.30pm, 5.45–10pm.

◊ **White House €**
Raheen (tel/fax: 061 301709).
5 rooms.
◊ **Woodfield House €€**
Ennis Road (tel: 061 453022, fax: 061 326755)
Closed 24–25 Dec.
27 rooms.

BALLYBUNNION, Co Kerry
◊ **Cashen Course House €€**
Golf Links Road (tel: 068 7351, fax: 068 28934).
Closed Nov–Feb.
9 rooms.
◊ **The Tides Guest House €€–€€€**
On the R551, near golf course (tel: 068 27980, fax: 068 27923).
5 rooms.

ADARE, Co Limerick
◊ **Adare Lodge €–€€**
Kildimo Road (tel: 061 396629, fax: 061 395060).
6 rooms.
◊ **Avona House €**
Kildimo Road (tel: 061 396323, fax: 061 396323).
Closed Nov–Mar.
4 rooms.
◊ **Berkeley Lodge €**
Station Road (tel: 061 396857, fax: 061 396857).
6 rooms.
◊ **Carrigane House €**
Rienroe (tel: 061 396778).
Closed 15 Dec–10 Jan.
6 rooms.
◊ ⁣◉ **Dunraven Arms €€€–€€€€**
Edge of village (tel: 061 396633, fax: 061 396541).
86 rooms.
Classic Irish cuisine, with such options as roast rib of beef with red wine jus, and pork and apricot terrine.
Daily 7–9.30pm, also 12.30–2.30pm Sun.

TOUR 3
LIMERICK, Co Limerick
(See also Tour 2)
◊ **Castle Oaks House €€€**
Castleconnel, 6 miles (10km) east off the N7 Dublin road (tel: 061 377666, fax: 061 377717).
66 rooms.

◊ **Clifton House €–€€**
Ennis Road (tel: 061 451166, fax: 061 451224).
Closed 21 Dec–2 Jan.
16 rooms.
◉ **Copper and Spice €€**
2 Cornmarket Row (tel: 061 313620).
Hailed by some as the best Indian restaurant in Ireland, where authentic dishes are cooked to perfection.
Daily 5–10.30pm, Wed–Fri 12.30–2pm.
◊ **Jurys Inn Limerick €–€€**
Lower Mallow Street (tel: 061 207000, fax: 061 400966).
Closed 24–26 Dec.
151 rooms.
◉ **Piccola Italia €€**
55 O'Connell Street (tel: 061 315844)
In the style of a traditional trattoria, serving pasta dishes, steaks and seafood with Mediterranean flair.
Mon–Sat 6–10.30pm.

TIPPERARY, Co Tipperary
◊ **Ach-na-Sheen €–€€**
Clonmel Road (tel: 062 51298, fax: 062 80467).
Closed 11 Dec–8 Jan.
8 rooms.

CASHEL, Co Tipperary
◊ ⁣◉ **Cashel Palace €€€–€€€€**
In the centre of town (tel: 062 62707, fax: 062 61521).
Closed 2 weeks Christmas–Jan.
23 rooms.
Modern Irish cooking in historic surroundings. Local salmon is the signature dish.
Mon–Fri 12.30–2.30, 6–9.30, Sat 12.30–2.30, 6–10, Sun 12–3, 6–9.30.
◊ **Dualla House €€**
Dualla, northeast of Cashel off the R691 (tel: 062 61487).
Closed Dec–Feb.
4 rooms.
◊ **Legends Guesthouse & Restaurant €–€€**
The Kiln (tel: 062 61292).
Closed 24–28 Dec.
7 rooms.

THURLES, Co Tipperary
◊ **Abbeyvale House €€**
Cashel Road, Holy Cross (tel: 0504 43032, fax: 0504 43032).
4 rooms.

◇ **The Castle** €€
Two Mile Borris (tel: 0504
44324, fax: 0504 44352).
4 rooms.

ROSCREA, Co Tipperary
◇ **Rackethall Country Golf
& Conference Hotel** €€
Dublin Road (tel: 0505 21748.
40 rooms.

NENAGH, Co Tipperary
◇ **Ashley Park House** €
On N52, 4 miles (6km) north
(tel: 067 38223, fax: 067 38013).
Closed 25 Dec.
5 rooms.
◇ **Coolbawn Quay** €€
Coolbawn, Lough Derg (tel: 067
28158, fax: 067 28162).
Closed 23–27 Dec.
80 rooms.

PORTUMNA, Co Galway
◇ **Shannon Oaks Hotel
& Country Club** €€€
St Joseph Road (tel: 090 974
1777, fax: 090 974 1357).
63 rooms.

MOUNTSHANNON
Co Galway
◇ **Clareville House** €
Tuamgraney, Scariff, 6 miles
(10km) southwest on the R352
(tel: 061 922925).
Closed 20–27 Dec.
4 rooms.
◇ **Lantern House** €€
Ogonnelloe, Scariff, 10 miles
(16km) south via the R352 and
R463 (tel: 061 923034 or 923123,
fax: 061 923139).
Closed Nov–Mar.
6 rooms.

TOUR 4
TRALEE, Co Kerry
◇ **Abbey Gate** €€–€€€€
Maine Street (tel: 066 712 9888,
fax: 066 712 9821).
Closed 25–26 Dec.
100 rooms.
◇ **Ballygarry House** €€€
Killarney Road (tel: 066 712
3322, fax: 066 712 7630).
Closed 20–26 Dec.
46 rooms.
◇ **Brianville** €
Clogherbrien, Fenit Road
(tel/fax: 066 712 6645).
5 rooms.

◇ **Meadowlands Hotel** €€€€
Oakpark (tel: 066 718 0444,
fax: 066 718 0964).
Closed 24–26 Dec.
57 rooms.
◎ **Restaurant David Norris**
€€–€€€
Ivy House, Ivy Terrace (tel: 066
718 5654).
*Pretty upstairs restaurant serving
modern Irish food and European
dishes.*
*Tue–Fri 5.30–9.30pm, Sat
7–9.30pm.*
◇ **Tralee Townhouse** €–€€
1–2 High Street (tel: 066 718
1111, fax: 066 718 1112).
Closed 24–28 Dec.
20 rooms.

CONNOR PASS, Co Kerry
◇ **O'Connor** €–€€
Cloghane, off Connor Pass road
(tel: 066 713 8113, fax: 066 713
8270).
20 rooms.

CASTLEGREGORY, Co Kerry
◇ **Beenoskee B&B** €–€€
Cappateige, Conor Pass Road
(tel/fax: 066 713 9263).
5 rooms.
◇ **Griffin's Palm Beach
Country House** €€
Goulane, Conor Pass Road (tel:
066 713 9147, fax: 066 713 9073).
Closed Dec–Feb.
8 rooms.
◇ **Sea-Mount House** €–€€
Cappatigue, Conor Pass Road
(tel/fax: 066 713 9229).
Closed Dec–Feb.
3 rooms.
◇ **Shores Country House**
€–€€
Cappatigue, Conor Pass Road
(tel: 066 713 9396 or 713 9195,
fax: 066 713 9196).
Closed mid-Nov to mid-Feb.
6 rooms.

DINGLE, County Kerry
◇ **Alpine** €–€€
Mail Road (tel: 066 915 1250,
fax: 066 915 1966).
10 rooms.
◎ **An Café Liteartha** €
Dykegate Street (tel: 066 915
2204).
*Soups, sandwiches, salads and
freshly baked cakes.*
Mon–Sat 9–6 (later in summer).

◇ **Bambury's** €–€€
Mail Road (tel: 066 915 1244,
fax: 066 915 1786).
12 rooms.
◇ **Castlewood House**
€€–€€€
The Wood (tel: 066 915 2788,
fax: 066 915 2110).
4 rooms.
◇ **Dingle Heights** €
Ballinaboola (tel: 066 915 1543).
4 rooms.
◇◎ **Doyle's Town House
and Seafood Bar** €
4 John Street (tel: 066 915 1174,
fax: 066 915 1816).
Closed mid-Nov to mid-Mar.
8 rooms.
*Serves the produce of Kerry's
offshore waters and onshore farms
(€€–€€€). Mon–Sat 6–9.30pm.*
Closed mid-Dec to mid-Feb.
◇ **Emlagh House** €€€
Edge of town (tel: 066 915 2345
or 915 2353, fax: 066 915 2369).
Closed 5 Nov–10 Mar.
10 rooms.
◇ **Gormans Clifftop House
& Restaurant** €€–€€€
Glaise Bheag, Ballydavid (tel:
066 915 5162, fax: 066 915 5003).
Closed 24–26 Dec.
9 rooms.
◇ **Heatons** €€
The Wood (tel: 066 915 2788,
fax: 066 915 2324).
Closed 5 Jan–1 Feb.
16 rooms.
◇ **Hurley's** €–€€
An Dooneen, Kilcooley, 6 miles
(11km) west on the R559
(tel: 066 915 5112).
Closed Nov–Mar.
4 rooms.
◎ **Lord Bakers** €€€
Main Street (tel: 066 915 1277).
*Historic pub serving good seafood
and steaks, including sole stuffed
with smoked salmon and spinach
in cheese sauce.*
Fri–Wed 12.30–2, 6–9.30.
◇ **Milltown House** €€–€€€
Milltown (tel: 066 915 1372,
fax: 066 915 1095).
Closed mid-Nov to mid-Mar.
10 rooms.

VENTRY, Co Kerry
◇ **Ard an Cháislean** €
Rathanane Castle (tel: 066 915
9846, fax: 066 915 9127).
4 rooms.

TOUR 5
KILLARNEY, Co Kerry

◇🍴 **Aghadoe Heights**
€€€–€€€€
3 miles (5km) north off the N22
Tralee road (tel: 064 31766,
fax: 064 31345).
74 rooms.
*The Lake Room restaurant has long
been considered one of Ireland's
finest restaurants, blending classical
European cuisine with superb Irish
fresh ingredients. (€€–€€€).
Daily 6.30–9.30pm, also
12.30–2pm Sun. Closed Jan–Mar,
residents only 25 Dec.*

◇ **Applecroft House** €€
Woodlawn Road (tel: 064 32782).
Closed Dec–Feb.
5 rooms.

◇🍴 **Arbutus** €€–€€€
College Street (tel: 064 31037,
fax: 064 34033).
Closed 12 Dec–30 Jan.
35 rooms.
*Traditional Irish dishes with a few
international elements (€€–€€€).
Daily 6.30–9pm.*

◇ **Ashville** €–€€
Rock Road (tel: 064 36405,
fax: 064 36778).
Closed 18–30 Dec.
10 rooms.

◇ **The Brehon** €€€
Muckross Road (tel: 064 30700,
fax: 604 30701).
125 rooms.

🍴 **Bricin** €€–€€€
26 High Street (tel: 064 34902).
*Great for boxty (potato pancakes
with various fillings), plus seafood,
pasta dishes and Irish stew. Above a
craft shop in one of the town's oldest
buildings.
Tue–Sat 10–4.30, also 6–9.30pm
Easter–Oct.*

◇🍴 **Cahernane House**
€€€–€€€€
Muckross Road (tel: 064 31895,
fax: 064 34340).
Closed 21 Dec–31 Jan.
38 rooms.
*Classic menu might include beef
fillet with champ mash and
parmesan tulle, or monkfish with
sweet potato puree and black grape
jus (€€€).
Daily noon–2.30, 7–9.30. Closed
for lunch Dec–Jan.*

◇ **Castlerosse** €€–€€€
1 mile (1.5km) from town on the
R562 Kilorglin road (tel: 064
31144, fax: 064 31031).
Closed Dec–Feb.
121 rooms.

◇ **Coffey's Loch Lein** €€–€€€
Golf Course Road, Fossa (tel:
064 31260, fax: 064 36151).
Closed 27 Oct–1 Apr.
16 rooms.

◇ **Crystal Springs** €–€€
Ballycasheen (tel: 064 33272
or 35518, fax: 064 35518).
7 rooms.

◇ **Darby O'Gills** €€
Lissivigeen, Mallow Road
(tel: 064 34168 or 34919,
fax: 064 36794).
42 rooms.

◇ **Earls Court House** €€
Woodlawn Junction, Muckross
Road (tel: 064 34009, fax: 064
34366).
Closed 13 Nov–11 Feb.
24 rooms.

◇ **Fairview** €€–€€€
College Street (tel: 064 34164,
fax: 064 71777).
18 rooms.

◇ **Foleys Town House** €€
22–23 High Street (tel: 064
31217, fax: 064 34683).
Closed 6 Nov–16 Mar.
28 rooms.

🍴 **Gaby's Seafood
Restaurant** €€–€€€
High Street (tel: 064 32519).
*Succulent lobster and other seafood
is cooked in a variety of ways.
Mon–Sat 6–10pm. Closed Christ-
mas week, late Feb to mid-Mar.*

◇ **Glena House** €–€€
Muckross Road (tel: 064 32705,
fax: 064 35611).
26 rooms.

◇ **Gleneagle** €€€
Muckross Road, 1 mile (1.6km)
south on the N71 (tel: 064
36000, fax: 064 32646).
250 rooms.

◇ **International** €€–€€€
East Avenue Road (tel: 064
31816, fax: 064 31837).
Closed 23–27 Dec.
90 rooms.

◇ **Kathleen's Country
House** €€
Tralee Road (tel: 064 32810,
fax: 064 32340).
Closed mid-Oct to mid-Mar.
17 rooms.

◇🍴 **Killarney Park**
€€€–€€€€
Kenmare Place, Killarney town
centre (tel: 064 35555, fax: 064
35266).
Closed 24–26 Dec.
68 rooms.
*A creative approach to traditional
favourites provides an interesting
choice of dishes (€€–€€€).
Daily 7–9.30pm.*

◇ **Killarney Royal** €€–€€€
College Street (tel: 064 31853,
fax: 064 34001).
29 rooms.

◇ **Killarney Villa** €€
Mallow Road (tel/fax: 064
31878).
Closed Nov–Easter.
6 rooms.

◇ **Kingfisher Lodge** €–€€
Lewis Road (tel: 064 37131,
fax: 064 39871).
Closed 15 Dec–31 Jan.
10 rooms.

◇ **Lake** €€–€€€
Muckross Road (tel: 064 31035,
fax: 064 31902).
Closed 18 Dec–18 Jan.
125 rooms.

◇ **Lime Court** €–€€
Muckross Road (tel: 064 34547,
fax: 064 34121).
Closed 24–25 Dec.
17 rooms.

◇ **Muckross Park Hotel** €€€
Muckross Village (tel: 064 31938,
fax: 064 31965).
Closed Dec–Feb.
27 rooms.

◇ **O'Donovans Farm and
Muckross Riding Stables** €
Mangerton Road, Muckross
(tel: 064 32238).
Closed 11 Nov–Feb.
6 rooms.

◇ **Old Weir Lodge** €€–€€€
Muckross Road (tel: 064 35593,
fax: 064 35583).
Closed 23–26 Dec.
30 rooms.

◇ **Quality Hotel Killarney
(Killarney Ryan)** €€
Cork Road (tel: 064 31555,
fax: 064 32438).
Closed Dec–Jan.
168 rooms.

◇ **Randles Court** €€€
Muckross Road (tel: 064 35333,
fax: 064 35206).
Closed 23–27 Dec.
52 rooms.

◊ **Redwood** €–€€
Tralee Road, 2 miles (3km) from town (tel: 064 34754 or 087 299 8924, fax: 064 34178).
6 rooms.

◊ **Scotts Garden Hotel** €€–€€€
College Street tel: 064 31060, fax: 064 36656).
Closed 24–25 Dec.
52 rooms.

◊ **Shraheen House** €
Ballycasheen, off the N22 Cork road (tel: 064 31286, fax: 064 37959).
Closed Christmas and New Year.
6 rooms.

◊ **White Gates** €€–€€€
Muckross Road (tel: 064 31164, fax: 064 34850).
Closed 25–26 Dec.

KILLORGLIN, Co Kerry
◊ **Carrig House Country House and Restaurant** €€€
Caragh Lake (tel: 066 976 9100, fax: 066 9766 9166).
Closed Oct–Feb.
16 rooms.

◊ **Dromin Farmhouse** €
Milltown Post Office, 2 miles (3km) from Killorglin off the N70 (tel: 066 976 1867).
Closed Nov–16 Mar.
4 rooms.

◊ **Grove Lodge** €€
Killarney Road (tel: 066 976 1157, fax: 066 976 2330).
Closed 22–30 Dec.
10 rooms.

◊ **O'Regan's Country Home** €
Bansha, 1 mile (1.5km) from Kilorglin off the N70 (tel/fax: 066 976 1200.
Closed 11–31 Dec.
4 rooms.

GLENBEIGH, Co Kerry
◊ **Ocean Wave** €–€€
Just outside village on Killorglin road (tel: 066 976 8249, fax: 066 976 8412).
Closed Nov–Feb.
6 rooms.

WATERVILLE, Co Kerry
◊ **Brookhaven House** €€
New Line Road (tel: 066 947 4431, fax: 066 947 4724).
Closed 21 Dec–Feb.
5 rooms.

◊ **Butler Arms** €€–€€€
In the centre of the village (tel: 066 947 4144, fax: 066 947 4520).
Closed Nov–Apr.
12 rooms.

◊ **Derrynane Bay House** €
Caherdaniel, south of Waterville on N70 (tel: 066 947 5404.
Closed Nov–23 Dec.
6 rooms.

SNEEM, Co Kerry
◊ ◉| **Parknasilla Hotel** €€€
On Kenmare road, 2 miles (3km) from Sneem (tel: 064 45122, fax: 064 45323).
83 rooms.

◊ **Tahilla Cove** €€
Tahilla, 5 miles (8km) east of Sneem just off the N70 (tel: 064 45204, fax: 064 45104).
Closed Nov–Easter.
9 rooms.

KENMARE, Co Kerry
(See also Tour 6)
◉| **d'Arcy's** €€
Main Street (tel: 064 41589)
One of the best restaurants in town, serving such classics as peppered fillet of beef plus more unusual combinations such as John Dory with salsa, and mussels in coconut and lime broth.
May–Sep Tue–Sun, noon–10pm; Oct–Apr Thu–Sun 6–10pm.

◊ **Davitts** €€
Henry Street (tel: 064 42741, fax: 064 42757).
Closed 1–14 Nov, 24–26 Dec.
11 rooms.

◊ **Lansdowne Arms** €€–€€€
Main Street (tel: 064 41368, fax: 064 41114).
Closed 25 Dec.
26 rooms.

◉| **Mulcahy's** €€
16 Henry Street (tel: 064 42383).
Excellent modern fusion cuisine, blending classical European cooking with Asian influences.
Jun–Sep daily 6–10pm; Oct–May Thu–Mon 6.15–10pm. Closed 24–26 Dec, 2 weeks end Jan.

◊ ◉| **Sheen Falls Lodge** €€€–€€€€
Off N71 Glengarriff road, first left after suspension bridge (tel: 064 41600, fax: 064 41386).
Closed 3 Jan–1 Feb.
66 rooms.

Leaning towards classical French cuisine, the menu changes monthly and might include Skeaghanore duck with pistachios or pan-fried Valentia scallop (€€€).
Daily 7–9.30pm. Closed Mon–Thu,3 weeks before Christmas, 2 Jan–1 Feb.

◊ **Virginia's Guesthouse** €–€€
36 Henry Street (tel: 064 41021, fax: 064 42415).
6 rooms.

TOUR 6
KENMARE, Co Kerry
(See also Tour 5)
◊ **Harbour Views** €–€€
Castletownbere Road, Dauros, about 5 miles (8km) southwest of Kenmare via the N71 and R571) (tel: 064 41755, fax: 064 42611).
Closed Nov–Feb.
4 rooms.

◊ ◉| **Park Hotel** €€€€
On the R569 at top of town (tel: 064 41200, fax: 064 41402).
Closed 1–23 Dec, 2 Jan–14 Feb.
46 rooms.
Classical dishes have a strong streak of creativity, such as baked hake wrapped in bacon on potato colcannon with mussel and clam chive cream sauce (€€€).
Daily 11–6, 7–9. Closed Nov–Apr, except Christmas and New Year.

◉| **Purple Heather** €
Henry Street (tel: 064 41016).
Classic tearoom fare, plus some excellent light meals such as wild smoked salmon salad, vegetarian omelette, homemade soups and Irish cheese patters.
Mon–Sat 10.45–6.

◊ **Sallyport House** €€–€€€
Glengariff Road (tel: 064 42066, fax: 064 42067).
Closed Nov–Mar.
5 rooms.

◊ **SeaShore Farm Guest House** €€–€€€
Tubrid, off the N70 Sneem road (tel: 064 41270 or 41675, fax: 064 41270).
Closed 15 Nov–Feb.
6 rooms.

TOUR 7
CORK, Co Cork
(See also Tour 8)
◇ **Ashley** €€€
Coburg Street (tel: 021 450 1518, fax: 021 450 1178).
Closed 22 Dec–5 Jan.
27 rooms.
🍴 **Crawford Gallery Café** €–€€
Emmet Place (tel: 021 427 4415).
Within the city's art gallery, this is a popular place serving traditional Irish food. It's run by the Allen family, of the famous Ballymaloe House cookery school.
Mon–Sat 10–5.Closed Sun, 24 Dec–3 Jan.
🍴 **Fenn's Quay Restaurant** €€
3 Fenn's Quay (tel: 021 427 9527).
Interesting combinations of food are expertly cooked here, such as spicy Toulouse sausages with sauerkraut, mashed potato and herb jus.
Mon–Sat 10–10.
◇ **Gamish House** €€
1 Aldergrove, Western Road (tel: 021 427 5111, fax: 021 427 3872).
26 rooms.
◇🍴 **Hayfield Manor** €€€–€€€€
Perrott Avenue, College Road (tel: 021 484 5900, fax: 021 431 6839).
88 rooms.
The chef here is a member of the Slow Food movement and uses organic ingredients wherever possible to produce his elaborate classical French dishes (€€€).
Daily 7–10pm, Sun–Fri 12.30–2pm.
🍴 **Ivory Tower** €€–€€€
Exchange Building, Princes Street (tel: 021 4274665)
American-born celebrity TV chef Seamus O'Connell presents diners here with unusual combinations of flavours (swordfish on banana ketchup with mango salsa, for instance).
Tue–Sat noon–3, 6.30–10.
🍴 **Jacobs** €
30a South Mall (tel: 021 425 1530).
Top quality ingredients are prepared with skill and creativity.
Mon–Sat 12.30–2.30, 6.30–10.

🍴 **Jacques** €€
9 Phoenix Street (tel: 021 427 7387).
A Cork favourite for more than 20 years, serving an interesting range of dishes with Mediterranean and Asian influences.
Mon–Sat 6–10pm.
◇ **Jurys Inn** €€–€€€
Anderson's Quay (tel: 021 494 3000, fax: 021 427 6144).
Closed 24–26 Dec.
133 rooms.
◇ **Killarney** €€
Western Road (tel: 021 427 0290, fax: 021 427 1010).
Closed 24–25 Dec.
19 rooms.
◇ **The Kingsley Hotel** €€€
Victoria Cross (tel: 021 480 0500, fax: 021 480 0527).
69 rooms.
◇ **Lancaster Lodge** €€–€€€
Lancaster Quay, Western Road (tel: 021 425 1125, fax: 021 425 1126).
Closed 22–26 Dec.
39 rooms.
◇ **Maryborough House and Spa** €€€–€€€€
Maryborough Hill, Douglas (tel: 021 436 5555, fax: 021 436 5662).
Closed 24–26 Dec.
93 rooms.
🍴 **Quay Co-op** €
24 Sullivan's Quay (tel: 021 431 7026).
Interesting vegetarian food, served in an upstairs restaurant above a wholefood shop.
Mon–Sat 9–9.
◇ **Rochestown Park Hotel** €€€–€€€€
Rochestown Road, Douglas (tel: 021 489 0800, fax: 021 489 2178).
Closed 25–26 Dec.
160 rooms.

BLARNEY, Co Cork
◇ **Ashlee Lodge** €€–€€€
Tower, 2.5 miles (4km) from Blarney on the R617 (tel: 021 438 5346, fax: 021 438 5726).
10 rooms.
◇ **Blarney Castle** €€
Village Green (tel: 021 438 5116, fax: 021 438 5542).
Closed 24–25 Dec.
13 rooms.

◇ **Blarney Vale House** €–€€
Cork Road (tel: 021 4381511).
Closed Dec–Jan.
4 rooms.
◇ **Killarney House** €
Station Road (tel: 021 438 1841, fax: 021 438 1841).
6 rooms.
◇ **White House** €
Shean Lower (tel: 021 438 5338).
6 rooms.

MALLOW, Co Cork
◇ **Ashfield B&B** €
Killarney Road (tel: 022 47979).
3 rooms.
◇ **Greenfield House** €
Navigation Road (tel: 022 50231).
6 rooms.
◇ **Longueville House** €€€–€€€€
3 miles (5km) west via the N72 (tel: 022 47156, fax: 022 47459).
Closed 10 Jan–15 Mar.
20 rooms.
◇ **Oaklands House** €
Springwood, off Killarney road (N72) (tel: 022 21127, fax: 022 21127).
4 rooms.
Closed Nov–Mar.
◇ **Springfort Hall Country House Hotel** €€€
Off the N20 Limerick road, on the R581 (tel: 022 21278, fax: 022 21557).
Closed 23 Dec–2 Jan.
49 rooms.

CAHIR, Co Tipperary
◇ **Caher House** €€
The Square (tel: 052 43000, fax: 052 42728).
Closed 25 Dec.
42 rooms.

LISMORE, Co Waterford
◇🍴 **Ballyrafter House** €€
Opposite Lismore Castle (tel: 058 54002, fax: 058 53050).
Closed Nov–Feb.
10 rooms.
Modern Irish food with a strong bias towards seafood (€€€).
Daily 1–2.30, 7.30–9.30. Closed Tue (except residents), 31 Oct–17 Mar.

Practical • Information

YOUGHAL, Co Cork

◊ ⁱ◎ **Aherne's** €€€
163 North Main Street
(tel: 024 92424, fax: 024 93633).
Closed 24–29 Dec.
13 rooms.
French-influenced treatment of the finest local seafood draws discerning diners (€€€).

◊ ⁱ◎ **Bay View** €€€
Ballycotton, southwest on coast; off the N25, via the R632 and R629 (tel: 021 464 6746; fax: 021 464 6075).
Closed Nov–Apr.
35 rooms.
Seafood is the speciality, but doesn't dominate the menu, which might also include braised pig cheeks with swede puree. Mon–Sat 7–9pm, Sun 1–2, 7–9.

◊ ⁱ◎ **Garryvoe Hotel** €€–€€€
Ballycotton Bay, Castlemartyr, west of Youghal, off the N25 (tel: 021 464 6718).
Irish country cooking here features lots of locally caught fish and notable meat dishes.
Daily 1–2.30, 6.45–8.45. Closed for dinner 24 Dec, 25 Dec.

TOUR 8
CORK, Co Cork
(See also Tour 7)
◊ **Abbeypoint House** €€
Western Road (tel: 021 427 5526, fax: 021 425 1955).
Closed 23 Dec–2 Jan.
8 rooms.

◊ **Antoine House** €–€€
Western Road (tel: 021 427 3494, fax: 021 427 3092).
7 rooms.

ⁱ◎ **Café Paradiso** €€
16 Lancaster Quay, (tel: 021 427 7939).
Vegetarians are certainly in paradise here, with gourmet treatment of the finest local produce (and you can buy the chefs' cookbook).
Tue–Sat noon–3, 6.30–10. Closed Christmas week.

◊ **Gresham Metropole** €€–€€€
MacCurtain Street (tel: 021 464 3777 fax: 021 450 6450)
113 rooms.

◊ **Imperial Hotel** €€€–€€€€
South Mall (tel: 021 427 4040, fax: 021 427 5375).
Closed 24–27 Dec.
130 rooms.

ⁱ◎ **Isaacs** €€–€€€
48 MacCurtain Street (tel: 021 450 3805).
Modern, understated cuisine incudes satisfying stews, pastas, grills and interesting salads.
Mon–Sat 12.3–2.30pm, Sun 6–10pm.

◊ **Lotamore House** €€
Tivoli (tel: 021 482 2344, fax: 021 482 2219).
Closed 21 Dec–6 Jan.
18 rooms.

◊ **Rose Lodge** €€
Mardyke Walk, off Western Road (tel: 021 427 2958, fax: 021 427 4087).
17 rooms.

◊ **Silver Springs Moran** €€–€€€
Tivoli (tel: 021 450 7533, fax: 021 450 7641).
Closed 24–26 Dec.
109 rooms.

KINSALE, Co Cork
◊ ⁱ◎ **Actons** €€
Pier Road (tel: 021 477 2135, fax: 021 477 2231).
Closed 24–27 Dec.
73 rooms.
Elegant cuisine might include canon of lamb wrapped in a black pudding mousseline and herb pancake. Daily 7–9.30pm, also 12.30–3pm Sun. Closed Jan.

◊ ⁱ◎ **Blue Haven Hotel and Restaurant** €€€
3 Pearse Street (tel: 021 477 2209, fax: 021 477 4268).
Closed 24–27 Dec.
17 rooms.
Excellent seafood is available in the atmospheric bar or lovely restaurant, with wine from French vineyards that were started by Irish exiles. Daily, bar: 12.15–3, 6.30–10; restaurant: 7–10pm.

◊ **Chart House Luxury Accommodation** €€–€€€
6 Denis Quay (tel: 021 477 4568, fax: 021 477 7907).
Closed Christmas.
3 rooms.

ⁱ◎ **Fishy Fishy Café** €€
Guardwell (tel: 021 477 4453).
Seafood café serving the freshest of fish in very interesting ways, such as John Dory with tomato and coriander salsa or tiger prawns with chick peas and bacon.
Daily noon–3.45pm.

◊ **Friar's Lodge** €€
5 Friars Street (tel: 086 289 5075 or 021 477 7384, fax: 021 477 4363).
18 rooms.

◊ **Harbour Lodge** €€€
Scilly (tel: 021 477 2376, fax: 021 477 2675).
10 rooms.

ⁱ◎ **Little Skillet** €€
Main Street (tel: 021 477 4202).
Lovely atmosphere and tasty Irish food, including stews and champ.
Daily 6–10.30pm.

◊ **Long Quay House** €€
Long Quay (tel: 021 477 4563 or 477 3201, fax: 021 477 4563).
Closed 15 Nov–26 Dec.
8 rooms.

◊ **Old Bank House** €€–€€€
11 Pearse Street (tel: 021 477 4075, fax: 021 477 4296).
Closed 22–27 Dec.
17 rooms.

◊ **Old Presbytery** €€–€€€
43 Cork Street (tel: 021 477 2027, fax: 021 477 2166).
Closed Dec–14 Feb.
6 rooms.

◊ **Rivermount House** €€
Knocknabinny, Barrells Cross (tel: 021 477 8033, fax: 021 477 8225).
Closed Dec–Jan.
6 rooms.

◊ ⁱ◎ **Trident** €€–€€€
Worlds End, on the waterfront, just beyond the pier (tel: 021 477 9300, fax: 021 477 4173).
Closed 24–26 Dec.
75 rooms.
Dishes with a modern edge are created using the finest local ingredients (€€–€€€).
Daily 7–9.30pm, also 1–2.30pm Sun. Closed 23–26 Dec.

◊ **Waterlands** €–€€
Cork Road (tel: 021 477 2318 or 087 276 7917, fax: 021 477 4873).
Closed Dec–Feb.
4 rooms.

◊ **The White House** €€
Pearse Street, The Glen (tel: 021 477 2125, fax: 021 477 2045).
Closed 24–25 Dec.
10 rooms.

◊ **Woodlands House B & B** €–€€
Cappagh (tel: 021 477 2633, fax: 021 477 2649).
6 rooms.

CLONAKILTY, Co Cork
◇ **An Garran Coir €**
Rathbarry, Rosscarbery Coast
Route (tel: 023 48236, fax: 023
48236).
5 rooms.
◇ **Desert House €**
Coast Road (tel: 023 33331,
fax: 023 33048).
5 rooms.
◇ **Duvane Farm €–€€**
Ballyduvane, 1.2 miles (2km)
southwest on N71 (tel: 023
33129, fax: 023 33129).
Closed Nov–Mar.
4 rooms.
◇ **Inchdoney Island Lodge
and Spa €€€–€€€€**
Edge of village (tel: 023 33143,
fax: 023 33229).
Closed 24–26 Dec.
67 rooms.
◇ **Kilkern House €–€€**
Rathbarry (tel: 023 40643,
fax: 023 40643)
5 rooms.
◇ **Springfield House €–€€**
Kilkern, Rathbarry, Castlefreke,
off the N71 Skibbereen road
(tel: 023 40622, fax: 023 40622).
Closed Dec.
4 rooms.

ROSS CARBERY, Co Cork
◇ **Celtic Ross €€–€€€**
On the N71, at the edge of the
village (tel: 023 48722, fax: 023
48723).
Closed mid-Jan to mid-Feb.
66 rooms.

GOUGANE BARRA, Co Cork
◇ **Gougane Barra €€**
Off the N22 (tel: 026 47069,
fax: 026 47226).
Closed mid-Oct to mid-Apr.
26 rooms.

MACROOM, Co Cork
◇ 🍴 **Castle Hotel €€–€€€**
Main Street, on the N22 (tel: 026
41074, fax: 026 41505)
Closed 24–28 Dec.
60 rooms.
*An occasional international influ-
ence creeps in here, on a menu that
might include lamb with spring
onion champ and roasted root
vegetables, or a starter of duck leg
confit with chilli dressing.
Daily noon–3, 6–8.30.*

TOUR 9
BANTRY, Co Cork
◇ 🍴 **Sea View House €€€**
Ballylickey, 5 miles (8km) north
on the N71 (tel: 027 50073 or 021
50462, fax: 027 51555).
Closed mid-Nov to mid-Mar.
25 rooms.
*Traditional Irish cuisine might
include warm scallop mousse and
grilled sea bass. Freshly baked bread
(try the courgette and walnut) is a
highlight (€€).
Daily from 7pm, also Sunday lunch.*
◇ **Westlodge €€–€€€**
On the outskirts of town overlooking the bay (tel: 027 50360,
fax: 027 50438).
Closed 23–27 Dec.
90 rooms.

SKIBBEREEN, Co Cork
◇ 🍴 **Baltimore Harbour
Hotel and Leisure Centre
€€–€€€**
Baltimore (tel: 028 20361,
fax: 028 20466).
Closed Jan.
64 rooms.
*The Clipper restaurant serves
accomplished cuisine using the very
best west Cork produce.
Daily 6.30–9.30pm (brasserie menu
available during the day in the bar).
Closed Sun–Thu, Nov–Mar.*
◇ 🍴 **Casey's of Baltimore
€€€**
Village centre, Baltimore
(tel: 028 20197, fax: 028 20509).
Closed 21–27 Dec.
14 rooms.
*Excellent seafood, served simply,
comes direct from Baltimore's fishing
fleet; the seafood chowder is
legendary (€€).
Daily 12.30–2.30, 6.30–9.*
◇ **Ilenroy House €**
10 North Street (tel: 028 22751
or 22193, fax: 028 23228).
5 rooms.

SKULL, Co Cork
🍴 **Adele's €–€€**
Main Street (tel: 028 28459).
*Lovely tearoom fare, plus a daily
changing menu of first-rate seafood
and pasta dishes.
Easter–Jun, Sep–Nov Wed–Sun
9.30–6; Jul–Aug daily 9.30–6.
Closed Nov–Easter.*

◇ **Rock Cottage €€**
Barnatonicane (tel: 028 35538,
fax: 028 35538).
3 rooms.

MIZEN HEAD, Co Cork
◇ **Carraig-Mor House €**
Toormore Bay, Goleen (tel: 028
28410, fax: 028 28410).
Closed 24–26 Dec.
5 rooms.
🍴 **Good Things Café €**
Ahakista Road, Durrus (tel: 027
61426).
*Unpretentious little bistro offering
the best of local produce, including
artisan cheeses, in creative dishes.
Wed–Mon 10.30–5, 6.30–8.30.*
◇ 🍴 **Heron's Cove €€**
The Harbour, Goleen (tel: 028
35225, fax: 028 35422).
Closed Christmas and New Year.
5 rooms.
*Casual restaurant specialising in
seafood such as Dunmanus Bay
scallops (€€).
May–Oct daily noon–10.*

TOUR 10
WATERFORD, Co Waterford
(See also Tour 15)
◇ **Arlington Lodge €€€**
John's Hill (tel: 051 878584,
fax: 051 878127).
Closed 24–27 Dec.
20 rooms.
◇ **Athenaeum House
€€–€€€**
Christendon, Ferrybank (tel: 051
833999, fax: 051 833977).
Closed 24–26 Dec.
29 rooms.
◇ **Belmont House €**
Belmont Road, Rosslare Road,
Ferrybank (tel: 051 832174,
fax: 051 832174).
Closed Nov–Apr.
6 rooms.
🍴 **Bodega! €€**
54 John Street (tel: 051 844177).
*Lively haunt of Waterfords
20-somethings, with loud music
and excellent continental cuisine.
Mon–Fri noon–2.30pm, Mon–Sat
6–10pm (10.30 Sat).*
◇ **Bridge Hotel €€**
1 The Quay (tel: 051 877222,
fax: 051 877229).
*Closed Christmas and first
2 weeks Jan.*
133 rooms.

◊ **Faithlegg House** €€€–€€€€
Faithlegg (tel: 051 382000,
fax: 051 382010).
82 rooms.

◊ **Granville** €€–€€€
The Quay (tel: 051 305555,
fax: 051 305566).
Closed 25–26 Dec.
100 rooms.

◊ **Sion Hill House and
Gardens** €€
Sion Hill, Ferrybank (tel: 051
851558, fax: 051 851678).
Closed mid-Dec to early Jan.
4 rooms.

◊ **Tower** €€–€€€
The Mall (tel: 051 875801 or 051
862300, fax: 051 870129).
Closed 24–28 Dec.
139 rooms.

◊ ◙ **Waterford Castle**
€€€–€€€€
The Island (tel: 051 878203,
fax: 051 879316).
19 rooms.
*Modern Irish cuisine with a classical
influence and strong emphasis on
seafood (€€€).*
*Daily 7–8.30pm, also
12.30–1.45pm Sun. Closed
Christmas, early Jan.*

◙ **Wine Vault** €–€€
High Street (tel: 051 853444).
*In a city famed throughout history
for its wine merchants, this restaurant matches wonderful bistro food
with great vintages.*
*Tue 5–10pm, Wed–Sat 12.30–2.30,
5–10.*

DUNMORE EAST,
Co Waterford
◊ **The Beach Guest
House** €€
Lower Village (tel: 051 383316,
fax: 051 383319).
Closed Nov–Feb.
7 rooms.

◙ **The Strand Seafood
Restaurant** €€€
(tel: 051 383174).
*Overlooking Waterford Harbour.
Intimate restaurant serving such
outstanding dishes as wild salmon
with green gooseberry sauce and
lemon sole stuffed with seafood
mousse.*
*Mar–Oct daily 6.30–10pm;
Nov–Dec and Feb Wed–Sun
6.30–10pm. Closed Jan.*

TRAMORE, Co Waterford
◊ **Cliff House** €–€€
Cliff Road (tel: 051 381497 or
391296, fax: 051 381497).
Closed 20 Dec–Jan.
6 rooms.

◙ **Coast** €€
Upper Branch Road (tel: 051
393646).
*Trendy gourmet restaurant serving
modern international cuisine such as
chargrilled Asian chicken and pan-
fried Barbary duck with honey and
sherry sauce.*
*Tue–Sun 6.30–10.30pm, Sun
1–2.30pm, also Sun evenings
Jul–Aug. Closed 24 Dec–1 Jan.*

◊ **Glenorney** €–€€
Newtown (tel: 051 381056,
fax: 051 381103).
Closed Christmas.
6 rooms.

◊ **Majestic** €€
(tel: 051 381761, fax: 051
381766).
60 rooms.

DUNGARVAN, Co Waterford
◊ **An Bohreen** €€
Killineen West (tel: 051 291010,
fax: 051 291011).
Closed Nov–mid-Mar.
4 rooms.

◊ **Castle Country House** €€
Millstreet, Cappagh (tel: 058
68049, fax: 058 68099).
Closed Dec–Feb.
5 rooms.

◊ **Gortnadiha House** €€
Ring (tel: 058 46142).
Closed Christmas and New Year.
3 rooms.

◊ **Lawlors** €€–€€€
Town centre (tel: 058 41122 or
41056, fax: 058 41000).
Closed 25 Dec.
89 rooms.

◊ **Powersfield House** €€
Ballinamuck West (tel: 058
45594, fax: 058 45550).
6 rooms.

◊ **Sliabh gCua Farmhouse**
€€
Touraneena, Ballinamult
(tel: 058 47120).
Closed Nov–Mar.
4 rooms.

◙ **The Tannery** €€
Quay Street (tel: 058 445420).
*Innovative chef Paul Flynn adds his
own special flair to traditional Irish
and European dishes.*
Tue–Sun 12.30–2.30, 6.30–9.30.
Closed Sat lunch, Mon.

CAPPOQUIN, Co Waterford
◊ **Richmond House** €€€
On Dungarvan road (tel: 058
54278, fax: 058 54988).
Closed 23 Dec–20 Jan.
10 rooms.

LISMORE, Co Waterford
(See Tour 7).

CASHEL, Co Tipperary
(See also Tours 3 and 14))
◊ **Baileys Guesthouse and
Restaurant** €€€
Main Street (tel: 062 61937,
fax: 062 63957).
Closed 24–28 Dec.
9 rooms.

◙ **Chez Hans** €€–€€€
Moor Lane (tel: 062 61177).
*This restaurant in a former
Wesleyan chapel is getting great
reviews for its menu of familiar
favourites, cooked to perfection.*
Open Tue–Sat 6–10pm.

◊ **Thornbrook House** €
Dualla Road (tel: 062 62388,
fax: 062 61480).
Closed Nov–Mar.
5 rooms.

CLONMEL, Co Tipperary
◙ **Angela's Wholefood
Restaurant** €
14 Abbey Street (tel: 052 26899).
*Satisfying lunch menu, including
soups, salads, sandwiches and such
dishes as spicy Moroccan lamb stew;
great for breakfast too.*
Mon–Fri 9–5.30, Sat noon–5pm.

◊ ◙ **Minella** €€€
South of the river (tel: 052
22388, fax: 052 24381).
Closed 24–28 Dec.
90 rooms.
*Traditional hotel-style menu using
local produce (€€).*
Daily 12.30–2.30, 6.30–9.30.

Mr Bumbles €€
Richmond House, Kickham
Street (tel: 052 29188).
*Bright, split-level bistro with a menu
of international dishes, including
superb fish and Tipperary beef.
Mon–Fri 5–9.30pm, Sat 6–10pm,
also noon–2.30pm Thu, Fri and
Sun.*

TOUR 11
ATHLONE, Co Westmeath
**Glasson Golf Hotel and
Country Club** €€€–€€€€
Glasson (tel: 090 648 5120,
fax: 090 648 5444).
65 rooms.
Hodson Bay €–€€€
Hodson Bay (tel: 090 644 2000,
fax: 090 644 2020).
182 rooms.
*Daily-changing menu might include
turf-smoked chicken breast or
Ballinstelligs Bay lobster (€€€).
Daily 12.30–2.30, 7–9.15.*
Left Bank Bistro €€€
Fry Place (tel: 090 649 4446).
*The cuisines of Italy, France and
Asia combine on a menu that ranges
from Thai spiced chicken to classic
beef fillet.
Tue–Sat 10.30–9.30.*
Riverview House €
Galway Road, Summerhill (tel:
090 649 4532, fax: 090 649 4532).
Closed 18 Dec–1 Mar.
4 rooms.
Shelmalier House €
Cartontroy, Retreat Road (tel:
090 647 2245 or 090 6472145,
fax: 090 647 3190).
Closed 20 Dec–31 Jan.
7 rooms.
Wineport Lodge €€€
Glasson (tel: 090 643 9010,
fax: 090 648 5471).
Closed 24–26 Dec.
29 rooms.
*Wholesome local produce, such as
Lissadel oysters or carved rack of
lamb, are served in generous
portions and there's an excellent
wine list (€€€).
Daily 6–10pm.*

MULLINGAR, Co Westmeath
Bloomfield House €€–€€€
Belvedere (tel: 044 40894,
fax: 044 43767).
Closed 24–26 Dec.
111 rooms.

Hilltop County House €
Delvin Road, Rathconnell
(tel: 044 9348958, fax: 044
9348013). *Closed Nov–Feb.*
5 rooms.
Mullingar Park €€€
Dublin Road (tel: 044 9344446,
fax: 044 9335937).
Closed 24–25 Dec.
95 rooms.

BIRR, Co Offaly
Aaron House €€
Kinitty (tel 057 9137040,
fax: 057 9137040).
5 rooms.

TOUR 12
DROGHEDA, Co Louth
**Boyne Valley Hotel &
Country Club** €€€
Stameen, Dublin Road. (tel: 041
983 7737, fax: 041 983 9188).
73 rooms.

SLANE, Co Meath
Conyngham Arms €€–€€€
Village Centre (tel: 041 988
4444, fax: 041 982 4205).
16 rooms.

NAVAN, Co Meath
Ardboyne €€–€€€
Dublin Road (tel: 046 902 3119.
Closed 24–26 Dec.
5 rooms.
Hudson's Bistro €€
Railway Street (tel: 046 29231).
*Bright and cheerful bistro with an
international menu, including Greek
kebabs and Thai curry.
Mon–Sat 6–11pm, Sun 6–9pm.*
Killyon €–€€
Dublin Road (tel: 046 907 1224,
fax: 046 907 2766).
Closed 24–26 Dec.
6 rooms.
Newgrange €€€
Bridge Street (tel: 046 907 4100,
fax: 046 907 3977).
Closed 25 Dec.
62 rooms.
Station House €€–€€€
Kilmessan (tel: 046 902 5239,
fax: 046 902 5588).
20 rooms.

TOUR 13
DUBLIN, Co Dublin
**Abberley Court Hotel
and Apartments** €€–€€€
Belgard Road, Tallaght (south of
city at junction of N81 Tallaght
by-pass and Belgard Road) (tel:
01 459 6000, fax: 01 462 1000).
Closed 25 Dec–2 Jan.
40 rooms.
Aberdeen Lodge €€–€€€
53 Park Avenue, Ballsbridge,
Dublin 4 (tel: 01 283 8155,
fax: 01 283 7877)
16 rooms.
Abrae Court €€
9 Zion Road, Rathgar (tel: 01 492
2242, fax: 01 492 3944).
Closed Christmas.
14 rooms.
Berkeley Court €€–€€€
Lansdowne Road, Dublin 4
(tel: 01 665 3200, fax: 01 661
7238).
186 rooms.
**Bewleys Hotel
Ballsbridge** €€
Merrion Road, Ballsbridge,
Dublin 4 (tel: 01 668 1111,
fax: 01 668 1999).
Closed 24–26 Dec.
304 rooms.
**Bewleys Hotel
Leopardstown** €€
Central Park, Leopardstown,
Dublin 18 (tel: 01 293 5000,
fax: 021 293 5099).
Closed 24–26 Dec.
352 rooms.
**Bewleys Hotel Newlands
Cross** €€
Newlands Cross, Naas Road, on
the N7, off the M50 junction 9
(tel: 01 464 0140, fax: 01 464
0900). *Closed 24–26 Dec.*
299 rooms.
Browne's €€€–€€€€
22 St Stephen's Green, Dublin 2
(tel: 01 638 3939, fax: 01 638
3900).
11 rooms.
Burlington €€€–€€€€
Upper Leeson Street, Dublin 4
(tel: 01 660 5222, fax: 01 660
8496).
500 rooms.
Buswells €€–€€€
23–25 Molesworth Street,
Dublin 2 (tel: 01 614 6500,
fax: 01 676 2090).
Closed 25–26 Dec.
67 rooms.

◇ **Camden Court** €€–€€€
Camden Street, Dublin 2 (tel: 01 475 9666, fax: 01 475 9677).
Closed Christmas/New Year.
246 rooms.

◇ **Carnegie Court** €€
North Street, Swords, off N1 north of Dublin Airport (tel: 01 840 4384, fax: 01 840 4505),
Closed 25–26 Dec.
36 rooms.

◇ **Cassidys** €€–€€€
Cavendish Row, Upper O'Connell Street, Dublin 1 (tel: 01 878 0555, fax: 01 878 0687).
Closed 24–26 Dec.
88 rooms.

◇ **Charleville Lodge Guest House** €€
268–272 North Circular Road, Phibsborough, Dublin 7 (tel: 01 838 6633, fax: 01 838 5854).
Closed 21–26 Dec.
30 rooms.

◇ 🍴 **The Clarence** €€€€
6–8 Wellington Quay, Dublin 2 (tel: 01 407 0800, fax: 01 407 0820).
Closed 24–27 Dec.
50 rooms.
Modern European cooking, using mostly organic ingredients (€€€).
Mon–Sat 12.30–2.15, 7–10.15, Sun–Fri 12.30–2.30pm.

◇ 🍴 **Clarion Hotel Dublin IFSC** €€€
North Wall Quay, Dublin 1 (tel: 01 433 8800; fax: 01 4338801).
147 rooms.
Modern Irish theme with interesting flavour combinations.
Daily noon–2.30, 6–9.30.

🍴 **Dobbins Wine Bistro** €€€
15 Stephen's Lane, off Upper Mount Street, Dublin 2 (tel: 01 676 4679).
Foodies' favourite serving innovative Continental cuisine.
Mon–Thu 6–9.30pm, Fri–Sat 7–9.30pm, Sun noon–3.

◇ **Eliza Lodge** €€–€€€
23–24 Wellington Quay, Temple Bar, Dublin 2 (tel: 01 671 8044, fax: 01 671 8362).
Closed 23 Dec–2 Jan.
18 rooms.

🍴 **Finnstown Country House** €€–€€€
Newcastle Road, Lucan (west of the city off the N4) (tel: 01 601 0700).
Victorian dining room with fixed price and à la carte menus of international food.
Mon–Sat 12.30–2.30, 7.30–9.30.

◇ 🍴 **Fitzwilliam Hotel** €€€–€€€€
St Stephen's Green, Dublin 2 (tel: 01 478 7000, fax: 01 478 7878).
12 rooms.
Thornton's, the hotel's restaurant, overlooks the green and produces contemporary dishes with intense flavours (€€).
Daily 12.30–2.30, 5.30–10.30.

◇ **Glenogra** €€
64 Merrion Road, Ballsbridge, Dublin 4 (tel: 01 668 3661, fax: 01 668 3698).
Closed 21 Dec–12 Jan.
13 rooms.

🍴 **Govinda's** €
4 Aungier Street, Dublin 2 (tel: 01 475 0309).
Vegetarian restaurant serving generous and satisfying dishes with European and Asian influences.
Mon–Sat noon–9.

◇ **Gresham** €€€–€€€€
23 Upper O'Connell Street, Dublin 1 (tel: 01 874 6881, fax: 01 878 7175).
287 rooms.

◇ **Harrington Hall** €
Harcourt Street, Dublin 2 (tel: 01 475 3497, fax: 01 475 4544).
28 rooms.

◇ **Herbert Park Hotel** €€€–€€€€
Ballsbridge, Dublin 4 (next to the RDS) (tel: 01 667 2200, fax: 01 667 2595).
153 rooms.

🍴 **Irish Film Centre Café Bar** €
Temple Bar, Dublin 2
Trendy place for an inexpensive meal, with Irish and international cuisine on the menu. Live music or comedy at weekends.
Daily 12.30–3, 6–9 (lunch from 1pm Sat–Sun).

🍴 **Jacob's Ladder** €€–€€€
4 Nassau Street, Dublin 2 (tel: 01 670 3865).
Punchy modern treatment of traditional Irish dishes with an emphasis on healthy eating. Possibly the best colcannon in Ireland.
Tue–Sat 12.30–2.30, 6–10, Sat 7–10pm. Closed 24 Dec–4 Jan.

◇ **Jurys Ballsbridge** €€€€
Pembroke Road, Ballsbridge, Dublin 4 (tel: 01 660 5000, fax: 01 6605540).
403 rooms.

◇ **Jurys Christchurch Inn** €€
Christchurch Place, Dublin 8 (tel: 01 454 0000, fax: 01 454 0012).
Closed 24–26 Dec.
182 rooms.

◇ **Jurys Inn Parnell Street** €€–€€€
Parnell Street, Dublin 1 (tel: 01 878 4900, fax: 01 878 4999).
Closed 24–26 Dec.
253 rooms.

◇ **Longfield's** €€–€€€
Fitzwilliam Street Lower, Dublin 2 (tel: 01 676 1367, fax: 01 676 1542).
26 rooms.

🍴 **Lord Edward** €€€
23 Christ Church Place, Dublin 8 (tel: 01 454 2420).
A lengthy menu of fresh fish and shellfish dishes.
Mon–Fri noon–2.30pm, Mon–Sat 6–10.30pm. Closed 24 Dec–3 Jan.

◇ **Lynch Green Isle** €€–€€€
Naas Road (6 miles/10km southwest) (tel: 01 459 3406, fax: 01 459 2178).
240 rooms.

◇ **McEniff Skylon** €€
Upper Drumcondra Road, Dublin 9, on the M1 between the airport and the city (tel: 01 837 9121, fax: 01 837 2778).
88 rooms.

◇ **Marine** €€
Sutton Cross, Dublin 13 (tel: 01 839 0000, fax: 01 839 0442).
Closed 25–27 Dec.
48 rooms.

◇ **Mercer** €€–€€€
Mercer Street Lower, Dublin 2 (tel: 01 478 2179 or 01 4774 4120, fax: 01 478 0328).
Closed 24–26 Dec.
41 rooms.

◇ **Merrion Hotel €€€€**
Upper Merrion Street, Dublin 2
(tel: 01 603 0600, fax: 01 603
0700).
143 rooms.

◇ **The Morrison €€€€**
Lower Ormond Quay, Dublin 1
(tel: 01 887 2400, fax: 01 878
3185).
Closed Christmas.
138 rooms.

◇ **Mount Herbert €€–€€€€**
Herbert Road, Lansdowne
Road, Dublin 4 (tel: 01 668 4321,
fax: 01 660 7077).
Closed 22–30 Dec.
168 rooms.

◇ **Plaza Hotel €€–€€€**
Belgard Road, Tallaght, Dublin
24 (6 miles/10km south, at end
of M50) (tel: 01 462 4200,
fax: 01 462 4600).
Closed 24–30 Dec.
122 rooms.

◇ **Red Cow Moran €€–€€€€**
Red Cow Complex, Naas Road,
Dublin 22 (tel: 01 459 3650,
fax: 01 459 1588).
Closed 24–26 Dec.
123 rooms.

◎ **Restaurant Patrick
Gilbaud €€€**
21 Upper Merrion Street,
Dublin 2 (tel: 01 676 4192).
*Ireland's finest restaurant. Expect
plenty of flair and innovation in the
French cuisine here.*
*Open Tue–Fri 12.30–2.15,
7–10.15, Sat 1–2.15.*

◎ **Restaurant 23 at The
Gresham Hotel €€–€€€**
O'Connell Street, Dublin 1
(tel: 01 817 6116 or 874 6881.
*Traditional fare with a modern
touch.*
*Mon–Fri noon–2.30, 5.30–10.30,
Sat–Sun 5.30–10.30. Closed bank
hols, 2 weeks at Christmas.*

◇ **Royal Dublin €€–€€€**
O'Connell Street, Dublin 1 (tel:
01 873 3666, fax: 01 873 3120).
Closed 24–25 Dec.
120 rooms.

◇ **The Shelbourne €€€–€€€€**
27 St Stephen's Green, Dublin 2
(tel: 01 663 4500, fax: 01 661
6006).
265 rooms.

◇ **Stillorgan Park €€–€€€**
Stillorgan Road, Dublin 4 (tel: 01
200 1800, fax: 01 283 1610).
150 rooms.

◇ **Temple Bar €€–€€€**
Fleet Street, Temple Bar,
Dublin 2 (tel: 01 677 3333,
fax: 01 677 3088).
Closed 23–25 Dec.
129 rooms.

◎ **Yamamori Noodles €–€€**
71–72 South Great George's
Street, Dublin 2 (tel: 01 475
5001).
*Lively Japanese restaurant with a
good choice of excellent and authentic
dishes.*
*Sun–Wed 12.30–11pm, Thu–Sat
12.30–11.30pm.*

KILLINEY, Co Dublin
◇ **Fitzpatrick Castle €€€**
On Killiney Hill (tel: 01 230
5400, fax: 01 230 5430).
113 rooms.

BRAY, Co Wicklow
◇ **Glenview Hotel €€–€€€**
Glen O' the Downs, Delgany
(south of Bray on N11) (tel: 01
287 3399, fax: 01 287 7511).
70 rooms.

◇ **Royal Hotel and Leisure
Guide €€–€€€€**
Main Street (tel: 01 286 2935,
fax: 01 286 7373).
130 rooms.

◎ **Tree of Idleness €€**
Seafront (tel: 01 286 3498)
*Greek Cypriot restaurant with all
the favourites on the menu, including moussaka, taramasalata and
roast sucking pig.*
Tue–Sun 7.30–11pm.

◇◎ **Woodville €€**
Ballywaltrim Lane (tel: 01 286
3103, fax: 01 286 3103).
Closed 15 Dec– 7 Jan.
5 rooms.

ROUNDWOOD, Co Wicklow
◎ **Roundwood Inn €–€€**
Main Street (R755) (tel: 01 281
8107)
*Lovely old coaching inn serving
superb food, including Irish stew
and fresh local lobster and salmon.*
Daily noon–9pm.

◇ **Wicklow Way Lodge €€**
Old Bridge (tel: 01 281 8489,
fax: 01 281 8189).
Closed Dec–Jan.
5 rooms.

GLENDALOUGH,
Co Wicklow
◇ **Glendalough €–€€**
Edge of village (tel: 0404 45135,
fax: 0404 45142).
Closed Dec–Jan.
44 rooms.

TOUR 14
KILKENNY, Co Kilkenny
◇ **Butler House €€–€€€**
Patrick Street (tel: 056 776 5707,
fax: 056 776 5626).
Closed 24–29 Dec.
13 rooms.

◎ **Café Sol €€–€€€**
6 William Street (tel: 056 776
4987.
*Brightly decorated café with basic
breakfast and lunch menus, and
some more interesting Southern
American and Mediterranean dishes
at dinner.*
Mon–Sat 6–10.

◎ **Kilkenny Design
Restaurant €**
The Parade (tel: 056 772 2118).
*Classy cafeteria with a good range
of salads, soups, platters and
pastries.*
*Mon–Sat 9–5, also Sun 10–5
May–Dec.*

◇◎ **Kilkenny River Court
Hotel €€–€€€€**
The Bridge, John Street (tel: 056
772 3388, fax: 056 772 3389).
Closed 24–26 Dec.
90 rooms.
*A Mediterranean twist is given to the
modern cooking here, producing such
dishes as wild mallard with a red
wine reduction.*

◇ **Langtons €–€€€**
69 John Street (tel: 056 776 5133,
fax: 056 776 3693).
Closed Good Fri, 25 Dec.
30 rooms.

◇ **Laragh House €€–€€€**
Smithsland North, Waterford
Road (tel: 056 776 4674, fax: 056
770 3605).
8 rooms.

◇ **Newpark €€€**
(tel: 056 776 0500, fax: 056 776
0555).
129 rooms.

◇ **Rosquil House €€–€€€**
Castlecomer Road (tel: 056 772
1419, fax: 056 775 0398).
7 rooms.

◊ **Shillogher House** €–€€
Callan Road (tel: 056 776 3249 or
776 4865, fax: 056 776 4865).
6 rooms.
🍴 **Zuni** €€–€€€
26 Patrick Street (tel: 056 772
3999).
*This restaurant offers international
specialities, such as tempura king
prawns with sesame toast and
Moroccan lamb.
Daily 6–9.30pm (closes at 9pm
Sun).*

THOMASTOWN, Co Kilkenny
◊ **Abbey House** €–€€
Jerpoint (tel: 056 772 4166,
fax: 056 772 4192).
Closed 31–30 Dec.
6 rooms.
◊🍴 **Mount Juliet Conrad**
€€€–€€€€
On N9 (tel: 056 777 3000,
fax: 056 777 3019).
59 rooms.
*Fresh vegetables and herbs from the
kitchen garden add to the imagina-
tive European dishes.
Daily 7–9.45pm.*
🍴 **Water Garden** €
On the Kilkenny road (tel: 056
772 4690).
*Nice little community/charity
tearoom serving home baked good-
ies, plus meals made with local
organic produce and meat.
Tue–Fri 10–5, Sun 12.30–5.
Closed Sun Christmas–Easter.*

NEW ROSS, Co Wexford
◊ **Brandon View** €
Ballyling Lower,
Graiguenamanagh, north on the
R705 (tel: 059 972 4625, fax: 059
972 4625).
6 rooms.
◊ **Woodlands House** €€
Carrigbyrne (tel: 051 428287,
fax: 051 428287).
4 rooms.

CARLOW, Co Carlow
◊ **Dolmen** €–€€€
Kilkenny Road (tel: 059 914
2002, fax: 059 914 2375).
93 rooms.
◊ **Seven Oaks** €€–€€€
Athy Road (tel: 059 913 1308,
fax: 059 913 2155),
Closed 25–26 Dec.
89 rooms.

PORTLAOISE, Co Laois
◊ **Comfort Inn** €€–€€€
Abbeyleix Road (tel: 057 869
5900, fax: 057 869 5901).
Closed 24–28 Dec.
90 rooms.
◊ **O'Sullivan Guesthouse** €€
8 Kelly Ville Park (tel: 057
8622774).
6 rooms.
◊ **The Portlaoise Heritage
Hotel** €€€
Jessop Street (tel: 057 8678588,
fax: 057 8678577).
Closed 23–27 Dec.
110 rooms.

ABBEYLEIX, Co Laois
◊ **Abbeyleix Manor Hotel** €€
South on the N8 (tel: 057
8730111, fax: 057 8730220).
Closed 25 Dec.
46 rooms.

THURLES, Co Tipperary
◊ **Inch House Country
House** €€
2.5 miles (4km) from Thurles on
the Nenagh road (tel: 0504
51348 or 51261, fax: 0504 51754).
5 rooms.

CASHEL, Co Tipperary
(See also Tours 3 and 10)
◊ **Aulber House** €€
Golden Road (tel: 062 63713,
fax: 062 63715).
Closed 23–27 Dec.
12 rooms.
◊ **Ashmore House** €–€€
John Street (tel: 062 61286,
fax: 062 62789).
5 rooms.

**TOUR 15
WEXFORD,** Co Wexford
◊ **Clonard House** €–€€
Clonard Great (tel: 053 9143141,
fax: 053 43141).
Closed Nov–Feb.
9 rooms.
◊🍴 **Ferrycarrig** €€€–€€€€
Ferrycarrig Bridge (tel: 053
9120999, fax: 053 9120982).
102 rooms.
*Classically inspired cuisine, with
eight choices per course (€€€).
Daily 7–10.15pm. Closed some
days; call for information.*

🍴 **Forde's Restaurant** €€
The Crescent (tel: 053 9123832).
*Elegant waterfront bistro with a
long menu of excellent, imaginative
dishes.
Mon–Sat 6–9.45pm.*
◊ **Killiane Castle** €€
Drinagh (tel: 053 9158885,
fax: 053 9158885).
Closed Dec–Feb.
8 rooms.
🍴 **Mange2** €€
100 South Main Street (tel: 053
9124419).
*Essentially French cuisine, but with
other influences here and there.
Daily 6–10.30pm, also
012.30–2.30pm Tue–Fri and Sun.*
◊ **Maple Lodge** €€
Castlebridge (tel: 053 9159195 or
053 9159 062).
Closed mid-Nov to mid-Mar.
4 rooms.
◊ **Newbay Country House**
€€
Newbay, Carrick (tel: 053 42779,
fax: 053 46318).
11 rooms.
◊ **Quality Hotel** €–€€€
Barntown Roundabout (tel: 053
917 2000, fax: 053 917 2001).
Closed 23–27 Dec.
107 rooms.
◊ **Rathaspeck Manor** €€
Rathaspeck (tel: 053 9141672).
Closed 8 Nov–Jun.
5 rooms.
◊ **River Bank House Hotel**
€€–€€€
By Wexford Bridge on the R741
(tel: 053 9123611, fax: 053
9123342).
Closed 24–25 Dec.
23 rooms.
◊ **Slaney Manor** €€–€€€
Ferrycarrig (tel: 053 9120051 or
9120144, fax: 053 9120510).
Closed Christmas week.
8 rooms.
◊ **Talbot** €€–€€€
The Quay (tel: 053 9122566, fax:
053 9123377).
Closed 24–25 Dec.
109 rooms.
◊ **White's** €€
Abbey Street (tel: 053 9122311,
fax: 053 9145000).
157 rooms.

⬦🍽 **Whitford House Hotel Health and Leisure Club** €€–€€€
New Line Road (tel: 053 9143444, fax: 053 9146399).
36 rooms.
French and other European dishes are produced with excellent Wexford produce (€€€).
Daily 7–9pm, also 12.30–3pm Sun.
Closed 23 Dec–2 Jan.

COURTOWN HARBOUR, Co Wexford
⬦ **Courtown** €€
(tel: 055 9425210, fax: 055 9425304)
Closed mid-Nov to early March.
21 rooms.

GOREY, Co Wexford
⬦🍽 **Ashdown Park** €€
The Coach Road (tel: 055 9480500, fax: 055 9480777).
Closed 25 Dec.
79 rooms.
Modern British cuisine, with Mediterranean accents, featuring local fish and game in season (€€).
Daily 6.30–9.30pm, also 12.30–2.30pm Sun.
⬦ **Hillside House** €–€€
Tubberduff (tel: 055 9421726, fax: 055 9422567).
Closed 20–28 Dec.
6 rooms.
⬦🍽 **Marlfield House Hotel** €€€
(tel: 055 9421124).
Closed 15 Dec–30 Jan.
20 rooms.
Daily changing menu of classical Mediterranean cuisine.
Daily 7–9pm, also 12.30–1.45 Sun.
⬦ **Woodlands Country House** €€
Killinierin (tel: 0402 37125, fax: 0402 37125).
Closed Sep–May.
6 rooms.

ENNISCORTHY, Co Wexford
⬦ **Ballinkeele House** €€–€€€
Ballymurn (tel: 053 9138105, fax: 053 9138468).
5 rooms.
⬦ **Lemongrove House** €–€€
Blackstoops (tel: 053 9236115, fax: 053 9236115).
Closed 20–31 Dec.
9 rooms.

⬦ **Riverside Park** €€€
The Promenade (tel: 053 9237800, fax: 053 9237900).
60 rooms.
⬦ **Treacys** €€–€€€
Templeshannon (tel: 053 9237789, fax: 053 9237733).
Closed 23–25 Dec.
59 rooms.

NEW ROSS, Co Wexford
(See also Tour 14)
⬦ **Cedar Lodge Hotel** €€€
Carrigbyrne, Newbawn (tel: 051 428386, fax: 051 428222).
Closed 21 Dec–31 Jan.
28 rooms.

WATERFORD, Co Waterford
(See also Tour 10)
⬦ **Brown's Town House** €€
29 South Parade (tel: 051 870594, fax: 051 871923).
Closed 20 Dec–29 Jan.
6 rooms.
⬦ **Diamond Hill Country House** €–€€
Diamond Hill, Slieverue (tel: 051 832855, fax: 051 832254).
Closed 22–27 Dec.
17 rooms.
⬦🍽 **Dooley's** €€–€€€
30 The Quay (tel: 051 873531, fax: 051 870262).
Closed 25–27 Dec.
113 rooms.
Broadly international menu might include cod fillet wrapped in cabbage leaves, with carrot and cardamom purée (€€€).
Daily 6–9.30pm, also 12.30–3pm Sun.
⬦ **Foxmount Country House** €€
Passage East Road, Dunmore Road (tel: 051 874308, fax: 051 854906).
Closed early Nov–early Mar.
4 rooms.
⬦ **Ramada Viking Hotel** €€
Cork Road (tel: 051 336933, fax: 051 336969).
100 rooms.
⬦ **Waterford Manor** €€–€€€
Killotteran, Butlerstown (tel: 051 377814, fax: 051 354545).
21 rooms.

BALLYHACK, Co Wexford
⬦ **Marsh Mere Lodge** €€
Near Ballyhack ferry (tel: 051 389186).
4 rooms.

KILMORE QUAY, Co Wexford
⬦ **Quay House** €€
On main street (tel: 053 9129988, fax: 053 9129808).
8 rooms.

ROSSLARE, Co Wexford
⬦ **Churchtown House** €€–€€€
On Rosslare–Rosslare Harbour link road (tel: 053 9132555, fax: 053 9132577).
Closed Nov–Feb.
12 rooms.
⬦ **Crosbie Cedars** €€–€€€
Rosslare village (tel: 053 9132124, fax: 053 9132243).
Closed 24–25 Dec.
34 rooms.
⬦ **Euro Lodge** €
(tel: 053 9135118 or 9133994, fax: 053 9135120).
Closed Nov–Mar.
38 rooms.
⬦🍽 **Kelly's Resort** €€€
On Wexford road (tel: 053 9132114, fax: 053 9132222).
Closed mid-Dec to late Feb.
118 rooms.
Smart, intimate restaurant with daily changing menu of steaks, seafood and more challenging conceptions. Local produce is handled with panache (€€€).
Daily 1–1.30, 7.30–9.30.
⬦ **Kilrane House** €
Kilrane village (tel: 053 9133135, fax 053 9133739).
Closed 25–28 Dec.
5 rooms.
⬦ **The Light House** €
Main Road (tgel: 053 9133214, fax: 053 9133214).
Closed Oct–Feb.
4 rooms.
⬦ **Oldcourt House** €
Rosslare Harbour, off N11 at St Patrick's Church (tel: 053 9133895 or 086 374 2568).
Closed Dec–Feb.
6 rooms.

TOUR 16
SLIGO, Co Sligo
◇ **Aisling €**
Cairns Hill (tel/fax: 071 916 0704).
Closed 24–26 Dec.
5 rooms.
🍽 **Austie's/The Elsinore €–€€**
Rosses Point Road, Rosses Point, 4 miles (6.5km) north-west) (tel: 071 917 7111).
Nautical-style pub restaurant over-looking Sligo Bay, with substantial pub food featuring local seafood, steaks and curry.
Daily 12.30–3, 5–8.45 (9.45pm Fri and Sat).
◇ **Clarion €€–€€€**
Ballinode (tel: 071 911 9000, fax: 071 911 9001).
Closed 24–26 Dec.
165 rooms.
🍽 **Crazy Jane's €**
Rockwood Parade (tel: 071 914 1976).
All-day breakfasts, pasta dishes, quiches, chicken supreme, snacks in a waterfront location.
Mon–Sat 9–6 (to 9pm Jun–Aug).
◇ **Radisson SAS Hotel and Spa Sligo €€**
Rosses Point Road, Ballincar (tel: 071 914 0008, fax: 071 914 0005).
132 rooms.
◇ **Sligo Park Hotel €€–€€€€**
Pearse Road (tel: 071 9190400, fax: 071 916 9556).
137 rooms.

LISSADELL, Co Sligo
◇ **Rowanville Lodge €€**
1 mile (1.5km) north of Grange on the N15 (tel: 071 916 3958).
Closed Nov–Apr.
3 rooms.

BUNDORAN, Co Sligo
◇ **Dùn Na Si €€€**
Bundoran Road, Ballyshannon (7 miles/11km northeast on the N15) (tel: 071 985 2322).
7 rooms.

TOUR 17
CARRICK-ON-SHAN-NON, Co Leitrim
◇ **Caldra House €€**
Caldragh, 1.5 miles (2.5km) north off the R280) (tel: 071 962 3040, fax: 071 962 3040).
3 rooms.
◇ **The Landmark Hotel €€€**
(tel: 071 962 2222, fax: 071 962 2233).
Closed 24–25 Dec.
50 rooms.

LONGFORD, Co Longford
◇ **Longford Country House €–€€€**
Ennybegs (tel: 043 23320, fax: 043 23516).
6 rooms.

ROSSCOMMON, Co Roscommon
◇ **Gleesons Townhouse €€**
Market Square (tel: 090 662 6954, fax: 090 662 7425).
19 rooms.

TOUR 18
WESTPORT, Co Mayo
◇ **Augusta Lodge €€**
Golf Links Road (tel: 098 28900, fax: 098 28995).
10 rooms.
🍽 **Bella Vita €€–€€€**
High Street (tel: 098 29771).
Cosy, friendly Italian wine bar/restaurant with great antipasti.
Tue–Sun 6–10pm.
◇ **Bertra House €**
Thornhill, Murrisk (southwest on R335 Louisburgh road) (tel: 098 64833, fax: 098 64833).
5 rooms.
◇🍽 **Carlton Atlantic Coast Hotel €€**
The Quay (tel: 098 29000, fax: 098 29111).
Closed 23–27 Dec.
85 rooms.
Modern international cuisine might include pan-roasted five-spice duck or black pudding stuffed guinea fowl supreme (€€€).
Daily 6.30–9.15pm.
◇ **Carrabaun House €**
Carrabaun, Leenane Road (tel: 098 26196, fax: 098 28466).
Closed 16–31 Dec.
6 rooms.

◇ **Hotel Westport Conference and Leisure Centre €€–€€€**
Newport Road (tel: 098 25122, fax: 098 26739).
129 rooms.
◇ **Knockranny House €€€**
Knockranny (tel: 098 28600, fax: 098 28611).
Closed 24–26 Dec.
97 rooms.
🍽 **Lemon Peel €–€€**
The Asgard, The Quay (tel: 098 26929).
Smart bistro serving tasty modern Irish cuisine with some international elements (Cajun crusted salmon; pork in black bean sauce on Chinese noodles).
Tue–Sat 6–9.30pm, Sun 6–9pm.
◇🍽 **The Olde Railway €€–€€€**
The Mall (tel: 098 25166 or 25606, fax: 098 25090).
24 rooms.
Simple but excellent food showing classic and traditional Irish roots. Fresh local lobster is a speciality (€€€).
Daily 6.30–9.30pm.
🍽 **Quay Cottage €€–€€€**
The Quay (tel: 098 26412).
Fresh, succulent fish, including wild local salmon, plus steaks and other daily specials.
Daily 6–10pm. Closed Sun & Mon Nov–Apr.
◇ **Park Inn Hotel €€€**
(tel: 098 36000, fax: 098 36899).
Closed 24–26 Dec.
61 rooms.
◇ **The Wyatt €€–€€€**
The Octagon (tel: 098 25027, fax: 098 26316).
Closed 25–26 Dec.
52 rooms.

ACHILL ISLAND, Co Mayo
◇ **Achill Cliff House €€**
Keel (tel: 098 43400, fax: 098 43007).
Closed 23–26 Dec.
10 rooms.
◇ **Fincorry House €**
Bleanaskill Bay, Atlantic Drive (tel: 098 45755 or 086 304 8039, fax: 098 45755).
Closed Nov–Feb.
6 rooms.

◇ **Gray's** €€
Dugort (tel: 98 43244 or 43315).
Closed 25 Dec–1 Jan.
15 rooms.
◇ **Lavelles Seaside House**
€–€€
Dooega (tel: 098 45116 or 01 282 8142).
Closed 2 Nov to mid-Mar.
14 rooms.

BALLINA Co Mayo
◇ ⦿ **Teach Iorrais** €€
Creesala (tel: 097 86888, fax: 097 86855).
31 rooms.
Modern European dishes, including pan-fried breast of duck with vanilla mash. Try the wonderful parsnip ice cream (€€€).
Daily 7–10pm.

KNOCK, Co Mayo
◇ **Belmont** €€–€€€
On the N17 Galway road (tel: 094 938 8122, fax: 094 938 8532).
Closed 25–26 Dec.
63 rooms.
◇ **Knock House Hotel**
€€–€€€
Ballyhaunis Road (tel: 094 938 8088, fax: 094 938 8044).
68 rooms.

TOUR 19
GALWAY, Co Galway
◇ **Almara House** €–€€
2 Merlin Gate, Merlin Park, Dublin Road (tel: 091 755345 or 086 245 1220, fax: 091 771585).
Closed 20–30 Dec.
4 rooms.
◇ **Ardawn House** €€
31 College Road (tel: 091 568833 or 564551, fax: 091 563454).
Closed 21–26 Dec.
8 rooms.
◇ **Ardilaun Hotel Club**
€€€–€€€€
Taylor's Hill (tel: 091 521433, fax: 091 521546).
Closed 24–26 Dec.
125 rooms.
◇ **Atlantic Heights** €€
2 Cashelmara, Knocknacarra Cross, Salthill (tel: 091 529466 or 528830.
Closed Nov–Mar.
6 rooms.

⦿ **The Cobblestone** €
Kirwan's Lane (tel: 091 567227).
Excellent vegetarian dishes, such as 'beanie shepherd's pie' or vegetable-and-walnut bake, plus some meat and fish dishes, and great baked goods.
Daily 9–7.
◇ **The Four Seasons** €–€€
23 College Road (tel: 091 564078, fax: 091 569765).
7 rooms.
◇ ⦿ **Galway Bay Hotel Conference and Leisure Centre** €€€
The Promenade, Salthill (tel: 091 520520, fax: 091 520530).
153 rooms.
Fresh fish majors on the modern French menu, and lobster is the signature dish (€€€).
Daily 6.30–9.30pm, also 12.30–2.30pm Sun.
◇ **Glenlo Abbey Hotel**
€€€–€€€€
Bushypark (tel: 091 526666, fax: 091 527800).
Closed 24–28 Dec.
46 rooms.
◇ **The Harbour** €€
New Dock Road (tel: 091 569466, fax: 091 569455).
Closed 23–27 Dec.
96 rooms.
◇ **The House Hotel** €€–€€€€
Lower Merchants Road (tel: 091 538900, fax: 091 568262).
40 rooms.
◇ **Jurys Galway Inn** €€
Quay Street (tel: 091 566444, fax: 091 568415).
Closed 24–26 Dec.
132 rooms.
◇ **Killeen House** €€–€€€
Killeen, Bushypark (on N59 towards Moycullen) (tel: 091 524179, fax: 091 528065).
Closed 23–28 Dec.
6 rooms.
⦿ **Kirwan's Lane** €€–€€€
Kirwan's Lane (tel: 091 568266).
One of Galway's best restaurants, offering a continental menu, including a superb mille-feuille of fresh crab and such meat dishes as stuffed guinea fowl.
Daily 12.30–2.30, 6–10.30. Closed Sun Sep–Jun.

◇ **Marian Lodge** €–€€
Knocknacarra Road, Salthill Upper (tel: 091 521678, fax: 091 528103).
Closed 23–28 Dec.
6 rooms.
◇ **Menlo Park Hotel** €€–€€€
Terryland (tel: 091 761122, fax: 091 761222).
Closed 24–25 Dec.
64 rooms.
⦿ **Nimmo's** €€
Long Walk, Spanish Arch (tel: 091 561114).
Trendy wine bar with seasonally changing menu.
Tue–Sun 12.30–3, 7–10.
◇ **Oranmore Lodge** €€–€€€
Oranmore (tel: 091 794400, fax: 091 790227).
Closed 22–27 Dec.
56 rooms.
◇ ⦿ **Park House Hotel and Park Room Restaurant**
€€–€€€€
Forster Street, Eyre Square (tel: 091 564924, fax: 091 569219).
Closed 24–26 Dec.
84 rooms.
Wide choice of dishes that are traditional, but not old-fashioned. Plenty of seafood (€€€).
Daily 6–10, Sun–Fri 12.30–2.30.
◇ ⦿ **Radisson SAS Hotel**
€€€–€€€€
Lough Atalia Road (tel: 091 538300, fax: 091 538380).
238 rooms.
Modern European menu features a different chef de partie each month (€€€).
Daily 6–10.30pm, also 12.30–3pm Sun.
⦿ **River God Café** €–€€
Quay Street (tel: 091 565811).
Satisfying comfort food, such as Connemara casserole of cod and potatoes.
Daily 5–10.30pm.
◇ **Victoria** €€
Victoria Place (tel: 091 567433, fax: 091 565880).
Closed 25 Dec.
57 rooms.
◇ **Westwood House Hotel**
€€–€€€
Dangan, Upper Newcastle, on the N6 (tel: 091 521442, fax: 091 521400).
Closed 24–25 Dec.
58 rooms.

CARNA, Co Galway

◇ **Carna Bay Hotel** €€–€€€
On the R340 (tel: 095 32255, fax: 095 32530).
Closed 23–26 Dec.
26 rooms.

◇ **Cashel House** €€€
Cashel, 8 miles (13km) beyond Carna on the R342 (tel: 095 31001, fax: 095 31077).
Closed 4 Jan–4 Feb.
32 rooms.

◇ **Hillside House B&B** €€
Kylesalia, Kilkieran, 5 miles (8km) east of Carna on the R340) (tel: 095 33420, fax: 095 33624).
Closed Oct–Mar.
4 rooms.

◇ **Zetland Country House** €€€–€€€€
Cashel Bay, 8 miles (13km) beyond Carna on the R342 (tel: 095 31111, fax: 095 31117).
Closed Nov–9 Apr.
19 rooms.

ROUNDSTONE, Co Galway

◇ ⌑ **Eldons** €€
On the main street (tel: 095 35933, fax: 095 35722).
Closed 4 Nov–16 Mar.
19 rooms.
Fish predominates on the menu, with chicken and steak dishes as an alternative – all accurately cooked with clear flavours.
Daily 6.30–9.30pm.

◇ **Ivy Rock House** €
Letterdyfe (tel: 095 35872, fax: 095 35959).
Closed Oct–Mar.
6 rooms.

⌑ **O'Dowd's Seafood Restaurant** €–€€
Roundstone Harbour (tel: 095 35809).
Traditional restaurant serving wonderful seafood, including chowder, crab claws in garlic butter, whole lobster, and fishermen's platters.
Easter to mid-Oct daily noon–10.

CLIFDEN, Co Galway

◇ **Abbeyglen Castle** €€€–€€€€
Sky Road (tel: 095 21201, fax: 095 21797).
Closed 6 Jan–1Feb.
45 rooms.

◇ ⌑ **Alcock and Brown Hotel** €€–€€€
Town centre (tel: 095 21206 or 21086, fax: 095 21842).
Closed 19–26 Dec.
19 rooms.
Plenty of fish from the local harbour on a menu of Irish cuisine with strong international influences (€€€).
Daily, lunch from 12.30, dinner from 6pm.

◇ ⌑ **Ardagh Hotel and Restaurant** €€€
Ballyconneely Road (tel: 095 21384, fax: 095 21314).
Closed Nov–Mar.
19 rooms.
Modern cuisine features some inspired combinations: pot-roast venison with sweet red cabbage, honey-roast monkfish on baby spinach, Thai-style mussels (€€€).
Daily 7.15–9.30pm.

◇ **Ardmore House** €–€€
Sky Road (tel: 095 21221, fax: 095 21100).
Closed Oct–Mar.
6 rooms.

◇ **Ben View House** €
Bridge Street (tel: 095 21256, fax: 095 21226).
10 rooms.

◇ **Buttermilk Lodge** €–€€
Westport Road (tel: 095 21951, fax: 095 21953).
Closed 3 Jan–10 Feb.
11 rooms.

◇ **Byrne Mal Dua House** €€–€€€
Galway Road (tel: 095 21171 or 0800 904 7532, fax: 095 21739).
14 rooms.

◇ **Dan O'Hara's Farmhouse** €
Lettershea, 5 miles (8km) east on the N59 (tel: 095 21246 or 21808, fax: 095 22098).
Closed Nov–Mar.
4 rooms.

◇ **Faul House** €
On the Ballyconneely road (tel: 095 21239, fax: 095 21998).
6 rooms.

◇ **Mallmore House** €
Ballyconneely Road (tel: 095 21460).
Closed Oct to mid-Mar.
6 rooms.

◇ ⌑ **Rock Glen Country House Hotel** €€€
1.5 miles (2km) from town (tel: 095 21035, fax: 095 21737).
Closed mid-Nov to mid-Feb, but open New Year.
26 rooms.
Lavishly furnished scenic restaurant serving intricate, creative Irish dishes with strong hints of Pacific Rim and French cuisine (€€).
Daily 7–9pm.

⌑ **The Signal** €€
Rear of Station House Hotel, on the N59 (tel: 095 22946).
Modern continental cuisine with plenty of originality and rich flavours, such as blackened turbot with smoked oysters.
May–Sep Wed–Sun 6–9.30pm.

⌑ **Two Dog Café** €
Church Street (tel: 095 22186).
Internet café serving wholesome soups, salads, baguettes and pastries with Italian coffee.

KYLEMORE ABBEY, Co Galway

◇ **Kylemore House** €€
On the shore of Lake Kylemore (tel: 095 41143, fax: 095 41143).
Closed Nov–Feb.
6 rooms.

◇ ⌑ **Renvyle House Hotel** €–€€€
Renvyle, west off the N59 (tel: 095 43511, fax: 095 43515).
Closed 6 Jan–14 Feb.
73 rooms.
Unusual combinations with clear flavours distinguish the menu here, including perfectly roasted monkfish (€€).
Daily 7–9pm.

LEENAUN, Co Galway

◇ **Leenane Hotel** €€
Killary Harbour (tel: 095 42249, fax: 095 42376).
34 rooms.

OUGHTERARD, Co Galway

◇ **The Boat Inn** €€
Village centre (tel: 091 552196, fax: 091 552694).
Closed 25 Dec.
11 rooms.

◇ **Midsummer Lake House House** €€
Portcarron Bay, off the N59 (tel: 091 552121 or 552146, fax: 091 552146).
Closed 10 Dec–16 Jan.
9 rooms.

◇ **Waterfall Lodge** €€
On the N59 (tel: 091 552168).
6 rooms.

TOUR 20
LONDONDERRY, Co Londonderry

◎ **Badger's** £
16–18 Orchard Street (tel: 028 7136 0763).
Cosy pub serving hot sandwiches ('damper melts') and such dishes as steak and Guinness casserole. Mon–Thu noon–6pm, Fri–Sat noon–9pm, Sun noon–4pm.

◇ **Beech Hill Country House** ££
32 Ardmore Road (tel: 028 7134 9279 fax: 028 7134 5366).
Closed 24–25 Dec.
27 rooms.

◎ **Brown's Bar & Brasserie** ££
1–2 Bond's Hill, Waterside (tel: 028 7134 5180).
Serves some of the best food in the city. Modern Irish cuisine blends with Italian and Thai. Tue–Fri noon–2.30, 5.30–10, Sat 5.30–10.30.

◇ **City Hotel** ££
Queen's Quay (tel: 028 7136 5800, fax: 028 7136 5801).
Closed 25 Dec.
145 rooms.

◇ **Clarence House** £
15 Northland Road (tel: 028 7126 5342, fax: 028 7126 5377).
9 rooms.

◇ **Quality Hotel Davincis** ££
15 Culmore Road (tel: 028 7127 9111, fax: 028 7127 9222).
Closed 25 Dec.
67 rooms.

◇◎ **Tower Hotel Derry** ££
Off the Diamond (tel: 028 7137 1000, fax: 028 7137 1234).
Closed 24–27 Dec.
93 rooms.
Modern menu inspired by Mediterranean and Pacific Rim cuisine (£). Daily 12.30–2.30pm, dinner from 6pm. Closed Christmas.

◇ **White Horse** ££
68 Clooney Road, Campsie (tel: 028 7186 0606, fax: 028 7186 0371).
57 rooms.

LETTERKENNY, Co Donegal
◇ **Ballyraine Guest House** £
Ramelton Road (tel: 074 912 4460 or 912 0851, fax: 074 912 0851).
8 rooms.

◇ **Downings Bay Hotel** ££
Downings (tel: 074 915 5586 or 915 5570, fax: 074 915 4716).
Closed 25 Dec.
40 rooms.

◇ **Mount Errigal** £££
Derry Road, Ballyraine (tel: 074 912 2700, fax: 074 912 5085).
82 rooms.

DUNFANAGHY, Co Donegal
◇ **Arnolds** €€–€€€
(tel: 074 913 6208, fax: 074 913 6352).
Closed Nov to mid-Mar.
30 rooms.

TOUR 21
LARNE, Co Antrim
◇ **Derrin** £
Prince's Gardens (tel: 028 2827 3269, fax: 028 2827 3269).
Closed 25–26 Dec.
7 rooms.

◇ **Manor** £
23 Oder Fleet Road, Harbour Highway (tel: 028 2827 3305, fax: 028 2826 0505).
Closed 25–26 Dec.
8 rooms.

CARNLOUGH, Co Antrim
◇ **Londonderry Arms** ££–£££
20 Harbour Road (tel: 028 2888 5255, fax: 028 2888 5263).
Closed Christmas.
35 rooms.

GLENARIFF, Co Antrim
◇ **Sanda** £
29 Kilmore Road (tel: 028 2177 1785).
2 rooms.

CUSHENDALL, Co Antrim
◇ **The Meadows** £
81 Coast Road (tel: 028 2177 2020).
6 rooms.

CUSHENDUN, Co Antrim
◇ **Drumkeerin** £
201A Torr Road (tel: 028 2176 1554, fax: 028 2176 1556).
3 rooms.

◇ **The Villa Farm House** £
185 Torr Road (tel: 028 2176 1252, fax: 028 2176 1252).
3 rooms.

BALLYCASTLE, Co Antrim
◇ **Marine** £–££
3 North Street (tel: 028 2076 2222, fax: 028 7076 9507).
30 rooms.

GIANT'S CAUSEWAY
Co Antrim
◎ **Smuggler's Inn** £–££
306 Whitepark Road, opposite entrance to Giant's Causeway (tel: 028 2073 1577).
Local ingredients, such as salmon, duck and game, are matched with creative sauces. Daily noon–2.30, 4–9.

BUSHMILLS, Co Antrim
◇ **Bayview** ££–£££
2 Bayhead Road, Portballintrae (north off A2) (tel: 028 2073 4100, fax: 028 2073 4330).
25 rooms.

◇ **Bushmills Inn** ££–££££
9 Dunluce Road (tel: 028 2073 3000, fax: 028 2073 2048).
32 rooms.

◇ **Whitepark House** ££
150 Whitepark Road, Balleycastle, east on the A2 (tel: 028 2073 1482).
3 rooms.

PORTRUSH, Co Antrim
◇ **Beulah Guest House** £–££
16 Causeway Street (tel: 028 7082 2413, fax: 028 7082 5900).
Closed 25–26 Dec.
9 rooms.

◎ **Café in the Centre** £
Dunluce Avenue (tel: 028 7082 4444)
Sandwiches, salads, omelettes and steaks are on the menu here, alongside the famous Ulster Fry. Jul–Aug daily 10–8, Easter–Jun and Sep daily noon–5, Oct Sat–Sun noon–5. Closed Nov–Easter.

◊ **Harbour Heights ££**
17 Kerr Street (tel: 028 7082
2765, fax: 028 7082 2558).
10 rooms.

◊ **Magherabuoy House
££–£££**
41 Magheraboy Road (tel: 028
7082 3507, fax: 028 7082 4687).
40 rooms.

◊ **Ramore £££**
6 The Harbour Road, (tel: 028
7082 4313).
*Pacific rim dishes encapsulate fresh,
vibrant flavours.*
*Daily 12.15–2.15, 5–10. Closed
25 Dec.*

◊ **Royal Court Hotel ££–£££**
Whiterocks (tel: 028 7082 2236,
fax: 028 7082 3176).
Closed 26 Dec.
18 rooms.

LIMAVADY, Co Londonderry
◊ **Gorteen House £–££**
Deerpark, Roemill Road
(tel: 028 7772 2333, fax: 028 7772
2333).
Closed 25 Dec.
26 rooms.

🍽 **The Lime Tree ££**
60 Catherine Street (tel: 028
7776 4300).
*Down-to-earth neighbourhood
restaurant serving generous portions
of excellent traditional Irish dishes.*
Tue–Sat 6–9pm.

◊ **Radisson SAS Roe Park
Resort £££**
1 mile (1.5km) outside the town
on the A2 (tel: 028 7772 2222,
fax: 028 7772 2313).
118 rooms.

BALLYMENA, Co Antrim
◊ **Galgorm Resort & Spa
£££**
1 mile (1.5km) outside
Ballymena on the A42, between
Galgorm and Cullybacky
(tel: 028 2588 1001, fax: 028 2588
0080).
75 rooms

**TOUR 22
BELFAST**
🍽 **Aldens ££**
229 Upper Newtownards Road
(tel: 028 9065 0079).
*Modern European cuisine in a chic
modern restaurant.*
*Mon–Fri noon–2.30pm, Mon–Sat
6–10pm. Closed Sun.*

◊ **Ash Rowan ££**
12 Windsor Avenue, between
Lisburn and Malone roads
(tel: 028 9066 1758, fax: 028 9066
3227).
5 rooms.

🍽 **Beatrice Kennedy ££**
44 University Road (tel: 028
9020 2290).
*Eclectic menu in Parisian brasserie-
style surroundings.*
*Tue–Sat 5–10.30pm, Sun
12.30–2.30, 5–8.30. Closed Mon,
24–26 Dec, 1 Jan.*

🍽 **Bourbon £–££**
60 Great Victoria Street (tel: 028
9033 2121).
*Modern European food, with such
interesting dishes as cinnamon
braised pork belly and duck and
ham hock crubeens.*
*Mon–Fri noon–3pm, daily
5–11pm.*

🍽 **Cayenne ££**
7 Ascot House, Shaftesbury
Square (tel: 028 9033 1532).
*Brash, lively restaurant of celebrity
chef, Paul Rankin, serving a mix
of Pacific, Oriental, Indian and
Mediterranean food.*
*Mon–Thu 6–10.15pm, Fri–Sat
6–11.15pm, Sun 5–8.45pm. Closed
25–26 Dec, 12 Jul.*

◊ **Crescent Townhouse
££–£££**
13 Lower Crescent (tel: 028
9032 3349, fax: 028 9032 0646).
*Closed 25–27 Dec, 1 Jan, part of
Jul.*
17 rooms.

◊ **Days Hotel Belfast £–££**
40 Hope Street Itel: 28 9024
2494, fax: 028 9024 2495).
250 rooms.

◊ **Jurys Inn Belfast ££**
Fisherwick Place, Great Victoria
Street (tel: 028 9053 3500,
fax: 028 9053 3511).
Closed 24–26 Dec.
190 rooms.

◊ **Malmaison Belfast £££**
34–38 Victoria Street (tel: 028
9022 0200).
64 rooms.

◊ **Malone Lodge Hotel £–££**
60 Eglantine Avenue (tel: 028
9038 8000, fax: 028 9038 8088).
51 rooms.

🍽 **Metro £–££**
13 Lower Crescent (tel: 028
9032 3349).
*Modern brasserie with casual
atmosphere and conttemporay
cooking.*
Daily 5.45–10pm.

🍽 **Nick's Warehouse £–££**
35–39 Hill Street (tel: 028 9043
9690).
*Trendy converted warehouse offering
hearty food with world-wide origins,
from Scandinavia to the
Mediterranean.*
*Mon–Fri noon–2.30, 6–9.30,
Sat 6–9.30pm.*

◊ **Ramada Belfast ££–£££**
117 Milltown Road, Shaws
Bridge (tel: 028 9092 3500,
fax: 028 9092 3600).
120 rooms.

🍽 **Restaurant Michael
Deane ££–£££**
38–40 Howard Street (tel: 028
9033 1134).
*Celebrity chef Deane maintains a
hands-on presence here, providing
accomplished renditions of modern
British and Irish dishes. Fine dining
upstairs; more relaxed brasserie
downstairs.*
*Mon–Sat noon–3, 5.30–9.30.
Closed Sun–Tue, Christmas, New
Year, Easter, 2 weeks Jul.*

🍽 **Shu £££**
253 Lisburn Road (tel: 028 9038
1655).
*Trendy eatery for discerning
gourmets, offering a globetrotting
menu of stylishly presented food.*
*Mon–Sat 12.30–2.30, 6–9.30.
Closed Sun, 24–26 Dec, 12–14 Jul.*

◊ **Tara Lodge ££**
36 Cromwell Road (tel: 028 9059
0900, fax: 028 9059 0901).
Closed 25–29 Dec, 9–14 Jul.
19 rooms.

◊ **TENsq £££**
10 Donegall Square (tel: 028
9024 1001, fax: 028 9024 3210).
22 rooms.

CULTRA, Co Down
♦️🍽 **Clandeboye Lodge Hotel ££–£££**
10 Estate Road, Clandeboye, southeast via theA2 and B170 (tel: 028 9185 2500, fax: 028 9185 2772).
Closed 25–26 Dec.
43 rooms.
In woodland surroundings, this hotel restaurant serves seasonally inspired modern classics (££).
Daily noon–2.30, 6.30–9.30.
🍽 **The Old Inn £££**
15 Main Street, Crawfordsburn, east off the A2 (tel: 028 9185 3255).
Modern British dishes, such as gratin of Dublin Bay prawns, pan-fried Ulster beef with red wine, and Finnebrogue venison with sweet potato.
Daily 12.30–2.30, 7–9.30. Closed 25 Dec.
🍽 **Shanks £££**
The Blackwood, Crawfordsburn (east off A2) (tel: 028 9185 3313).
Award-winning restaurant offering essentially classical cooking with restrained international influences; exceptional seafood.
Tue–Fri lunch and dinner, Sat dinner only. Closed Sun–Mon, 25–26 Dec, Easter Tue and 2 weeks mid-Jul.

NEWTOWNARDS, Co Down
♦️ **Ballynester House £**
1a Cardy Road, off the Mount Stewart Road, Greyabbey (tel: 028 4278 8386, fax: 028 4278 8986).
3 rooms.
♦️ **Edenvale House ££**
130 Portaferry Road (tel: 028 9181 4881, fax: 028 9182 6192).
Closed 24–26 Dec.
3 rooms.

PORTAFERRY, Co Down
♦️ **The Narrows £££**
8 Shore Road (tel: 028 4272 8148, fax: 028 4727 8105).
13 rooms.
♦️ **Portaferry £££**
10 The Strand (tel: 028 4272 8231, fax: 028 4272 8999).
Closed 24–25 Dec.
14 rooms.

TOUR 23
ENNISKILLEN, Co Fermanagh
♦️ **Dromard House £**
Tamlaght, 3 miles (5km) east on the A4 (tel: 028 6638 7250).
Closed 24–26 Dec.
4 rooms.
♦️ **Killyhevlin £££**
2 miles (3km) south off the A4 (tel: 028 6632 3481; fax: 028 6632 4726).
Closed 24–25 Dec.
70 rooms.
♦️ **Willowbank House £**
60 Bellevue Road (tel: 028 6632 8582, fax: 028 6632 8582).
Closed Christmas.
5 rooms.

FLORENCE COURT, Co Fermanagh
♦️ **Arch House Tullyhona Farm £–££**
Marble Arch Road, Florencecourt (tel: 028 6634 8452, fax: 028 6634 8452).
6 rooms.

TOUR 24
ARMAGH, Co Armagh
♦️ **Charlemont Arms Hotel ££**
57–65 English Street (tel: 028 3752 2028, fax: 028 3752 6979).
Closed 25–26 Dec.
30 rooms.

DUNGANNON, Co Tyrone
♦️ **Cohannon Inn £–££**
212 Ballynakilly Road (tel: 028 8772 4488, fax 028 8775 2217).
42 rooms.
♦️ **Grange Lodge ££**
7 Grange Road (tel: 028 8778 4212, fax: 028 8778 4313).
Closed 21 Dec–9 Jan.
5 rooms.
♦️ **Millbrook Bed and Breakfast £**
46 Moy Road (tel: 028 8772 3715).
3 rooms.

OMAGH, Co Tyrone
🍽 **Hawthorn House ££**
72, Old Mountfield Road (tel: 028 8225 2005, fax: 028 8225 2005).
Exciting contemporary cooking and innovative seafood dishes.
Daily, lunch from noon, dinner from 7pm.

TOUR 25
CASTLEWELLAN, Co Down
♦️ **Slieve Croob Inn ££**
119 Clonvaraghan Road, 1 mile (1.5km) from town on the A25 (tel: 028 4377 1412, fax: 028 4377 1162).
7 rooms.

NEWCASTLE, Co Down
♦️ **Briers Country House £**
39 Middle Tollymore Road, off the B180 (tel: 028 4372 4347, fax: 028 4372 6633).
8 rooms.
♦️ **Burrendale Hotel and Country Club £££**
51 Castlewellan Road (tel: 028 4372 2599, fax: 028 4372 2328).
69 rooms.
♦️ **Enniskeen House ££**
98 Bryansford Road (tel: 028 4372 2392, fax: 028 4372 4084).
Closed 12 Nov–14 Mar.
12 rooms.
♦️ **Grasmere £**
16 Marguerite Park, Bryansford Road (tel: 028 4372 6801; fax: 028 4372 6801).
3 rooms.
♦️ **Slieve Donard ££**
Downs Road (tel: 028 4372 1066. 028 4372 4830).
130 rooms.

ANNALONG, Co Down
♦️ **Glassdrumman Lodge £££**
85 Mill Road (tel: 028 4376 8451, fax: 028 4376 7041).
10 rooms.

WARRENPOINT, Co Down
🍽 **The Duke ££**
7 Duke Street, above the Duke Bar (tel: 028 4175 2084).
Creative cooking here has won critical acclaim for such dishes as seared chilli beef with crunchy vegetables and Thai rice and excellent seafood.
Tue–Sat 6–10, Sun 5.30–9.

FESTIVALS AND EVENTS

JANUARY
Funderland
This event beats the winter weather by constructing a temporary theme park inside the Royal Dublin Society, complete with white-knuckle rides, stalls and such entertainment as a high-wire motorcycle act.
Boxing Day to mid January.
For information: tel: 061 419 988; www.funfair.ie/www.rds.ie).

Yeats Winter School
The writer's home town, Sligo, plays host to this weekend of lectures and tours of the countryside that inspired his work.
Late January.
For information: tel: 071 9142693; www.yeats-sligo.com

FEBRUARY
Tradfest
University College Cork has a year-round society promoting Irish traditional music, and their annual festival features many of the best musicians in Ireland over five days of concerts, lectures, seminars and sessions.
Early February.
For information: tel: tel: 087 9209795 or 086 3753533; www.ucc.ie/tradmusic/tradfest.htm

Six Nations Rugby Tournament
The national teams of Ireland, England, Scotland, Wales, France and Italy compete at the 50,000-capacity Lansdowne Road rugby ground in Dublin, with its great atmosphere, and in the surrounding pubs.
Certain Saturdays, early February–April.
For information: tel: 01 668 4601; www.6-nations-rugby.com

Antiques and Collectibles Fair
Newman House, on St Stephen's Green, Dublin hosts this event, with antiques dealers specialising in small pieces and collectors' items.
Four Sundays in February.

For information: tel: 01 716 7422.

Jameson Dublin International Film Festival
Showcasing around a hundred full-length and short films from more than 30 countries.
Mid-February.
For information: tel: 01 661 6216; www.dublin.iff.com

MARCH
St Patrick's Day
The patron saint of Ireland is commemorated across the country on 17 March, and most major cities will have lively celebrations and perhaps a parade (see also St Patrick's Festival, below).

St Patrick's Festival
St Patrick's Day is celebrated throughout Ireland. Dublin's event stretches to a full-scale five-day festival with concerts, fireworks, street theatre and, of course, the St Patrick's Day Parade through the city.
Starts 16 March.
For information: tel: 01 676 3205; www.stpatricksday.ie

Limerick Spring Festival
A highlight of this lively festival is the International Marching Band Parade and Competition, with 20 or so bands from several countries taking part.
Mid- to late March.
For information: tel: 061 400255; www.limerickcityfestivals.com

Connemara Four Seasons Walking Festival
This is the springtime event – there are also summer, autumn and winter festivals, and all feature organised walks to explore Connemara and the Aran Islands. The festival is based at the Connemara Walking Centre in Clifden.
Late March.
For information: tel: 095 21492 or 21379; www.walkingireland.com

Wexford Book Festival
Six days of adults' and children's events, featuring the best of Irish and European authors, including a popular Sports Writers Night.
Late March.
For information: tel: 053 9122226; www.wexfordbook.com

Pan Celtic International Festival
Celebrating the music, dance and culture of the Celtic nations. Held in a different location each year.
March/April, during week after Easter.
For information: tel: 074 9723760; www.panceltic.ie

Titanic – Made in Belfast
A week-long festival recalling the positive aspects of the *Titanic* era in Belfast's shipyards and factories, including living history events, exhibitions, boat trips, talks, storytelling for children, concerts and a memorial service for those who died when *Titanic* sank.
Late March–early April.
For information: www.titanic.com

Irish Grand National
The highlight of the Easter Festival at Fairyhouse racecourse is the Irish Grand National, the most valuable and prestigious National Hunt race in the country.
March or April, Easter weekend.
For information: tel: 01 825 6167; www.fairyhouseracecourse.ie

APRIL
Belfast Film Festival
Movies are screened over 11 days at this celebration of the moving image, with premieres, classics and short films.
Early April.
For information: tel: 028 9032 5913; www.belfastfilmfestival.org

Cork International Choral Festival

This four-day festival brings an international line-up of top quality choral music to the west of Ireland. Events include public performances, competitions, gala concerts, educational events in local schools and fringe events.
Late April–early May
For information: tel: 021 4215125; www.corkchoral.ie

MAY

Ballydehob International Jazz Festival

Devotees flock to this little West Cork town to enjoy Irish and other European jazz musicians over the four-day festival. In addition to concerts in various venues, there are music workshops and busking competitions for adults and children. A market lines the main street daily, adding to the festival spirit.
Early May.
For information: tel: 028 37663; wwwballydehobjazzfestival.com

Carlsberg Kilkenny Rhythm n' Roots Festival

A big line-up of bands from Ireland and America, playing blues, bluegrass, appalachian, cajun, country-rock and traditional Irish music.
Early May.
For information: tel: 056 779 4664; www.kilkennyroots.com

Cathedral Quarter Arts Festival

Cutting edge and culturally diverse events in and around Belfast's Cathedral Quarter cover performing and visual arts, with such innovative ideas as graffiti art and comic-book culture; Irish, world and rock music; plus world-class comedy, modern theatre and circus arts.
Early to mid-May.
For information: tel: 028 9023 2403; www.cqaf.com

Wicklow Gardens Festival

Co Wicklow is known as the 'Garden of Ireland', and this festival provides the chance for visitors to tour some private gardens in addition to those always open to the public. Around 40 gardens are involved.
Beginning of May to mid-August.
For information: tel: 0404 20070; www.wicklow.ie/tourism

Heineken Green Energy International Music Festival

Big names from the world of pop music feature in concerts at Dublin Castle.
Early May.
For information: tel: 01890 925100; www.heinekenmusic.ie

Belfast City Marathon

Celebrating its 27th year in 2006, this event attracts thousands of runners, and there's also a wheelchair event, a marathon walk, a relay race and a fun run.
Early May.
For information: tel: 028 2587 2828; www.belfastcity-marathon.com

Northwest 200

Motorcycle road race from Portrush to Portstewart along Co Antrim's country lanes – one of Northern Ireland's biggest sporting events, drawing an international crowd.
Mid- to late May.
For information: tel: 028 7035 5800; www.northwest200.org

Lord Mayor's Show

Marking the end of each Lord Mayor's term of office, there's a big parade through Belfast city centre, starting from Writer's Square.
21 May.
For information: tel: 028 9024 6609.

Galway Early Music Festival

Celebrating European music and dance of the 12th to 18th centuries, this four-day festival attracts the finest exponents from Ireland and elsewhere to the medieval streets of Galway city. There are concerts, workshops and masterclasses in medieval, renaissance and baroque music.
Mid to late May.
For information:
tel: 087 930 5506;
www.galwayearlymusic.com

Fleadh Nua

A week-long festival of traditional music and dancing, held in Ennis, Co Clare, including concerts, workshops, informal sessions, ceilis, exhibitions, lectures and film shows.
Late May.
For information: tel: 065 682 4276; www.fleadhnua.com

Wexford Opera Festival

Nearly 20 evening events and double that amount during the day, with performers from all over the world taking part in productions staged exclusively for the festival.
Late May–early June.
For information: tel: 053 22400; www.wexfordopera.com

JUNE

Dublin Writers Festival

Writers from many countries converge on Dublin for readings, discussions, lectures, music, film and children's events.
Mid-June.
For information: tel: 01 679 6622 or 670 7788; www.dublinwriters festival.com

Smithwick's Cat Laughs Comedy Festival

A front-runner for the title of best comedy festival in the world, held in Kilkenny, Co Kilkenny, featuring an international line-up of comedians in stand-up, skits, improv and film.
Early June.
For information: tel: 056 776 3837; www.smithwickscat laughs.com

Listowel Writers' Week

A lively literary festival drawing a number of internationally known writers to this Co Kerry town to give readings and talks, conduct workshops and launch new books. Also film and music events, competitions and children's events.
Early June.
For information: tel: 068 21074; www.writersweek.ie

Bloomsday

Dublin celebrates its James Joyce heritage by commemorating the 24 hours in the life of Leopold Bloom that are the subject of his *Ulysses*. There are special ceremonies at the Joyce Museum. Restaurants and pubs join in with their own festivities.
Mid-June.
For information: tel: 01 878 8547; www.jamesjoyce.ie

Budweiser Irish Derby

The most historic horse racing event of the year, held at Ireland's premier track, The Curragh in Co Kildare.
Late June.
For information: tel: 045 441205; www.curragh.ie

Strawberry Festival

A long-time favourite in the Co Wexford calendar, this festival features entertainment, arts and crafts, funfair, demonstrations and exhibitions… but, most of all, fresh strawberries in profusion.
Late June.
For information:
www.strawberryfestival.ie

Spancil Hill Fair

This is one of the oldest horse fairs in the country, and buyers come from around the world to check out as many as 2,000 horses up for sale. There's a famous traditional song about the event, near Ennis, Co Clare.
Late June.
For information: tel: 065 682 8366.

Drogheda Samba Festival

A carnival atmosphere prevails during this celebration of Brazilian dance, with dancing, international bands, street theatre and a parade.
Late June/early July.
For information: tel: 041 983 8332; www.solo.ie/samba/

JULY
Killarney Summerfest

A comprehensive range of family entertainments includes big-name stadium rock concerts, classical music, busking and other street entertainment, comedy, theatre and dance.
Early July.
For information: tel: 064 71560; www.killarneysummerfest.com

American Independence Celebrations

Ireland's strong links with the US are reflected in the existence of the Ulster American Folk Park and they celebrate the Fourth of July in style, with living history enactments, bluegrass, jazz and folk music and traditional American games.
2–4 July.
For information: tel: 028 8224 3292; www.folkpark.com

Clonmel Junction Festival

A mix of theatre, art, concerts and free daytime events.
Early to mid-July.
For information: tel: 052 29339; www.junctionfestival.com

Oxegen

A mammoth two-day rock music festival at Punchestown Racecourse, with five stages and more than 80 bands, including the biggest names of the moment.
Early July.
For information: www.oxegen.ie
Ticket hotline: 0818 719300 (Republic of Ireland) or 0870 243 4455 (Northern Ireland).

Hooves 'n' Grooves Festival

Exactly what it sounds like, this festival features horseracing and music – a perfect combination for the Irish in particular. As well as harness racing and masses of gigs, there's street theatre, street markets and water sports.
Early July.
For information: tel: 053 52900 (Wexford Tourism); www.hoovesandgrooves.com

Battle of the Boyne Commemoration

In Belfast and other cities of Northern Ireland, the Protestant community remembers the historic battle with parades and other celebrations. It's also known as Orangemen's Day.
12 July.

For information: tel: 028 9032 2801.

Volvo Dun Laoghaire Regatta

This biennial event (in odd-numbered years) is Ireland's largest regatta, featuring four days of racing within the region in many classes.
Mid-July.
For information: tel: 01 280 1881; www.dlregatta.org

Galway Arts Festival

Hailed as Ireland's biggest and most exciting arts festival, this is a two-week event covering both visual and performing arts.
Mid- to late July.
For information: tel: 091 509700; www.galwayartsfestival.com

Rose Week

A fragrant festival in which rose breeders from across the globe submit entries for judging at Sir Thomas and Lady Dixon Park in Belfast. In addition to the flowers and garden walks, there are plant and craft stalls and entertainment.
Mid- to late July.
For information: tel: 028 9032 0202.

Croagh Patrick Pilgrimage

More than 25,000 pilgrims climb Ireland's holy mountain to honour the patron saint.
Last Sunday in July.
For information: tel: 098 64114; www.croagh-patrick.com

Galway Races

The summer festival meeting is one of the great events of the social calendar, with much more going on than horse racing.
Late July/early August.
For information: tel: 091 753870; www.galwayraces.com

Lughnasa Fair

A medieval extravaganza, based at the great waterfront castle at Carrickfergus, Co Antrim, with traditional food and entertainment, crafts, medieval games and participants in medieval costume.
Late July.

For information: tel: 028 4336 6455.

Belfast Pride
A week of parties, drama, music, dance and other evens culminates in a spectacular parade around the city centre, ending with a party in Writer's Square.
Late July/early August.
For information:
www.belfastpride.com

AUGUST
Dublin Horse Show
This event at the RDS is an acknowledgement of the Irish love of horses and a great social event. In addition to the show jumping and other competitions, there are lots of exhibitors, an arts and crafts exhibition, music and children's entertainment.
For information: tel: 01 240 7213; www.dublinhorseshow.com

Ballyshannon Music Festival
Ireland's oldest and biggest traditional music festival, attracting top bands and soloists.
Early August.
For information: tel: 086 2527400; www.ballyshannon folkfestival.com

Matchmaking Festival
Famous traditional festival (the original singles event) in the spa town of Lisdoonvarna, Co Clare, with music, dancing and perhaps romance.
Late August–early October.
For information: tel: 065 707 4005;
www.matchmakerireland.com

Baltimore Regatta
Waterborne events in Roaringwater Bay, Co Cork.
First Monday in August.
For information: www.baltimore-sailingclub.com

Puck Fair
Ancient festival honouring a goat that reputedly alerted the town of Killorglin to impending danger. There's music, theatre, a procession and a ceremony in which a goat is crowned.
10th–12 August.

For information: tel: 066 976 2366www.puckfair.ie

Kilkenny Arts Festival
A comprehensive festival of all the arts, including theatre and dance, visual arts, literature and all kinds of music – world, jazz, classical, traditional Irish.
Mid-August.
For information: tel: 056 775 2175 or 056 776 3663;
www.kilkennyarts.ie

Connemara Pony Show
The premier event (among several) that showcase the sturdy little breed of pony that originated in and still comes from Co Galway.
Mid-August.
For information: tel: 095 21863; www.cpbs.ie

Rose of Tralee Festival
Much more than just a beauty pageant, though entrants of Irish descent come to Tralee, Co Kerry, from across the globe to take part. Lots of other events and festivities.
Mid- to late August.
For information: www.roseoftr alee.ie

Fleadh Cheoil na hEireann
The grandaddy of all traditional music festivals in Ireland, at a different location each year.
Late Aug.
For information: tel: 074 912 5133.

Festival of World Cultures
Bringing internationally renowned performers of music, theatre, dance, circus and film together with local acts, amid a real carnival atmosphere in Dun Laoghaire, Co Dublin.
Late August.
For information: tel: 01 271 9555.

Ould Lammas Fair
Held in Ballycastle, on the north Co Anrim coast, this is one of the oldest fairs in Ireland, with a huge street market, various entertainments and the chance to try the local delicacies, such as dulce (edible seaweed) and

yellow man (a type of confectionery).
Last Monday and Tuesday in August.
For information: tel: 028 2076 2024 (Ballycastle Tourist Information Centre).

Appalachian & Bluegrass Music Festival
The Ulster American Folk Park in Co Tyrone stages this popular event, the largest of its kind in Europe, with musicians from North America and Europe.
Late August/early September.
For information: tel: 028 8224 3292; www.folkpark.com

SEPTEMBER
Clarenbridge Oyster Festival
Heralding the start of the oyster season in Co Galway, this is a nine-day feast of oysters (and other seafood) and entertainment.
Early September.
For information: 091 796 6766; www.clarenbridge.com

Cork Art Fair
Cork's City Hall plays host to a contemporary art fair featuring original paintings and sculptures by Irish and foreign artists.
Late September.
For information: tel: 01 499 2244 or 087 617 5418; www.corkart fair.com

Heritage Week
Ireland's contribution to European Heritage Days consists of a week of nationwide events at various historic properties, parks and gardens and other venues. Sunday events are usually free of charge.
Early to mid-September.
For information: tel: 056 7770777; www.heritageweek.ie or contact local tourist offices.

All-Ireland Hurling and Gaelic Football Finals
Two of Ireland's best-loved sports reach their annual pinnacle at Croke Park in Dublin. It's comparable to the Super Bowl and if you can't get tickets, soak up the atmosphere in a pub.

*Hurling Final, early September;
Gaelic Football, mid-September.*
For information: tel: 01 836
3222; www.gaa.ie

Cape Clear International Storytelling Festival

An ancient art form is kept alive
at this lively event on Cape
Clear Island, Co Cork, proving
conclusively that the Irish really
do have a way with words.
For information: tel: 028 39116;
http://indigo.ie/~stories/

Blackstairs Blues Festival

Enniscorthy, Co Wexford, is
jumping during this festival,
which features a good range of
blues, from acoustic guitar and
harmonica duos to big bands.
Mid-September.
For information: tel: 087 622
1589; www.blackstairsblues.com

Galway Art Fair

Brings together exhibitions from
around 40 Irish and foreign
artists and galleries, totalling
thousands of original art works
to see and buy, hosted by the
Corrib Great Southern, Galway.
Late September.
For information: tel: 01 499 2244
or 087 617 5418;
www.galwayartfair.com

Galway International Oyster Festival

Parties, parades, concerts,
beauty contests, the World
Oyster Opening Champion-
ships, and lots of oyster-eating
and Guinness-drinking.
Late September.
For information: tel: 091 522066;
www.galwayoysterfest.com

Dublin Theatre Festival

Features the best of Irish and
international drama, including
classics and new works, staged
by every major Irish company.
Late September to mid-October.
For information: tel: 01 677
8439, www.dublintheatre
festival.com

Ballinasloe Horse Fair

Originating in 1700, this is one of
the oldest Horse Fairs in
Europe.

Late September/early October.
For information: tel: 0909
644793 www.ballinasloe.com

OCTOBER
Kinsale International Gourmet Festival

The village of Kinsale, Co Cork,
has a reputation for good eating
all year round, culminating in
this culinary celebration.
Early October.
For information: tel: 021 477
2847;
www.kinsalerestaurants.com

Cork Film Festival

Running for more than 50 years,
this festival is internationally
renowned for is eclectic mix of
screenings and events, including
short films, blockbusters, independent and foreign-language
films and documentaries.
Mid-October.
For information: tel: 021 427
1711; www.corkfilmfest.org

Ideal Homes Exhibition

A showcase for everything that's
new and exciting in home
design and lifestyle. Held at the
Royal Dublin Society's
Simonscourt Pavilion.
Late October.
For information: tel: 01 490
0600; www.idealhome.ie

Belfast Festival at Queens

Ireland's largest arts festival with
world-class concerts of all types
of music, dance, comedy, literature and visual arts.
Late October–early November.
For information: tel: 028 9097
1034; www.belfastfestival.com

Adidas Dublin Marathon

Dublin's Georgian streets are
thronged by enthusiastic crowds
cheering on the thousands of
runners in this long-established
event, which attracts serious
international athletes as well as
amateurs and celebrity fundrais-
ers. It's known world-wide as
'the friendly marathon'.
Late October.
For information: tel: 01 623
2250;
www.dublincitymarathon.ie

Guinness Jazz Festival

40,000 music fans gather in Cork
for Europe's friendliest jazz
festival, which features the
biggest international names over
a four-day period.
Late October.
For information: tel: 021 425
5100 (Cork Kerry Tourism);
www.corkjazzfestival.com

NOVEMBER
Patrick Kavanagh Weekend

Iniskeen, in Co Monaghan, was
the birthplace of Patrick
Kavanagh, one of Ireland's fore-
most literary figures. His body of
work is celebrated with this
weekend of readings, songs,
stories, walks and tours, and the
annual Patrick Kavanagh Poetry
Awards.
Late November.
For information: tel: 042 937
8560; www.patrickkavanagh-
country.com

DECEMBER
National Crafts Competition

Perfect for Christmas shopping,
this show brings together craftspeople and craft shops and
galleries from all over Ireland at
Dublin's RDS exhibition hall.
Early December.
For information: tel: 01 240
7255; www.rds.ie

Limerick Christmas Racing Festival

Three days of post-Christmas
horse-racing at Limerick
Racecourse.
26–28 December.
For information: tel: 061 320000;
www.limerick-racecourse.com

Leopardstown National Hunt Festival

Thoroughbred National Hunt
(over jumps) racing at
Leopardstown Racecourse, just
south of Dublin.
26–28 December.
For information: tel: 01 289
2888; www.leopardstown.com

PRACTICAL INFORMATION

TOUR INFORMATION

The addresses, telephone numbers and opening times of the attractions mentioned in the tours, including the telephone numbers of the Tourist Information Centres are listed below tour by tour.

TOUR 1

ⓘ Arthur's Row, Ennis.
Tel: 065 6828366.
ⓘ Cliffs of Moher.
Tel: 065 7081171.

Ennis
Riches of Clare Museum
Arthur's Row, Ennis, Co Clare. Tel: 065 6823382.
Open Jun–Sep, Mon–Sat 9.30–5, Sun 9.30–1; Oct–May, Tue–Sat. 9.30–1, 2–5
Ennis Friary
Ennis, Co Clare. Tel: 065 682 9100. *Open Jun to mid-Sep, daily 10–6, rest of year Tue–Sun 10–5*

⑤ Cliffs of Moher
O'Brien's Tower and New Visitor Experience
Liscannor, Co Clare.
Tel: 061 360788. *Open daily 9.30–5.30 (9–7 Jun–Aug)*

⑥ Kilfenora
The Burren Centre
Kilfenora, Co Clare.
Tel: 065 7088030. *Open mid-Mar to May, Sep–Oct, daily 10–5; Jun–Aug, daily 9–6; last tour half an hour before closing.*

⑦ Kinvarra
Dunguaire Castle
Kinvarra, Co Clare.
Tel: 091 637108. *Open May/Apr to Sep, daily 9.30–5; last admission 4.30pm.*

Thoor Ballylee
Gort, Co Galway. Tel: 091 631436. *Open Jun–Sep, daily 9.30–5.*

Coole Park & Visitor Centre
Coole, Gort, Co Galway.
Tel: 091 631804. *Open, park: all year daily; Visitor Centre: Apr–Sep, daily 10–5 (6 Jun–Aug). Last admission 4.45, last audio-visual show 4.*

⑧ Quin
Knappogue Castle
Quin, Co Clare.
Tel: 061 360788. *Open mid-Apr to mid-Oct, daily 9.30–5.15; last admission 4.30pm.*
Craggaunowen Project
Kilmurry, Sixmilebridge, Co Clare. Tel: 061 360788. *Open Apr–Oct, daily 10–6; last admission 5pm.*

⑨ Bunratty
Bunratty Castle and Folk Park
Bunratty, Co Clare.
Tel: 061 360788. *Telephone for opening times.*

Special to...
Castle Banquets and Traditional Irish Nights, Shannon Heritage, Bunratty Folk Park, Co Clare. Tel: 061 360788. *Times and seasons vary; call for information.*
Dromore Wood and Visitor Centre
Ruan, Ennis, Co Clare.
Tel: 065 6837166. *Open Visitor Centre daily 10–6; last admission 5.15pm; wood: all year, daylight hours.*

For children
Aillwee Cave
Ballyvaghan. Tel: 065 707 7036. *Open daily 10–6.30.*
Doolin Cave
Minibus pick-up from Bruach na nAille Restaurant in Doolin village, Co Clare. Tel: 065 707 5761. *Open Apr–Nov, daily 9–6.*

TOUR 2

ⓘ Arthur's Quay, Limerick. Tel: 061 317522.
ⓘ St John's Church, Listowel. Tel: 068 22590.
ⓘ Heritage Centre, Adare. Tel: 061 396255.

Limerick
The Georgian House
2 Pery Square, Limerick, Co Limerick, Tel: 061 314130. *Open Mon–Fri 10–4.30 or by appointment at weekends.*
The Hunt Museum
The Custom House, Rutland Street, Limerick, Co Limerick. Tel: 061 312833. *Open Mon–Sat 10–5, Sun 2–5.*
Askeaton
Celtic Park and Gardens
Kilcornan. Tel: 061 394243 *Open mid-Mar to mid-Oct, daily 9.30–6; other times by arrangement..*

⑤ Foynes
Flying Boat Museum
Foynes, Co Limerick.
Tel: 069 65416. *Open Mar–Sep, daily 10–6; Oct–Nov 10–4; last admission one hour before closing.*

⑤ Glin
Glin Castle and Gardens
Glin, Co Limerick.
Tel: 068 34173. *Open late Mar–Nov. Telephone for information.*

⑤ Newcastle West
Desmond Banqueting Hall
The Square. Tel: 069 77408. *Open mid-Jun to mid-Sep, daily 10–6; last admission 5.15.*

⑨ Rathkeale
Castle Matrix
Rathkeale, Co Limerick.
Tel: 087 792 1702. *Open Apr–Sep, Sat–Thu, (visitors are requested to telephone before visiting).*

⑩ Adare
Heritage Centre
Main Street, Adare, Co Limerick. Tel: 061 396666. *Open Apr–Sep, daily 9–6.*

For history buffs
King John's Castle
Limerick, Co Limerick.
Tel: 061 360788. *Open May–Oct, daily 9.30–5.30, Mar and Apr, 9.30–5; Nov–Feb, 10–4.30; last admission one hour before closing.*
Irish Palatine Heritage Centre
Rathkeale, Co Limerick.
Tel: 069 63511. *Open Jun–Sep, Mon–Sat 10–5, Sun 2–6, closed 12–2.*

TOUR 3

ⓘ Arthur's Quay, Limerick. Tel: 061 317522.
ⓘ Heritage Centre, Main Street, Cashel. Tel: 062 2511.
ⓘ Heritage Centre, Nenagh. Tel: 067 31610.
ⓘ Killaloe Heritage Centre, The Bridge, Killaloe. Tel: 061 376866.

② Cashel
Rock of Cashel
Cashel, Co Tipperary.
Tel: 062 61437. *Open daily, mid-Sep to mid-Mar, 9–4.30; mid-Jun to mid-Sep, 9–4.30; mid-Mar to mid-Jun, 9–5.30.*
Bru Boru Heritage Centre
Cashel, Co Tipperary.
Tel: 062 61122. *Open: centre daily, 9–5. Theatre Jun–Sep, Tue–Sat 9am–midnight, Sun–Mon 9–5.*

⑤ Thurles
Famine Museum
St Mary's Church, Thurles, Co Tipperary. Tel: 0504 21133. *Open May–Sep, daily 10–12.30, 1.30–5.*

Practical • Information

$\boxed{i}$ Tourist Information Centre
$\boxed{12}$ Number on tour

❹ Roscrea
Roscrea Heritage Centre and Damer House
Castle Street, Roscrea, Co Tipperary. Tel: 0505 21850. *Open Apr–Oct, daily, 10–6; last admission 5.15pm.*

❺ Nenagh
Nenagh District Heritage Centre
The Governor's House, Nenagh, Co Tipperary. Tel: 067 33850. *Open Mon–Fri 9.30–5, also Sat mid-May to mid-Sep; last admission 4.30.*

❻ Portumna
Portumna Castle
Portumna, Co Galway. Tel: 090 974 1658. *Open late Mar to mid-Apr, daily 10–5; mid-Apr to Oct, daily 10–6.*

❼ Mountshannon
Lough Derg Holy Island
Mountshannon, Co Clare. *Open daily. Tel: 061 921615 for boat trip.*

❽ Killaloe
Brian Boru Heritage Centre
Killaloe, Co Clare. Tel: 061 360788. *Open May–Sep, daily 10–6.*

Special to...
Bolton Library
Cashel, Co Tipperary. Tel: 062 62511. *Open May–Sep daily.*
Irish Seed Saver Association
Capparoe, Scariff, Co Clare (west of Scariff off A461). Tel: 061 921866. *Open Mon–Fri (with 24-hours notice).*

TOUR 4

$\boxed{i}$ Ashe Memorial Hall, Denny Street, Tralee. Tel: 066 7121288.
$\boxed{i}$ Dingle Quay. Tel: 066 9151188.

Tralee
Kerry County Museum
Tralee, Co Kerry. Tel: 066 7127777. *Open all year; telephone for information.*

Siamsa Tíre
Town Park, Tralee, Co Kerry. Tel: 066 712 3055. *Open May–Aug 8.30pm.*
Tralee–Blennerville train
Tralee, Co Kerry. Tel: 066 712 1064. *Open May–Sep daily, trains on the hour 11–5.*

❹ An Daingean (Dingle)
Dolphin Boat Trips
Dingle Boatmen's Association, Dingle Pier, Dingle, Co Kerry. Tel: 066 915 1967. *Sailings depart daily, weather permitting.*

❻ Dunbeg
Dunbeg Fort
Fahan, Ventry, Co Kerry. Tel: 066 9159070 (tourist information centre). *Open all year. Call for details.*

❼ Fahan
Famine Cottage
Fahan, Co Kerry. Tel: 066 915 6241. *Open Apr–Oct, daily 10–6.*

❽ Ceann Sléibhe (Slea Head)
Blasket Centre
Dún Chaoin, Dingle Peninsula, Co Kerry. Tel: 066 915 6444. *Open Easter–Oct, daily 10–6 (Jul–Aug 10–7).*

❿ Ballyferriter
Chorca Dhuibhne Museum
Old Schoolhouse, Ballyferriter, Co Kerry. Tel: 066 915 6333. *Open Apr–Oct, daily 10–6*

For children
Aqua Dome
Tralee, Co Kerry. Tel: 066 712 8899. *Open daily 10–10 (may vary Sep–May).*
Blennerville Windmill
Tralee, Co Kerry. Tel: 066 712 1064. *Open Apr–Oct, daily 9.30–5.30 (9–6 Jun–Aug).*
Freshwater Experience
Emlagh, Lispole, Co Kerry. Tel: 066 9151045. *Open daily 9–5 (Jul–Aug 9–6).*

Dingle Oceanworld
The Wood, Dingle, Co Kerry. Tel: 066 915 2111. *Open daily 10–5.*

⓫ Gallarus Visitor Centre
Dingle, Co Kerry. Tel: 066 915 5333. *Open Apr–Sep, 9–9; Oct–Mar, 9–5.*

For history buffs
Celtic and Prehistoric Museum
Kilvicadownig, Dingle, Co Kerry. Tel: 066 915 9191. *Open daily 10–5.30.*

TOUR 5

$\boxed{i}$ Beech Road, Killarney. Tel: 064 31633.
$\boxed{i}$ Kenmare Heritage Centre, Kenmare. Tel: 064 41233.

❷ Glenbeigh
Kerry Bog Village Museum
Ballincleave, Glenbeigh, Co Kerry. Tel: 066 9769184. *Open Mar–Nov, daily 8.30–7; Nov–Mar on request.*

❸ Cahersiveen
The Barracks Heritage Centre
Bridge Street, Cahersiveen, Co Kerry. Tel: 066 9472589. *Open all year, daily 11–5.*

❺ Sneem
Derrynane House
Caherdaniel, Co Kerry. Tel: 066 9475113. *Open Nov–Mar, Sat–Sun 1–5; Apr, Oct, Tue–Sun 1–5; May–Sep, Mon–Sat 9–6, Sun 11–7; last admission 45 minutes before closing.*

Kerry Alternative Technology
Sneem (take coast road towards Kenmare, turning off at Tahilla Church). Tel: 064 45563. *Open May–Oct, daily 10–6.*

❽ Ladies' View
Killarney National Park Centre
Muckross House, Muckross, Co Kerry. Tel: 064 31440. *Open mid-Mar to Oct, daily 9–6 (Jul–Aug 9–7).*

Muckross House, Gardens and Traditional Farms
Killarney, Co Kerry. Tel: 064 31440. *Open: House and Garden: daily 9–5.30 (9–7 Jul–Aug); Traditional Farms: Mar–Apr and Oct Sat–Sun and holidays 1–6, Jun–Sep daily 10–6.*

Recommended walks
Ross Castle
Ross Road, Killarney, Co Kerry. Tel: 064 35851. *Open daily, Apr 10–5; May, Sep 10–6; Jun–Aug 9–6.30; Oct, Tue–Sun 10–5.*

Back to nature
Skellig Experience Heritage Centre
Skellig, Co Kerry. Tel: 066 9476306. *Open daily Apr, May, Sep–Nov 10–6; Jun–Aug 10–7; last admission one hour before closing.*

TOUR 6

$\boxed{i}$ Kenmare Heritage Centre, Kenmare. Tel: 064 41233.
$\boxed{i}$ Town Centre, Glengarriff. Tel: 027 63084.

❶ Glengarriff
Garinish Island
Reached by boat from Blue Pool, Glengarriff, Co Cork. Tel: 027 63040. *Open Mar, Oct, Mon–Sat 10–4.30, Sun 1–5; Apr, Mon–Sat 10–6.30, Sun 1–6.30; May–Jun, Sep, Mon–Sat 10–6.30, Sun 11–6.30; Jul, Aug, Mon–Sat 9.30–6.30, Sun 11–6.30.*

Bamboo Park
N71, Glengarriff, Co Cork. Tel: 027 63570. *Open daily 9–7.*

❸ Castletown Bearhaven
Call of the Sea
North Road, Castletown Bearhaven, Co Cork. Tel: 027 70835. *Open Mon–Fri 10–5, Sat–Sun 1–5; last admission 4.15. Call for hours in low season.*

Dursey Island Cable Car
Castletown Bearhaven,
Co Cork. Tel: 027 73017.
*Cable car operates all year,
weather permitting, Mon–
Sat 9–11, 2.30–5, 7–8, Sun
9–10.30, 1–2.30, 7–8 (also
Sun 4–5, Jun–Aug). Arrive 30
minutes before departure.*

For history buffs
Kenmare Heritage Centre
Kenmare. Tel: 064 41233.
Open Easter–Sep.

TOUR 7

[i] Grand Parade, Cork
City. Tel: 021 4255100.
[i] Town Centre, Blarney.
Tel: 021 4381624.
[i] Heritage Centre,
Lismore. Tel: 058 54975.
[i] Heritage Centre,
Market Square, Youghal.
Tel: 024 20170.

Cork
Cork City Gaol and Radio
Museum
Sundays Well, Cork, Co
Cork. Tel: 021 4305022.
*Open Mar–Oct, daily
9.30–6; Nov–Feb 10–5.*
Crawford Art Gallery
Emmet Place, Cork, Co
Cork. Tel: 021 4907855.
*Open Mon–Sat 10–5; last
admission 4.45pm.*

1 Blarney
Blarney Castle
Barney, Co Cork. Tel: 021
4385252. *Open all year,
Mon–Sat 9–6.30 (to 7
Jun–Aug), Sun 9.30–5.30
(sunset in winter).*

4 Mitchelstown
Mitchelstown Caves
Burncourt, Cahir, Co
Tipperary. Tel: 052 67246.
Open all year, daily 10–6.

5 Caher
Caher Castle
Caher, Co Tipperary.
Tel: 052 41011. *Open mid-
Mar to mid-Oct, daily
9.30–5.30 (to 7.30pm mid-
Jun to mid-Sep); mid-Oct to
mid-Mar, 9.30–4.30; last
admission 45 minutes before
closing.*

7 Lismore
Lismore Castle Gardens
and Castle Arts
Lismore, Co Waterford.
Tel: 058 54424. *Open mid-
Apr to early Oct, daily
1.45–4.45 (from 11am
Jun–Aug).*
Lismore Heritage Centre
Lismore, Co Waterford. Tel
058 54975 or 54855. *Open
Mon–Fri, 9.30–5.30,
(May–Oct also Sat
10–5.30), Sun 12–5.30.*

8 Youghal
Heritage Centre
Market Square, Youghal,
Co Cork. Tel: 024 20170
or 92447. *Open Apr–Oct,
Mon–Fri 9–5.30, Sat–Sun
9.30–5. Call for winter open-
ing hours.*

For history buffs
Queenstown Story
Cobh Heritage Centre,
Cobh, Co Cork. Tel: 021
4813591. *Open Feb–Dec,
daily 10–6; last admission
5pm.*

For children
Fota Wildlife Park
Carrigtwohill, Co Cork.
Tel: 021 4812678. *Open
Mon–Sat from 10am, Sun
from 11am.*

Special to...
Lifetime Lab
Lee Road, Cork City.
Tel: 021 494 1500. *Open
Apr–Sep, Mon–Fri 9.30–5,
Sat–Sun 10–4; Oct–Mar
Mon–Fri 9.30–3.30.*

TOUR 8

[i] Grand Parade, Cork.
Tel: 021 4255100.
[i] Pier Road, Kinsale.
Tel: 021 4772234.
[i] 25 Ashe Street,
Clonakilty. Tel: 023 33226.
[i] Castle Gates, The
Square, Macroom. Tel: 0236
43280.

Cork
Cork Public Museum
Fitzgerald Park, Cork, Co
Cork. Tel: 021 4270679.
*Open Mon–Fri 11–1,
2.15–5 (to 6 Jun–Aug), Sat
11–1, 2.15–4. Also Sun 3–5
Apr–Sep.*

1 Kinsale
International Wine
Museum
Desmond Castle, Cork
Street, Kinsale, Co Cork.
Tel: 021 4774855. *Open
mid-Apr to late Oct, Tue–Sun
10–6 (also Mon mid-Jun to
late Oct).*
.Charles Fort
Summercove, Kinsale,
Co Cork. Tel: 021 772263.
*Open mid-Mar to Oct, daily
10–6, Nov to mid-Mar, daily
10–5; last admission 45
minutes before closing.*

2 Clonakilty
Timoleague Castle
Gardens
Clonakilty, Co Cork. Tel:
023 46116. *Open Jun–Aug,
Mon–Sat 11–5.30, Sun
2–5.30; other times by
arrangement.*
Michael Collins Centre
Castle View, Clonakilty,
Co Cork. Tel: 023 46107.
*Open mid-Jun to mid-Sep,
Mon–Sat 10.30–5.*

**6 Gougane Barra
Forest Park**
Gougane Barra, Co Cork.
Tel 026 20277. *Open all
year daily, except during tree
harvesting times.*

For children
Splashworld
Tramore, Co Waterford.
Tel: 051 390176. *Open daily
10–10; phone to check
winter hours.*

TOUR 9

[i] The Old Courthouse,
The Square, Bantry.
Tel: 027 50229 (seasonal) .
[i] Town Hall, North
Street, Skibbereen. Tel: 028
21766.

Bantry
Bantry House, Gardens
and French Armada
Centre
Bantry, Co Cork. Tel: 027
50047. *Open 17 Mar–Oct,
daily 10–6.*

2 Skibbereen
Skibbereen Heritage
Centre
Upper Bridge Street,
Skibbereen, Co Cork. Tel:
028 40900. *Open mid-Mar
to Oct, Tue–Sat 10–6 (daily
late May to mid-Sep).*
Cape Clear Heritage
Centre
Cape Clear Island,
Co Cork. Tel: 028 39119.
Telephone for opening times.

3 Skull
Skull Planetarium
Skull Community College,
Skull, Co Cork. Tel: 028
28552. *Telephone for
opening times.*

4 Mizen Head
Mizen Head Visitor
Centre
The Harbour Road,
Goleen, Co Cork. Tel: 028
35115 or 35225. *Open
mid-Mar to Oct, daily
10.30–5 (Jun–Sep 10–6);
Nov to mid-Mar, weekends
11–4.*

TOUR 10

[i] The Quay, Waterford.
Tel: 051 875823.
[i] Railway Square,
Tramore, Co Waterford.
Tel: 051 381572.
[i] The Courthouse,
Dungarvan. Tel: 058 41741.
[i] Heritage Centre,
Lismore. Tel: 058 54975.
[i] Castle Car Park, Cahir.
Tel 052 41453.
[i] Heritage Centre,
Cashel. Tel: 062 62511.
[i] Heritage Centre, Main
Street, Carrick-on Suir.
Tel: 051 640200.

Waterford
Waterford Crystal Visitor
Centre
Waterford, Co Waterford.
Tel: 051 332500.

Open Jan–Feb, Nov–Dec, daily 9–5; Mar–Oct, daily 8.30–6. Factory tours Mar–Oct, daily 8.30–4.15; Nov–Feb, Mon–Fri 9–3.15.

Reginald's Tower
The Quay, Waterford, Co Waterford. Tel: 051 858958. *Open Easter–Oct, daily 10–6; Nov–Easter, Wed–Sun 10–5.*

[3] Tramore
Surf and Wildlife Visitor Centre
The Beach, Tramore. Tel: 051 391297. *Call for details.*

[4] Dungarvan
Waterford County Museum
St Augustine Street, Dungarvan, Co Waterford. Tel: 058 45960. *Open all year, Mon–Fri, 10–1, 2–4.30 (5 in summer); also Sat in summer.*

[5] Cappoquin
Cappoquin House and Gardens
Cappoquin, Co Waterford. Tel: 058 54004. *Open Apr–Jul, Mon–Sat, 9–1.*

[6] Lismore
Lismore Castle Gardens
Lismore, Co Waterford. Tel: 058 54424. *Open Apr–Sep, 1.45–4.45 (from 11 in high season).*

Lismore Heritage Centre
The Courthouse, Lismore, Co Waterford. Tel: 058 54975. *Open Apr–Oct, daily 9.30–5.30, Sun 12–5.30.*

[7] Cahir
Cahir Castle
Cahir, Co Tipperary. Tel: 052 41011. *Open mid-Mar to mid-Oct, daily 9.30–5.30 (7pm mid-Jun to mid-Sep); mid-Oct to mid-Mar, 9.30–4.30; last admission 45 minutes before closing.*

Swiss Cottage
Kilcommon, Co Tipperary. Tel: 052 41144 or 41011. *Open mid-Mar to Apr, Tue–Sun 10–1, 2–4.30 (till 6 in Apr).*

[8] Cashel
Rock of Cashel, Co Tipperary. Tel: 062 61437. *Open daily, mid-Sep to mid-Mar, mid-Jun to mid-Sep 9–4.30; mid-Mar to mid-Jun 9–5.30.*

[9] Clonmel
South Tipperary County Museum
Mick Delahunty Square, Clonmel, Co Tipperary. Tel: 052 34551. *Open all year, Tue–Sat 10–5.*

Clonmel Museum of Transport
Emmet Street, Clonmel, Co Tipperary. Tel: 052 29727. *Open all year, Mon–Sat 10–6; also Sun Jun–Aug 2.30–6.*

[10] Carrick-on-Suir
Ormond Castle
Off Castle Street, Carrick-on-Suir, Co Tipperary. Tel: 051 640787. *Open mid-Jun to early Sep, daily 9.30–6.30.*

Heritage Centre
Main Street, Carrick-on-Suir, Co Tipperary. Tel: 051 640200. *Open daily 10–4 (5 Jun–Sep; may vary weekends).*

Tipperary Crystal
Ballynoran, Carrick-on-Suir, Co Tipperary. Tel: 051 640543. *Open Mon–Sat 9.30–6, Sun 10–6. Tours Mon–Fri 10–3.30.*

For children
Splashworld
Tramore, Co Waterford. Tel: 051 390176. *Open daily 10–10; phone for winter hours.*

[i] Athlone Castle, Athlone. Tel: 090 94630.
[i] Dublin Road, Mullingar. Tel: 044 9348650 (seasonal).
[i] Clonmacnoise. Tel: 090 9674134 (seasonal).
[i] Bury Quay, Tullamore. Tel: 057 9352617.
[i] Brendan Street, Birr. Tel: 057 9120110 (seasonal).
[i] Bridge Street, Ballinasloe. Tel: 090 964 2604 (seasonal).

Athlone
Athlone Castle and Visitor Centre
St Peters Square, Athlone, Co Westmeath. Tel: 090 6472107 or 6492912. *Open Easter, May–Sep, daily 10–4.30.*

[1] Mullingar
Belvedere House, Gardens and Park
Mullingar, Co Westmeath. Tel: 044 9349060. *Open Mar–Apr, Sep–Oct daily 10.30–7; May–Aug 10–5; Nov–Feb 10.30–4.30; last admission 1 hour before closing. Times may be subject to change.*

Tullynally Castle and Gardens
Castlepollard, Co Westmeath. Tel: 044 9661159. *Gardens May–Jun Sat–Sun 2–6; Jul–Aug. daily Castle: groups only.*

[2] Tullamore
Locke's Distillery Museum
Kilbeggan, Co Westmeath. Tel: 0506 32134. *Open Nov–Mar, 10–4; Apr–Oct 9–6.*

Tullamore Dew Heritage Centre
Bury Quay, Tullamore, Co Offaly. Tel: 0506 9325015. *Open May–Sep Mon–Sat 9–6, Sun 12–5; Oct–Apr, Mon–Sat 10–5, Sun 12–5.*

[3] Birr
Birr Castle Demesne and Historic Science Centre
Birr, Co Offaly. Tel: 05791 20336. *Open daily 9–6.*

[4] Clonmacnoise
Shannonbridge, Co Offaly. Tel: 0905 74195. *Open mid-Mar to mid-May, early Sep–Oct, daily 10–6; mid-May to early Sep, 9–7; Nov to mid-Mar, 10–5.30; last admission 45 minutes before closing.*

For Children
Clonmacnoise and West Offaly Railway Bog Tour
Blackwater Works, Shannonbridge, Co Offaly. Tel: 090 9674450. *Open*

Apr–Sep, daily 10–5; trains run on the hour.

[i] Mayoralty Street, Drogheda. Tel: 041 98370370.
[i] Bru na Boinne, Donore. Tel: 041 9880305.

Drogheda
Millmount
Drogheda, Co Louth. Tel: 041 9833097. *Open Mon–Sat 10–6 (last tour 5.30), Sun and bank hols 2.30–5.30.*

[2] Mellifont
Old Mellifont Abbey
Tullyallen, Co Louth. Tel: 041 9826053. *Open May–Sep, daily 10–5.15pm.*

[3] Newgrange
Brú na Boinne Visitor Centre
Dunore, Co Meath. Tel: 041 9880300. *Open daily from 9 or 9.30, closing time varies. Knowth open early Apr–Oct only.*

[4] Slane
Slane Castle
Slane, Co Meath. Tel: 041 9884400. *Open early May–early Aug, Mon–Thu noon–5.*

[5] Kells
Kells Heritage Centre
Headfort Place, Kells, Co Meath. Tel: 046 9247840. *Open Oct–Apr, Mon–Sat 10–5; May–Sep, Mon–Sat 10–5, Sun & bank hols 2–6.*

[7] Tara
Hill of Tara Visitor Centre
Hill of Tara, Co Meath. Tel: 046 9025903. *Open mid-May to mid-Sep, daily 10–6; last admission 5.15pm.*

For history buffs
Trim Castle
Trim, Co Meath. Tel: 046 9438619. *Open Easter–Oct, daily 10–6; Nov–Easter, Sat–Sun 10–5.*

[i] Tourist Information Centre
[12] Number on tour

Practical • Information

For children
Newgrange Farm
Newgrange, Slane, Co
Meath. Tel: 041 9824119.
Open Easter Sat–Aug. 10–5.

TOUR 13

[i] Suffolk Street, Dublin.
Tel: 02 605 7700.

❶ Dun Laoghaire
National Maritime
Museum of Ireland
Haigh Terrace, Dun
Laoghaire, Co Dublin.
Tel: 01 2800969. *Open
May–Sep, Tue–Sun, 1–5.*
James Joyce Tower
Sandycove, Co Dublin.
Tel: 01 2809265. *Open
Mar–Oct, Mon–Sat 10–1,
2–5, Sun & bank hols, 2–6.*

❸ Bray
Heritage Centre
Old Courthouse, Bray, Co
Wicklow. Tel: 01 28667796.
*Open Jun–Aug, Mon–Fri,
9.30–1, 2–5, Sat 10–3;
Sep–May, Mon–Fri
9.30–4.30, Sat 10–3.*
National Sea Life Centre
Strand Road, Bray,
Co Wicklow. Tel: 01 286
6939. *Open May–Sep, daily
10–6; Oct–Apr, Mon–Fri
11–5, Sat, Sun & bank hols
11–6; last admission 1 hour
before closing.*
Kilruddery House and
Gardens
Bray, Co Wicklow. Tel: 0404
46024. *Open Gardens:
Apr–Sep, daily 1–5; House:
May–Jun , Sep 1–5*

❹ Enniskerry
Powerscourt Gardens and
House Exhibition
Enniskerry, Co Wicklow.
Tel: 01 2046000. *Open daily
9.30–5.30; last admission 5.
Gardens close at dusk in
winter.*

❺ Roundwood
Mount Usher Gardens
Ashford, Co Wicklow.
Tel: 0404 40205. *Open late
Apr–Oct, daily 10.30–6.*

❻ Glendalough
Visitor Centre
Glendalough, Co Wicklow.
Tel: 0404 45352. *Open daily
9.30–6 (5 winter).*
Avondale House and
Forest Park
Rathdrum, Co Wicklow.
Tel: 0404 46111. *Open all
year, daily 11–6 (last admis-
sion 5); other times by
appointment.*

❽ Blessington
Russborough House
Blessington, Co Wicklow.
Tel: 045 865239. *Open Apr
& Oct, Sun & bank hols
10–5; May–Sep, daily 10–5.*

❿ Killakee
Rathfarnham Castle
Rathfarnham, Dublin 14.
Tel: 01 4939462. *Open May–
Oct, daily 9.30–5.30. May be
closed for renovation.*

Special to...
Guinness Storehouse
St James Gate, Dublin 8.
Tel: 01 4084800. *Open all
year, daily 9.30–5; Jul, Aug
9.30–7.*

For children
Clara Lara Funpark
Vale of Clara, Rathdrum,
Co Wicklow. Tel: 0404
46161. *Open May–early
Sep, daily 10–6.*

For history buffs
Pearse Museum
St Enda's Park, Grange
Road, Rathfarnham,
Dublin 16. Tel: 01 4934208.
*Open all year, daily 10–4
(5 or 5.30 in summer).*

TOUR 14

[i] Shee Alms House,
Rose Inn Street, Kilkenny.
Tel: 056 7751500.
[i] Dunbrody Heritage
Centre, The Quay, New
Ross. Tel: 051 421857.
[i] Tullow Street, Carlow.
Tel: 059 9131554.
[i] Market House, Kildare.
Tel: 045 521240.
[i] James Fintan Lawlor
Avenue, Portlaoise. Tel: 057
8621178.

Kilkenny
Kilkenny Castle
The Parade, Kilkenny, Co
Kilkenny. Tel: 056 7721450.
*Open Apr–May, daily
10.30–5; Jun–Aug, daily
9.30–7; Sep, 10–6.30;
Oct–Mar, 10.30–12.45,
2–5; last tour 45 minutes
before closing.*

❶ Thomastown
Jerpoint Abbey
Thomastown, Co Kilkenny.
Tel: 056 24623. *Open
Mar–May, mid-Sep to Oct,
daily 10–5; Jun to mid-Sep,
daily 9.30–6.30; Nov, 10–4;
last admission one hour
before closing.*

❹ Kildare
Irish National Stud,
Japanese Gardens and
St Fiachras Garden
Tully, Co Kildare. Tel: 045
521617. *Open Feb–Nov,
daily 9.30–6; last admission
5pm.*

❺ Portlaoise
Emo Court
Emo, Co Laois. Tel: 0502
26573. *Gardens open all
year daily during daylight
hours. House open for
guided tours mid-Jun to
mid-Sep 10.30–5; last tour
4.30pm.*

❼ Portlaoise
Abbeyleix
Abbeyleix Heritage House
Abbeyleix, Co Laois.
Tel: 057 8731653. *Open
all year, Mon–Fri 9–5, also
Sat–Sun May–Sep 1–5.*

❾ Fethard
Fethard Folk and
Transport Museum
Cashel Road, Fethard. Co
Tipperary. Tel: 052 31516.
Phone for opening times.

Back to nature
John F Kennedy Park and
Arboretum
New Ross, Co Wexford.
Tel: 051 388171. *Open
daily 10–5 (6.30 Apr; 8
May–Aug); last admission
45 minutes before closing.*

TOUR 15

[i] Crescent Quay,
Wexford. Tel: 053 9123111.
[i] Main Street, Gorey.
Tel: 055 9421248.
[i] Castle Museum,
Enniscorthy. Tel: 054
9234699.
[i] Dunbrody Heritage
Centre, The Quay, New
Ross. Tel: 051 421857.
[i] 41, The Quay, Water-
ford. Tel: 051 875823.

❸ Enniscorthy
Wexford County Museum
Enniscorthy Castle,
Enniscorthy, Co Wexford.
Tel: 053 9235926. *Open
Jun–Sep, Mon–Sat 10–5.30,
Sun 2–5.30; Oct–Nov, daily
2–5; Dec–May call for
details.*
National 1798 Rebellion
Centre
Millpark Road, Enniscorthy,
Co Wexford. Tel: 053
9237596. *Open Mon–Fri
9.30–5, Sat–Sun 11–9.30–4
winter; last admission 3pm.*

❹ New Ross
The *Dunbrody*
The Quay, New Ross,
Co Wexford. Tel: 051
425239. *Open Apr–Sep,
daily 9–6; Oct–Mar, daily
10–5.*
Dunbrody Abbey Visitor
Centre
Campile, Co Wexford.
Tel: 051 388603. *Open May
to mid-Sep, daily 10–6.*

❺ Waterford
Waterford Treasures
Merchant's Quay,
Waterford. Tel: 051
304500. *Open Apr–May,
Sep daily 9.30–6; Jun–Aug
9.30–9; Oct–Mar 10–5.*

❼ Ballyhack
Ballyhack Castle
Ballyhack, Co Wexford.
Tel: 051 389468. *Call for
details.*
Duncannon Fort
Duncannon, Co Wexford.
Tel: 051 389990. *Open
Jun–Sep, daily 10–5.30.*

Practical • Information

[i] Tourist Information Centre

[12] Number on tour

[8] Hook Head
Hook Lighthouse
Hook Head, Co Wexford.
Tel: 051 397055. *Open
Mar–Oct, daily 9.30–5.30;
Nov–Feb, some Sun.*

[9] Fethard
Tintern Abbey
Saltmills, Co Wexford.
Tel: 051 562650. *Open mid-
Jun to late Sep, 9.30–6.30;
last admission 5.45pm.*

For children
Irish National Heritage
Park
Ferrycarrig, Co Wexford.
Tel: 053 9120733. *Open,
daily 9.30–6.30.*

For history buffs
Kennedy Homestead
Dunganstown, New Ross,
Co Wexford. Tel: 051
388264. *Open Jul–Aug, daily
10–5; May–Jun, Sep,
Mon–Fri 11.30–4.30.*

TOUR 16

[i] Temple Street, Sligo.
Tel: 071 9161201.
[i] The Bridge, Bundoran.
Tel: 071 9842539.

[2] Lissadell
Lissadell House
Drumcliffe, Co Sligo.
Tel: 071 9163150. *Open
early Apr–Sep daily 10.30–6
(last tour at 5pm); Mar
some weekends.*

[7] Lough Gill
Parkes Castle
Fivemile Bourne, Co
Leitrim. Tel: 071 9164149.
*Open mid-Mar to Oct, daily
10–6; last admission
5.15pm.*

[10] Strandhill
Carrowmore Megalithic
Cemetery
Strandhill, Co Sligo. Tel: 071
9161534. *Open Easter–Oct,
daily 10–5.*

TOUR 17

[i] King House, Boyle.
Tel: 071 9662145.

[i] Marina, Carrick-on-
Shannon. Tel: 071 9620170.
[i] 45 Dublin Street,
Longford. Tel: 043 46566.
[i] Harrison Hall,
Roscommon. Tel: 090
6626342.

Boyle
King House
Main Street, Boyle, Co
Roscommon. Tel: 071
9663242. *Open Apr–Sep,
daily 10–6; last admission
5pm.*

[2] Longford
Carrigglas Manor
Longford, Co Longford.
Tel: 043 45165. *Telephone
for details of tours and open-
ing times.*

[3] Roscommon
Roscommon County
Museum
The Square, Roscommon,
Co Roscommon. Tel: 090
6625613. *Open Jun–Aug,
Mon–Sat 10–5.30;
Sep–May, Mon–Fri 10–4.*

[4] Castlerea
Clonalis House
Castlerea, Co Roscommon.
Tel: 094 9620014. *Open
Jun–Aug, Mon–Sat 11–4.*

TOUR 18

[i] James Street, Westport.
Tel: 098 25711.
[i] Cashel, Achill Island.
Tel: 098 47384 (seasonal).
[i] Cathedral Road, Ballina.
Tel: 096 70848.
[i] Village Centre, Knock.
Tel: 094 9388193.
[i] Mill Museum, Tuam.
Tel: 093 25486 or 24463.
[i] Town Centre,
Castlebar. Tel: 094 9021207.

Westport
Westport Heritage
Centre
James Street, Westport,
Co Mayo. Tel: 098 25711.
Call for opening hours.
Westport House
Westport, Co Mayo. Tel:
098 25430 or 27766. *Open
Apr–Sep daily 11.30–5.30;
Mar–Oct weekends only.*

[4] Knock
Knock Shrine
Knock, Co Mayo. Tel: 0990
9388100. *Open all year,
main ceremonies Mon–Sat
2, Sun 2.30, 7 Masses daily.*
Knock Folk Museum
Knock, Co Mayo. Tel: 094
9388100. *Open May–Oct,
10–6 (to 7pm Jul–Aug).*

[5] Tuam
Tuam Mill Museum
Shop Street, Tuam,
Co Mayo. Tel: 093 25486.
Open Mon–Sat 10–5.30.

[6] Castlebar
Museum of Country Life
Turlough Park, Castlebar,
Co Mayo. Tel: 094
9031773. *Open all year,
Tue–Sat 10–5, Sun 2–5.*

For history buffs
Ballintobber Abbey,
Ballintobber, Claremorris,
Co Mayo. Tel: 094
9030934. *Telephone for
opening times and tours.*
Ceide Fields Visitor
Centre and Site
West of Ballycastle, Co
Mayo. Tel: 096 43325.
*Open early Apr–Nov, 10–5
(Jun–Sep, 10–6).*

TOUR 19

[i] Forster Street, Galway.
Tel: 091 537700.
[i] Main Street, Oughter-
ard. Tel: 091 552808.

Galway
Galway City Museum
Spanish Arch, Galway, Co
Galway. Tel: 091 532460.
*Open Tue–Sat 10–5, also
Sun 2–5 Jun–Sep.*
Nora Barnacle House
Museum
Bowling Green, Galway,
Co Galway. Tel: 091
564743. *Phone for opening
times.*

[2] Rossaveel
Aran Island Ferries
Rossaveel, Co Galway.
Tel: 091 568903. *Sailings
daily; call for details.*

[4] Gortmore
Patrick Pearse's Cottage
Rosmuck, Co Galway. Tel:
091 574292. *Open Easter,
early Jun–Sep, daily 10–6.*

[7] Clifden
Connemara Heritage and
History Centre
Lettershea, Clifden, Co
Galway. Tel: 095 21808.
*Open Apr–Oct daily 10–6;
other times on request.*

[8] Kylemore Abbey
Connemara, Co Galway.
Tel: 095 41146. *Open all
year, daily Mar–Nov
9.30–5.30; Dec–Feb
10.30–4.30*

[11] Oughterard
Aughnanure Castle
Oughterard, Co Galway.
Tel: 091 552214. *Open late
Mar–Oct, daily 9.30–6.*
Glengowla Mines
Oughterard, Co Galway.
Tel: 091552360 or 552021.
*Open Mar–Nov, daily
10–5.30.*

Back to nature
Connemara National Park
Visitor Centre
Letterfrack, Co Galway.
Tel: 095 41054. *Open mid-
Mar to Oct, daily 10–5.30;
(last admission 4.45).*

TOUR 20

[i] 44, Foyle Street,
Londonderry. Tel: 028
71267284.
[i] Neil T Blaney Road,
Letterkenny. Tel: 074
9121160.

[2] Letterkenny
Newmills Corn and Flax
Mills
Churchill Road,
Letterkenny, Co Donegal.
Tel: 074 25115. *Open mid-
Jun to late Sep, daily
10–6.30.*

[4] Rathmullan
The Flight of the Earls
Heritage Centre
Tel: 074 9158131.
*Open Jun–Sep, Mon–Sat
10–6, Sun 12.30–6.30.*

11 Glenveagh
Glenveagh National Park
Churchill, Co Donegal.
Tel: 074 9137090. *Open
mid-Mar to early Nov, daily
10–6; last admission 5pm.*
Glebe House and Gallery
Churchill. Tel: 074 9137071.
*Open Easter, mid-May–Sep,
daily, except Fri 11–6.30.*
Columcille Heritage Centre
Gartan, Churchill. Tel: 074
9137306. *Open Easter, & 1st
Sun May–last Sun Sep, Mon–
Fri 10.30–6.30, Sun 1–6.30.*

TOUR 21

|i| Narrow Gauge Road,
Larne. Tel: 028 28260088.
|i| Sheskburn House,
7 Mary Street, Ballycastle.
Tel: 028 20762024.
|i| Giant's Causeway, 44
Causeway Road, Bushmills.
Tel: 028 20731855.
|i| Dunluce Centre,
Sandhill Drive, Portrush.
Tel: 028 70823333.
|i| 7 Connell Street,
Limavady. Tel: 028 77760307.

Larne
Carnfunnock Country
Park
Coast Road, Larne, Co
Antrim. Tel: 028 28270541
(out of season: 028
28260088). *Open daily
9–dusk (to 9pm Jul–Aug).*

5 Glenariff
Glenariff Forest Park
Glenariff, Co Antrim.
Tel: 028 29556000. *Open
daily, 10–sunset.*

7 Ballycastle
Ballycastle Museum
59 Castle Street. Tel: 028
20762942. *Open Jul, Aug
Mon–Sat 12–6 or by
arrangement.*

8 Carrick-a-Rede
Carrick-a-Rede Rope
Bridge
Larrybane, Co Antrim.
Tel: 028 2069839. *Open
Mar–Oct, daily 10–6 (7pm
Jun–Aug).*

9 Giant's Causeway
44 Causeway Road,
Bushmills, Co Antrim.
Tel: 028 20731582. *Open
all year. Visitor Centre daily
from 10am.*
Causeway School
Museum
Causeway Road, Bushmills,
Co Antrim. Tel: 028
20731777. *Open Jul–Aug,
daily 11–5.*

10 Bushmills
Bushmills Distillery
2 Distillery Road, Bushmills,
Co Antrim. Tel 028
20731521. *Open Apr–Oct,
Mon–Sat, 9.30–5.30, Sun
12–5.30. daily reduced
hours.*

11 Portrush
Dunluce Castle
87 Dunluce Road,
Bushmills, Co Antrim.
Tel: 028 20731938. *Open
Apr–Sep, Mon–Sat, 10–6,
Sun 2–6; Jul, Aug, Sun 12–6;
Oct–Mar, Tue–Sat 10–4,
Sun 2–4.*

12 Downhill
Downhill and Mussenden
Temple
Mussenden Road, Castle-
rock, Co Londonderry.
Tel: 028 20731582.
*Grounds daily, dawn to dusk;
Temple: phone for details.*

13 Limavady
Roe Valley Country Park
Limavady, Co London-
derry. Tel: 028 77722074.
*Open Apr–Sep, daily 9–6;
Oct–Mar, Mon–Fri 9–5.*

14 Ballymoney
Leslie Hill Open Farm
Ballymoney, Co Antrim.
Tel: 028 27666803. *Open
Easter–May, Sun and bank
hols 2–6; Jun Sat–Sun 2–6;
Jul, Aug, Mon–Sat 11–6,
Sun 2–6.*

For children
Portrush Countryside
Centre
8 Bath Road, Portrush, Co
Antrim. Tel: 028 70823600.
Open Jul–Sep, 10–5.

Dunluce Centre
10 Sandhill Drive, Portrush,
Co Antrim. Tel: 028
70824444. *Open Easter,
May–Aug, daily; Apr,
Sep–Oct, weekends.*

TOUR 22

|i| Belfast and Northern
Ireland Welcome Centre,
47 Donegall Place, Belfast.
Tel: 028 90246609.
|i| 31 Regent Street,
Newtownards. Tel: 028
91826846.
|i| The St Patrick Centre,
53A, Market Street,
Downpatrick. Tel: 028
44612233.

Belfast
City Hall
Donegall Square, Belfast.
Tel: 028 90270456. *Open
for tours Mon–Fri 11, 2, 3,
Sat 2, 3.*
Botanical Gardens
Stranmillis Road/Botanic
Avenue, Belfast. Tel: 028
90314762. Open *all year
daily from 7.30am. Closing
times vary seasonally.*

1 Cultra
Ulster Folk and Transport
Museum
Cultra, Co Down. Tel: 028
90428428. *Open at 10
Mon–Sat, 11 on Sun. Closing
times vary from 4 to 6
according to season.*

2 Newtownards
Scrabo Tower and
Country Park
Scrabo Road,
Newtownards, Co Down.
Tel: 028 91811491. *Country
Park open daily. Scrabo Tower
open Apr–late Sep, Sat–Thu
10.30–6.*

3 Mount Stewart
Mount Stewart
Co Down. Tel: 028
42788387. *Call for opening
times.*

6 Portaferry
Exploris
The Rope Walk, Castle
Street, Portaferry, Co
Down. Tel: 028 42728062.

*Open Apr–Aug, Mon–Fri
10–6, Sat 11–6, Sun 12–6;
Sep–Mar, Mon–Fri 10–5,
Sat 11–5, Sun 1–5.*

7 Strangford
Castle Ward
Strangford, Downpatrick,
Co Down. Tel: 028
44881204. *Open mid-Mar
to Jun, Sep, weekends 10–6;
Easter week, Jul–Aug, daily
1–6. Grounds all year daily
10–4 (8pm Apr–Sep).*

8 Downpatrick
Down Cathedral
English Street,
Downpatrick, Co Down.
Tel: 028 44614922. *Open
Mon–Sat 9.30–4.30, Sun
2–4.30.*
Down County Museum
The Mall, English Street,
Downpatrick, Co Down.
Tel: 028 44615218. *Open
Mon–Fri 10–5, Sat–Sun
1–5.*
St Patrick Centre
53A Market Street,
Downpatrick, Co Down.
Tel: 028 44612233. *Open
Apr–May, Sep, Mon–Sat
9.30–5.30, Sun 1–5.30;
Jun–Aug, Mon–Sat 9.30–6,
Sun 10–6; Oct–Mar,
Mon–Sat 10–5, Sun on
request, St Patrick's Day
9.30–7.*

**10 Nendrum
Monastic Site**
Mahee Island, Comber, Co
Down. Tel: 028 91811491.
*Open Apr–Sep, Tue–Sat
10–7, Sun 2–7; Oct–Mar,
Sat 10–4, Sun 2–4.*

Back to nature
Castle Espie Wildfowl and
Wetlands Centre
Ballydrain Road, Comber,
Co Down. Tel: 028
91874146. *Open Mar–Oct,
Mon–Fri 10.30–5 (5.30 Jul,
Aug), Sat–Sun 11–5.30;
Nov–Feb, Mon–Fri 11–4,
Sat–Sun 11–4.30.*

TOUR 23

|i| Wellington Road,
Enniskillen. Tel: 028
66323110.

Enniskillen
Enniskillen Castle and Museums
Castle Barracks, Enniskillen, Co Fermanagh. Tel: 028 66325000. *Open Mon 2–5, Tue–Fri 10–5; also Sat 2–5 May–Sep, Sun 2–5 Jul–Aug.*
Castle Coole
Enniskillen, Co Fermanagh. Tel: 028 66322690. *Open Apr–May, Sep, Sun and bank hols 1–6; Easter, daily 1–6; Jun, Fri–Wed 1–6; Jul–Aug, daily 12–6; last tour 5pm.*

1 Devenish
Devenish Island
Co Fermanagh. Tel: 028 90546518 *Ferry operates Good Friday to mid-Sep, daily; call for times.*

2 Castle Archdale
Kesh, Co Fermanagh. Tel: 028 68621588. *Park open all year 9am–dusk. Museum and Visitor Centre open Easter Sat–Sun 12–6, May bank hol, 11–6; Jul–Aug, Tue–Sun 11–7.*

5 Belleek
Belleek Pottery Visitor Centre
Belleek, Co Fermanagh. Tel: 028 68658501. *Open Mar–Oct, Sep, Mon–Fri 9–6, Sat 10–6, Sun 2–6; Nov–Feb, Mon–Fri 9–5.3, Sat 10–5.30; no tours Sat, Sun.*

8 Marble Arch
Marble Arch Caves European Geopark
Marlbank, Florencecourt, Co Fermanagh. Tel: 028 66348855. *Open late Mar–Sep, 10–4.30 (to 5pm Jul–Aug); may close after heavy rain.*

9 Florence Court
Florencecourt village, Co Fermanagh. Tel: 028 66348249. *Open mid-Mar to May, Sep, Sat, Sun & bank hols 1–6; Jun, Wed–Mon 1–6; Jul–Aug, daily 12–6.*

10 Bellanaleck
Crom Estate
Newtownbutler, Co Fermanagh. Tel: 028 67738118. *Open mid-Mar to Apr, mid- to end Sep, Sat–Sun 10–6; May to mid-Sep daily 10–6.*
Sheelin Irish Lace Museum
Bellanaleck, Co Fermanagh. Tel: 28 66348052. *Open Mon–Sat 10–6.*

TOUR 24

i 40 English Street, Armagh. Tel: 028 37521800.
i 190 Ballygawley Road, Dungannon. Tel: 028 87767259.
i Burn Road, Cookstown. Tel: 028 86769949
i 1 Market Street, Omagh. Tel: 028 82247831.

Armagh
Emain Macha, Navan Fort
81 Killylea Road, Armagh, Co Armagh. Tel: 028 3752 1801. *Open Apr–May, Sep, Sat 10–5, Sun noon–5; Jun–Aug, Mon–Sat 10–5, Sun 12–5 (closed 12 Jul).*

1 Loughgall4
6Ardress House
Ardress Road, Co Armagh. Tel: 028 87784753. *Open mid-Mar–Sep, Sat–Sun 2–6.*

2 Moy
The Argory
Derrycaw Road, Moy, Dungannon, Co Tyrone. Tel: 028 87784753. *Open Grounds: daily 10–4 (7pm May–Sep). House: closed for refurbishent until Mar 2008.*

3 Dungannon
Tyrone Crystal
Killybrackey, Coalisland Road, Dungannon, Co Tyrone. Tel: 028 87725335. *Open daily, seasonal times; call for details.*
Grant Ancestral Home
45 Dergna Road, Dungannon, Co Tyrone. Tel: 028 85557133. *Open all year; call for times.*

4 Cookstown
Wellbrook Beetling Mill
20 Wellbrook Road, Corkhill, Cookstown, Co Tyrone. Tel: 028 86748210. *Open mid-Mar–Jun, Sep, Sat, Sun & bank hols 2–6; Easter, Jul, Aug, daily 12–6.*

6 Omagh
Ulster-American Folk Park
Mellon Road, Castletown, Omagh, Co Tyrone. Tel: 028 82243292. *Open Apr–Sep, Mon–Sat 10.30–6, Sun & bank hols 11–6.30; last admission 1.5 hours before closing.*

8 The Clogher Valley
Fivemiletown Coach and Carriage Museum
Fivemiletown, Co Tyrone. Tel: 028 89521221. *Open by appointment only.*

For children
Benburb Valley Heritage Centre
Milltown Road, Benburb, Dungannon, Co Tyrone. Tel: 028 37549885. *Open Easter–Sep, daily 10–5.*

Back to nature
Peatlands Park
33 Derryhubbert Road, Dungannon, Co Tyrone. Tel: 028 3885 1102. *Open daily 9–5 (9pm in summer).*

For history buffs
Springhill House
20 Springhill Road, Moneymore, Co Londonderry. Tel: 028 86748210. *Open mid-Mar to Jun, Sep, Sat–Sun 1–6; Easter, Jul–Aug daily 1–6.*

TOUR 25

i 200 Newry Road, Banbridge. Tel: 028 40623322.
i Newcastle Centre, Central Promenade, Newcastle. Tel: 028 43722222.

1 Rathfriland
Brontë Interpretive Centre
Church Hill Road, Drumballyroney, Co Down. Tel: 028 40623322. *Open mid-Mar to late Sep, Fri–Sun & bank hols, 12–4.30, or by appointment.*

5 Dundrum
Dundrum Castle
Dundrum, Co Down. Tel: 028 90543037. *Open Apr–Sep, Tue–Sat, 10–7, Sun 2–7; Oct–Mar, Sat 10–4, Sun 2–4.*

6 Newcastle
Mourne Heritage Trust
87, Central Promenade, Newcastle, Co Down. Tel: 028 43724059. *Open all year, Mon–Fri, 9–5.*
Tollymore Forest Park
Bryansford Road, Newcastle, Co Down. Tel: 028 43722428. *Open 10–dusk.*

7 Annalong
Annalong Corn Mill
Marine Park, Annalong, Co Down. Tel: 028 41752256. *Telephone for details.*

8 The Silent Valley Visitor Centre
Head Road, Kilkeel, Co Down. Tel: 028 90741166. *Open Apr–Sep, 10–6.30; Oct–Mar 10–4.*

For children
Seaforde Gardens and Butterfly House
Seaforde, Co Down. Tel: 028 44811225. *Open Apr–Sep, Mon–Sat 10–5, Sun 1–6; gardens also open in winter, Mon–Sat..*

Back to Nature
Murlough National Nature Reserve Visitor Centre
Dundrum, Co Down. Tel: 028 43751467. *Open access daily, visitor facilities mid-Mar to May, Sat–Sun & bank hols; Jun to mid-Sep, daily.*

INDEX

Index & Acknowledgements

The Automobile Association
wishes to thank the following libraries and photographers for their assistance in the preparation of this book.

ALAMY 18; MICHAEL DIGGIN 59, 151; NORTHERN IRELAND TOURIST BOARD 123, 147, 149.

The remaining transparencies are held in the Association's own library (AA WORLD TRAVEL LIBRARY) and were taken by:

L BLAKE 40, 82, 99, 102, 104, 109, 112, 114/5, 118; J BLANDFORD 6, 28, 31, 32/3, 35, 36, 37, 52, 56, 56/7, 58, 106; C COE 5, 79; S L DAY 7, 12, 45, 50, 63, 65, 70, 96/7, 98, 120/1, 121, 146; M DIGGIN 8, 17, 27, 114, 117; D FORSS 49, 110, 130; C HILL 100, 101, 102/3, 105, 107, 111, 113, 116, 127, 160; S HILL 9, 10/11, 13, 26, 34, 48, 50, 51, 54, 129; J JENNINGS 135, 141, 144, 171; C JONES 30, 71; S MCBRIDE 90; G MUNDAY 122, 125, 128, 131, 133, 137, 138, 140, 142, 143, 145, 148, 153, 154/5, 156, 157; M SHORT 2, 38/9, 41, 42, 44, 46, 47, 53, 55, 61, 69, 73, 74, 75, 76, 77, 80, 81, 84, 85, 86, 87, 88, 89, 92, 94, 95; A STONEHOUSE 29; P ZOELLER 14, 15, 16, 19, 21, 22/3, 24, 25, 60, 62, 64, 66, 78, 90/1, 93, 97, 166.

Contributors
Verifier: Penny Phenix **Designer:** Jo Tapper **Indexer:** Marie Lorimer

Atlas

Londonderry/
Derry
Ballymena
Larne
Donegal
198-199 NORTHERN
BELFAST
IRELAND
Omagh
Enniskillen
Armagh
Downpatrick
Sligo
Newry
Ballina
Dundalk
Castlebar
REPUBLIC
Navan
Drogheda
Roscommon
Mullingar
200-201 Athlone
DUBLIN
Galway
OF
Dún Laoghaire
Birr
Portlaoise
204
Ennis
Wicklow
Limerick
Kilkenny
Carlow
Arklow
IRELAND
Enniscorthy
Tralee **202-203**
Wexford
Waterford
Cork
Bantry

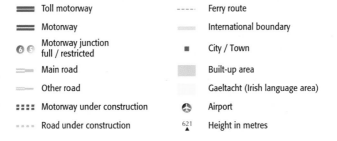

	Toll motorway		- - - -	Ferry route
	Motorway			International boundary
	Motorway junction full / restricted		■	City / Town
	Main road			Built-up area
	Other road			Gaeltacht (Irish language area)
	Motorway under construction			Airport
	Road under construction		621	Height in metres

0	10	20	30	40 km
0		10		20 miles

ATLAS INDEX

Atlas Index